Health and Saf

Health and Safety Law

Health and Safety Law

Brenda Barrett
Richard Howells

THE M & E HANDBOOK SERIES

Pitman Publishing
128 Long Acre, London WC2E 9AN

A Division of Longman Group UK Limited

First published in 1993

© Longman Group UK 1993

A CIP catalogue record for this book can be obtained from the British Library.

ISBN 0 7121 0847 5

Typeset by FDS Ltd, Penarth
Printed and bound in Singapore

Contents

Part three Compensation for industrial accidents

Part four Systems and procedures at the workplace

Part three Compensation for industrial accidents

Part four Systems and procedures at the workplace

Preface

It is appropriate to publish a book about occupational health and safety given the European Community's interest in this subject. Nevertheless, the enthusiasm with which the Community has adopted Directives relating to health and safety under Article 118A of the Treaty of Rome, for implementation in Member States by 1993, is so impacting on health and safety law in the United Kingdom that it has proved difficult to produce a volume with confidence that it will have lasting value. However, the authors believe that the European Community's activity will be reflected in the detail rather than the framework of the common law and they hope that they have emphasised the concepts which have been and, in their view, will continue to be inherent in this aspect of the national legal system.

This book is primarily intended for persons who have a special interest in occupational health and safety although they may not have studied law in depth. It may be useful to students undertaking HND or undergraduate courses in areas such as business studies, environmental studies or engineering, and to students undertaking postgraduate vocationally oriented courses, such as in personnel management or business management. It may also be of value to law students studying special topics such as employment law.

Finally the authors believe it is so structured that it may be of value to managers who have special responsibilities for occupational health and safety.

1992

BB
RH

Table of cases

Table of statutes

Table of statutory instruments

EC Directives

Official reports

1
Introduction

1. General

The importance of maintaining efforts to achieve safe and healthy workplaces in Great Britain is demonstrated by official statistics. It is estimated that every year 350 are killed at work, 1.5 million suffer injury, 2 million people suffer from work-related ill-health, 30 million working days are lost, and employers pay over £570 in insurance premiums.

Historical background

2. Legal responsibility for accidents

The practice of attributing legal responsibility for work-related injuries and ill-health is essentially a characteristic of industrial societies. Although people must always be prone to suffer injury when working in the home or in the fields, the need to attribute blame for such injuries does not seem to arise until society reaches the point of industrial development at which small-scale work activity at home is replaced by larger-scale activity carried out in special workplaces. England reached this stage of industrialisation in the nineteenth century and it was then that questions of occupational health and safety first came before Parliament and the law courts.

3. Early compensation law

Today, everyone agrees that it is preferable to prevent injuries rather than to mitigate their consequences. In the *laissez-faire* climate of earlier times, however, there was a belief that if employers had to pay compensation to workers for the injuries they suffered as a result of work this would be sufficient to motivate them to minimise the opportunity for injury. However, although it was acknowledged, after the case of *Priestley* v. *Fowler* (1837), that someone who suffered an injury at the workplace might claim damages from the wrongdoer who had caused the injury, in practice it was very difficult for any industrial accident victims to bring a claim in the common law courts, and few obtained compensation.

Even today, it is sometimes argued that in a free market economic forces should be sufficient to ensure safety at the workplace. Those who use this argument maintain that any organisation having such a disregard for safe systems of operation that it failed to manage its activities so as to protect its plant, equipment and workers from being damaged or destroyed in the course of production would incur such heavy replacement and compensation costs that it would be bankrupt. The argument is highly questionable and Western society is unwilling to put the theory to the test!

4. Employer's liability insurance

Unfortunately, the free market theory fails to ensure that those who are injured are adequately compensated. It can be small comfort for the victim to know that the accident has put the organisation out of business; moreover, the bankrupt organisation may not be able to compensate the victims of its unsafe practices. Before the end of the nineteenth century it was realised that it was more important to compensate the injured than to punish the wrongdoer by inflicting the cost of compensation on the wrongdoer personally. After the introduction of employer's liability insurance, the argument that safety might be achieved through making wrongdoers pay personally for the injuries they had caused was seriously weakened.

5. Growth of health and safety legislation

Towards the middle of the nineteenth century Parliament intervened to specify minimum standards for certain workplaces, and to empower the making of detailed regulations to cover particular hazards in those workplaces because economic forces were not operating to ensure healthy and safe working environments, particularly in factories and mines. It was, however, only 150 years later, with the passing of the Health and Safety at Work Act 1974, that there was legislation for general application in relation to health and safety in every workplace in Great Britain. The Health and Safety (Northern Ireland) Order 1978 brought similar provisions into effect in that part of the United Kingdom.

Purpose of modern legislation

6. Prevention of injury

The era which opened with the Health and Safety at Work Act finally shifted the emphasis from compensation of the injured to prevention of injury. Legislation nowadays demands the installation and maintenance of safe systems intended to ensure that accidents do not occur and health is not endangered. The decline of the 'smoke stack industries', and the introduction of advanced technology, has now shifted the concerns over safety away from the traditional problems of a dirty working environment and dangerous machinery. The emphasis now is upon protection of the worker from the health hazards associated with use of chemicals and also from the stress of the workplace — both mental stress, and the physical stress of repetitive and rapid physical activity.

Twentieth-century legislation stipulates safety standards, provides for inspectors to monitor that these standards are observed, and provides, in the last instance, for criminal sanctions on those who do not observe the legislative requirements; but accidents still happen. The necessity remains, therefore, for mechanisms to compensate accident victims. Much income maintenance is now provided through the social security system, but the common law action for damages remains important.

7. Scope of this text

The United Kingdom is generally regarded as a single state, and indeed it is so regarded by the EC, but, as its name suggests, there is more than one component. There are three jurisdictions in the UK, namely England and Wales, Scotland, and Northern Ireland, and the laws of these three jurisdictions are not necessarily the same.

This book will focus on English law and endeavour to explain how it operates today in relation to both the prevention of workplace accidents and the compensation of accident victims. In order to explain this law, however, it must be put into context, and to achieve this it is necessary to consider the following matters:

(a) first, the legal system within which occupational health and safety laws are enforced;
(b) second, the historical context from which current law has developed;
(c) third, other similar systems of regulatory control to which occupational health and safety laws relate — such as environmental protection, road traffic and employment protection laws.

Part one

Occupational health and safety in context

2
Health and safety in the English legal system

1. Introduction

Laws have been formulated to improve workplaces; when these laws are not observed, or if someone suffers personal injury at the workplace, the law may be invoked and there may be a trial in a court. Most of this book will be concerned with health and safety laws; it will therefore be helpful to begin by outlining the ways in which laws are made in England, and also to describe, in equally broad outline, the system of courts in which health and safety disputes are heard. The chapter will conclude with a short discussion of principles of liability.

2. Sources of law

There are, in the English legal system, two principal sources of law: decided cases and Acts of Parliament.

Case law

3. Common law system

The English legal system is a common law system. In any legal system it is the task of the judge to identify and apply the relevant rules of law. When the English common law system first began, at least 500 years ago, judges made their decisions by reference to what people normally did — thus elevating custom into law. There have now been so many judicial decisions that judges do not often have to investigate custom to find rules of law; they look instead to the decisions of other judges.

4. Law reports

For hundreds of years there has been a system of recording the details of cases and the judgments given in them. For over a hundred years these reports have been of a very high standard. While law reporting remains largely in the hands of commercial publishing houses, it is now common practice for the publishers to use typescripts supplied to them by judges themselves.

In recent years law reports have become readily accessible, for example in university law libraries, and through special 'on-line' and other data retrieval systems. The most authoritative printed law reports are those produced by the Incorporated Council of Law Reporting. These publishers produce *The Law Reports*, a series including Appeal Cases (cited as AC) and Queen's/King's Bench Division (QBD/KBD), and the Weekly Law Reports (WLR). Other major series are All England Reports (All ER), Industrial Case Reports (ICR) and, in employment law, Industrial Relations Law Reports (IRLR). To facilitate reference, libraries shelve reports by series and, within a series, in chronological order. Cases are cited thus: name of case, year of decision, series reference and page within the volume. For example, the famous product liability case about the snail in the ginger beer bottle is *Donoghue* v. *Stevenson* [1932] AC 562.

5. Use of case law

Barristers usually have little difficulty in finding several cases sufficiently like that of their client for them to be able to refer the judge to them and invite him to follow these earlier decisions. The judge has then to decide whether the earlier cases are *binding precedents* which have to be followed or whether the present case can be *distinguished* from them. A case may be distinguished on its facts.

Additionally, whether an earlier case is a binding precedent depends on the authority of the court in which it was decided. Broadly courts are bound by decisions of courts which are of senior status and within the same jurisdiction.

Subject to the hierarchy of the courts, judicial statements will be of binding authority when they are central to the reasoning of the decision (*ratio* of the case — short for *ratio decidendi*) whereas propositions made in passing (*obiter* — short for *obiter dicta*) are only of persuasive authority; statements made in courts in other jurisdictions are normally also of only *persuasive* authority. However, if an *obiter* statement is made by a senior judge in an appeal court it is likely to be treated with almost as much respect as if it were a binding authority.

6. Criminal prosecutions

Almost all criminal prosecutions on safety issues are for breaches of the special health and safety legislation which will be the main subject of this book, but it is possible, where unsafe conduct has caused death, for the ordinary law of homicide, which is almost entirely case law, to be invoked. The charge most usually brought is manslaughter. Catastrophies, such as the capsising of the *Herald of Free Enterprise*, and the King's Cross fire, have made it a matter of some controversy whether homicide charges ought to be laid against industrial organisations, managers or other employees whose acts, or omissions, cause death. In principle such charges could be brought, but it is difficult to prove that individuals have displayed sufficient fault to secure a conviction for such a serious offence as manslaughter. It is less clear that a corporate employer could be convicted of homicide, even supposing it were established that the corporate body had committed what for individuals might be criminal offences.

7. Strengths and weaknesses of case law

The system of developing the law through decided case has both strengths and weaknesses. Its main strength is that it enables law to be built on practical experience. Its weaknesses are that until judges have considered an issue, the law is uncertain. Alternatively, outdated rulings may remain in the law long after changes in society have made them inappropriate.

Acts of Parliament

8. Regulatory legislation

Today society is largely shaped by 'regulatory legislation'. Parliament enacts statutes to redirect the common law, or to provide for matters which have never been addressed by case law. The system of regulating society through Acts of Parliament had its origins in the nineteenth century, as industrialisation made fundamental changes in the way in which people lived and worked, and indeed in the way in which industrial activity was financed and managed. Acts of Parliament, and the detailed regulations made under their authority, are very useful tools for laying down minimum standards of behaviour, to protect the health and safety of people at work, and the public generally. Today we have major regulatory Acts of Parliament, and subordinate regulations, on a number of topics such as occupational health and safety, road safety, consumer safety, public health and environmental protection.

9.   The Health and Safety at Work Act 1974

The principal statute for occupational health and safety today is the Health and Safety at Work Act 1974. It is an 'enabling' (or framework) Act: it sets up a system for dealing with the problems of occupational health and safety but creates only broad rules for the workplace. An important aspect of the legislation is that it enables the making of regulations to provide detailed standards for particular work situations. Regulations made in accordance with the procedures set out in, and for the purposes allowed by, an Act of Parliament have the same authority, and may carry the same or similar penalties as any rules written into the parent Act itself.

10.   Role of legislation

In the UK today safety standards (i.e. accident prevention laws) are entirely statutory in origin and are enforced, in the last resort, through the criminal courts. Sometimes, however, where statutory provisions which are intended by Parliament primarily to ensure safety have not been followed and personal injury has occurred, the victim may rely on the breach of that statutory duty in a civil court to claim damages.

11.   Role of the judges

It is a feature of the common law system that while Parliament can, by statute, alter the common law, it falls to judges to interpret the words of Parliament. The role of the judges is very powerful, especially if Parliament has failed to express itself clearly within the text of the legislation. Judicial interpretations of Parliament's words can, if they do not accord with the legislator's intentions, result in amending legislation to re-state Parliament's intention and overrule the judicial interpretation of the original Act.

However, in most instances, judicial interpretations become an important addition to the body of law on the subject. For example, the words 'reasonably practicable' often appear in health and safety legislation and the accepted interpretation of them is that provided by Asquith LJ in *Edwards* v. *National Coal Board* [1949]. The work of the judiciary in sympathetic interpretation of occupational health and safety legislation has played a vital part in the development of the law.

Criminal and civil law

12. Criminal and civil law distinguished

There are two branches of the law: the criminal law and the civil law. Behaviour which falls short of the standard required for the protection of society is criminal behaviour and is punished by the state. Claims between individuals for the settlement of grievances by awards of compensation (such as damages) are civil claims. The division between criminal and civil law is reflected in the system of courts: criminal cases are heard in criminal courts and civil cases are heard in civil courts. In the last resort, therefore, safety standards legislation is interpreted in criminal courts and civil claims for compensation following accidents are heard in civil courts.

In both accident prevention law and accident compensation law, however, going to court is the last resort. Whenever possible steps will be taken to get hazards removed without laying criminal charges and in many instances accident victims are able to settle their claims without litigation.

13. Civil law and compensation

The civil law relating to compensation for personal injuries is largely the product of decided cases. Apart from civil actions for breach of statutory duty, liability for personal injury arises either in contract (where the parties have a legally binding agreement), or, where they do not rely on a contract, in tort (delict in Scotland).

The criminal courts

14. Magistrates' courts and the Crown Court

All criminal prosecutions start in a magistrates' court. There are three categories of criminal offence. The most serious (indictable) offences have to be tried upon indictment; that is to say when the magistrates have decided that there is a charge to answer a bill of indictment is framed and the case is sent for trial in the Crown Court. At the other extreme the least serious offences, which are termed summary offences, have to be dealt with in the magistrates' court, which is otherwise known as a court of summary jurisdiction. There is a third category of offences of some severity, known as 'either way offences', which, as their name suggests, can be tried either summarily or upon indictment.

15. Procedure in the magistrates' court

When the accused appears before magistrates, therefore, the first task of the magistrates is to consider which way the case is to be tried. If the charge is of an either way offence the magistrates have to make a choice, but there is an overriding right for the accused to elect to be tried by jury. Traditionally occupational health and safety offences have been summary offences. Since the Health and Safety at Work Act 1974, however, many health and safety offences have been either way offences, though in practice the great majority of cases are still tried summarily.

When magistrates decide whether either way offences are to be tried summarily or upon indictment they take into account the apparent severity of the offence: magistrates have not normally been empowered to award fines of over £2,000 for any one offence, but this general limit is now raised, by s.17 of the Criminal Justice Act 1991, to £5,000 for 'level 5' and 'either way' offences, and even higher in relation to some offences governed by enviromental pollution legislation. Additionally, some health and safety offences committed after March 1992 carry penalties of up to £20,000 or six months' imprisonment (Offshore Safety Act 1992, s.4). There is no upper limit to the powers of the Crown Court when imposing fines for offences under the 1974 Act. Even though most occupational safety cases are tried summarily, having the power to set serious cases down for trial in the Crown Court may lead magistrates to make use of the higher range of their summary powers.

If the case is intended for trial upon indictment the magistrates conduct a preliminary enquiry, taking statements (called depositions) from the prosecution witnesses to make sure that there is some evidence to support the charge. If the magistrates are not satisfied that there is a case to be tried, they terminate the proceedings. In most cases, however, they will arrange for the case to be tried in the Crown Court.

A major part of the trial court's task will be to receive the evidence in order to establish the facts. Once the evidence has been heard the magistrates, or, in the Crown Court, the jury, decide where the truth lies as between the prosecution's and the accused's stories. In the Crown Court the judge has first to sum up, informing the jury as to the significance in terms of presence or absence of guilt of the various possible interpretations of factual evidence with which they have been presented.

Courts in which cases are first heard, and the evidence is evaluated, are known as courts of first instance; the magistrates' courts and the Crown Court are both courts of first instance.

16. Appeal procedure from the magistrates' court

It is generally possible for the accused to appeal to the Crown Court against a magistrates' court's verdict of guilty. Such an appeal takes the form of a re-trial. Sometimes appeal may be by way of case stated. That is, either the accused or the prosecution may ask the magistrates to state a case for the opinion of a divisional court of the Queen's Bench Division: this is a valuable route by which the prosecution may appeal against an acquittal.

Appeal by way of case stated is a technical procedure which only lies where some irregularity in the trial is alleged such as that the magistrates exceeded their jurisdiction or wrongly interpreted the law — for example, it might be contended that they have applied the provisions of the Factories Act 1961 to circumstances to which they are not applicable (e.g. *Haygarth* v. *J & F Stone Lighting & Radio Ltd* [1965]).

Appeal against a decision of the divisional court is to the Appellate Committee of the House of Lords.

17. Appeal procedure from the Crown Court

Appeals from the Crown Court, on the other hand, go first to the Court of Appeal Criminal Division; from that court there is a right of final appeal to the House of Lords. Most appeals are about points of law rather than matters of fact, i.e. generally about the application of the law to the facts determined in the trial court. It may be necessary to get permission to appeal; it will always be necessary to get leave to appeal to the House of Lords from the Court of Appeal and this leave will not be granted unless a point of public importance is involved.

In practice it is unusual for health and safety cases to reach the Court of Appeal. Indeed the majority of these cases do not go beyond the magistrates' courts; this means that few of the cases which are prosecuted are reported in the law reports because the decisions of magistrates cannot create precedents. Even Crown Court decisions are of little precedential value and are rarely reported.

Civil courts

18. County courts and the High Court

Compensation cases will go to trial, according to the size of the claim and the complexity of the issues, in either the county court or the High Court.

The county court system was established in the nineteenth century as a system of local courts where small claims might be dealt with swiftly and relatively cheaply and informally. Its jurisdiction is still governed by statute, but it has failed to achieve all the original objectives, to the extent that it has proved necessary to make further provision for small claims. Since the implementation of the Law Courts and Legal Services Act 1990 district judges have been attached to the small claims courts, which now underpin the county court system, and they are empowered to deal with personal injury cases where less than £5,000 is claimed.

The county court's jurisdiction is technically limited, when hearing cases in contract and tort (which are the areas of law in which personal injury claims are founded), to claims in which the amount claimed is small. In practice the cost of litigation and the work load of the High Court has meant in recent years that most personal injury claims have been started in the local county court, or referred back there by the High Court. The High Court and

County Courts Jurisdiction Order 1991 abolished many of the limits on the county court's jurisdiction with effect from 1 July 1991. Cases are now allocated for trial according to substance, importance and complexity. All personal injury claims for less than £50,000 are nowadays started in a county court. Very large claims or complicated ones are heard at first instance in the Queen's Bench Division of the High Court.

19. Appeal procedure

Appeal lies from both the county courts and the High Court to the Court of Appeal and there is a further and final appeal to the House of Lords. The decisions of county courts do not create precedents and therefore they are not published in the law reports.

Tribunals

20. Tribunals in general

There are, within the English legal system, institutions known as tribunals which have many of the attributes of law courts, and perform a function similar to courts, in that they hear and resolve disputes. Many of these tribunals are created by, and take their jurisdiction from, statute. For example, there are tribunals to determine disputes over social security claims and these may be referred to by persons who, having suffered an industrial injury, seek one of the various forms of income maintenance which the social security system provides for persons who are physically incapacitated.

21. Industrial tribunals

Industrial tribunals were created by statute in the 1960s and, by further statutes, many of which date from the 1970s, they have acquired a wide and complex jurisdiction. Most of their work is the hearing of complaints by employees that their employers have dismissed them unfairly or for redundancy, or failed to award them the floor of rights to which statute entitles them during the contract of employment. The majority of this employment protection law is contained in the Employment Protection (Consolidation) Act 1978. Some aspects of this legislation, and the work of industrial tribunals more widely, is relevant to safety. For example, industrial tribunals have jurisdiction to hear employers' appeals against notices served on them by health and safety inspectors.

22. Appeal from industrial tribunals

Appeal lies on a point of law from an industrial tribunal, in employment protection cases, to the Employment Appeal Tribunal (a special body of High Court status) and thence to the Court of Appeal. Appeal lies from decisions concerning safety notices to a specially constituted High Court. In both instances appeal may ultimately be to the House of Lords.

Impact of the EC

23. The European Community

The European Communities Act 1972 took the UK into membership of the European Community in 1973 and committed the UK to the Treaty of Rome and other Community treaties. The purpose of the European Community is a common market between the Member States and the Treaty of Rome has that objective. A common market requires free movement of goods and people and the prevention of unfair trading at the expense of the workforce.

24. The EC and product standards

Articles 100 and 100A of the Treaty, concerned with the 'approximation of laws', are important to health and safety in that they enable harmonisation of standards in relation to the working environment, including standards for plant and equipment and personal protective clothing. In due course plant and equipment, including personal protective equipment used at the workplace in Member States of the EC, will have to meet relevant European standards, i.e. those of the Comité Européen de Normalisation (CEN) and, for electrical goods, of the Committee for Electrotechnical Standardisation (CENELEC), rather than British (BSI) standards. Equipment complying with these standards is likely to be marked by the manufacturer with the Community Mark. The UK's Health and Safety Commission is committed to making a major contribution to the development of standards at the national, European and international levels. (*See Policy Statement on Standards* (1991).)

25. The EC and workplace safety

The Community had, by the mid-1980s, already made stipulations on matters, such as dangerous substances used at work, classification packaging and labelling of substances, and the control of installations which created a major hazard. After the Treaty of Rome was amended (*see* the Single European Act 1986) which added Article 118A specifically concerned with occupational health and safety, the Community's efforts in this area were substantially increased. Article 118A provides:

1. Member States shall pay particular attention to encouraging improvements, especially in the working environment, as regards the health and safety of workers, and shall set as their objective the harmonisation of conditions in this area, while maintaining the improvements made.

Some Articles of the Treaty are directly enforceable by the EC but Article 118A merely enables the legislative machinery of the Community to make Directives on health and safety. Paragraph 2 of Article 118A describes how this shall be done:

2. In order to help achieve the objectives laid down in the first paragraph, the Council acting by a qualified majority on a proposal from the Commission, in cooperation with the European Parliament and after consulting with the Economic and Social Committee, shall adopt, by means of directives, minimum requirements for gradual implementation, having regard to the conditions and technical rules obtaining in each of the Member States.

In June 1989 Article 118A was used to enable the adoption of a Framework Directive on the introduction of measures to encourage improvements in the safety and health of workers at work and this was soon followed by five individual Directives concerning:

(a) the minimum safety and health requirements for the workplace;
(b) the minimum safety and health requirements for the use of work equipment by workers;

(c) the minimum health and safety requirements for the use by workers of personal protective equipment at the workplace;
(d) the minimum health and safety requirements for the manual handling of loads where there is a risk particularly of back injury to workers;
(e) on the minimum safety and health requirements for work with display screen equipment.

All these Directives must be read in the context of paragraph 3 of Article 118A which states that Member States shall not be prevented from maintaining or introducing more stringent measures for the protection of working conditions. However, plant and equipment used in order to comply with these measures must conform to, and not exceed, CEN standards.

A further Directive of 25 June 1991 makes special provision for encouraging improvements in the safety and health of workers with a fixed duration employment relationship or a temporary employment relationship.

Member States are required to implement these particular Directives by the end of 1992. However, there are some instances where the EC does not require existing workplaces to achieve the stipulated standards before 1997.

The Consultative Document introducing UK proposals for the implementation of the Framework Directive estimates that compliance with that Directive will impose on employers ongoing annual costs of about £70 million.

26. The Social Charter
Perhaps because Directives made under Article 118A may be adopted on a qualified majority (i.e. without the unanimous agreement of all the Member States) the Community now has a heavy programme of work stemming from the so called Commission's Community Charter of Fundamental Social Rights. Although the UK is not committed to this Charter, the Commission has published a first programme of work to implement it. Proposals for Directives related to safety feature largely in this programme: there are, for example, proposals to complement the five individual Directives with other Directives for particular industries such as those relating to the extractive industries and to construction sites. It might be argued that some

of the programme goes beyond Article 118A, or indeed the Treaty of Rome itself.

27. Compliance with EC Directives

A Member State may implement a Directive by whatever legislative techniques are appropriate to its legal system, but if it fails to implement it at all, or implements it imperfectly, that state will be in breach of its Treaty obligations and may be subject to proceedings in the European Court of Justice by the Commission (Article 169) or another Member State (Article 170). Moreover, in some instances, a citizen of the State in question may bring an action if that citizen is being deprived of personal rights as a result of the State's breach of Treaty obligation.

Article 177 makes provision for the European Court of Justice to give preliminary rulings on the interpretation of the Treaty itself or of acts of the institutions of the Community: this empowers the court to interpret Directives. Article 177 requires that when the final court of appeal in a member state needs clarification of Community provisions in order to make a decision on the case before it, it must make a reference to the European Court. As long ago as *Macarthys* v. *Smith* [1979] the Court of Appeal was prepared to find for a plaintiff when, as a result of a reference under Article 177, it appeared that English law, which was unfavourable to her case, was in fact contrary to an EC provision. Subsequently, and somewhat controversially, in order to avoid the time and expense of reference to the European Court of Justice, English courts have presumed to read the intention of the Community and interpret UK statutes 'purposively' to make them comply with the Community's intention (e.g. *Pickstone* v. *Freemans plc* [1988]). The European Court has now decided that even statutes which pre-date a relevant EC Directive must be purposively interpreted (*SA Marleasing* v. *La Commercial Internacional de Alimentacion* [1990]). Thus, in the situation where there was a conflict between the Health and Safety at Work Act 1974 and the EC Framework Directive of 1989, the 1974 Act would have to be interpreted to give effect to the Directive. Moreover, even an industrial tribunal is empowered to hear a claim based solely on EC law (*Secretary of State for Scotland and Greater Glasgow Health Board* v. *Wright and Hannah* [1991]).

Nevertheless it is not always easy for a lawyer trained in

common law to relate to Directives and other statements emanating from the Community. There is frequently a generality and lack of precision in them which it is difficult for the common lawyer to understand.

Again the legal significance of EC statements of policy is by no means clear. It would appear that UK law may be subordinated even to policy statements; EC case law appears to have laid down that UK judges ought not to enforce UK statutes which are not in harmony with EC intentions. (*See R v. Secretary of State for Transport, ex parte Factortame Ltd* [1991].)

Strict and fault liability

28. Liability in general

There are two fundamental principles of liability in the English legal system: no person shall be liable unless he has personally brought about a wrongful state of affairs, and no person shall be liable except that his state of mind in relation to the wrongful conduct has been to some extent reprehensible. Neither of these principles is without exception and indeed they are not necessarily suitable principles on which to base liability in the circumstances in which society functions today.

29. Criminal liability

General rules

The basic principles of criminal liability are that persons shall not be found guilty of crimes unless the prosecution can establish both that they have by their acts or omissions brought about a prescribed state of affairs (the *actus reus* of the crime) and that they have brought about this state of affairs when in a wrongful state of mind, i.e. showing the necessary *criminal* intent (*mens rea*).

It is never easy for the prosecution to establish the wrongful intent of an accused person. That task is much more difficult when the wrongful situation has occurred in an organisational context.

Status and responsibility

Much regulatory legislation places duties on the organisation itself often by virtue of its status, for example as an employer, a manufacturer, or as the occupier of premises. If a person is, for example, the occupier of premises where many people are present, when a wrongful situation occurs, it certainly may not be the occupier who has personally brought this about. The legislature often deals with such situations by creating strict duties making the person on whom the duty is imposed liable if the statutory standard is not achieved without proof of how the situation arose, much less that the accused had a guilty mind. Thus s.14 of the Factories Act 1961, a provision of fundamental importance in factory law for many years, imposed a duty of strict liability on the occupier of premises providing that the occupier would be liable if dangerous machinery were found there without secure guarding.

30. Corporate and personal liability

Regulatory duties of this description can be used to attach liability not only to human persons but also to corporate entities. While the law deems a corporation to be a person capable of incurring legal rights and duties, there are — offences of strict liability apart — nevertheless problems of attaching criminal liability to a corporate body, since there are practical and conceptual problems in attributing the necessary *mens rea* to anything other than human persons.

If Parliament has not expressly required proof of *mens rea* the courts will be willing to accept that duties are strict, provided that the offence is a summary one. On the other hand, if Parliament has created an offence, which is triable upon indictment, without stipulating that it is a *mens rea* offence, there is a presumption that the common law principle applies, and the prosecution must prove the defendant had a guilty mind. (*See Sweet* v. *Parsley* [1969].)

Many regulatory statutes contain a clause providing that where it can be established that a corporation has been caused to commit an offence because of the 'neglect' of a director, secretary or senior manager, or with the 'consent or connivance' or one of these senior persons, the human wrongdoer may be prosecuted, as well as or in place of the company. (*See* s.37 of the Health and Safety at Work Act.)

There remain problems, however, as to whether the company may itself be liable where the *mens rea* is that of a director or other person employed by the company. While in principle the courts are prepared to regard senior personnel as the 'brains' of the company and hold the company liable for their wrongful behaviour, this will only be so where the wrongdoer is at least a senior manager. (*See Tesco Supermarkets Ltd* v. *Nattras* [1971].) It remains unclear whether a series of, what may individually be minor, lapses by individual employees or managers may be totted up, and, in sum, attributed to the company, to give it the necessary state of mind required for an offence. This uncertainty is at the heart of the debate as to whether or not there can be corporate manslaughter when death has resulted from the cumulative effects of a series of lapses in the systems operating within an organisation.

31. Civil liability

Liability for negligence
Actions for compensation for personal injury are usually founded in negligence: thus the plaintiff (the victim) must, in order to win the case, prove that the defendant's conduct was negligent. There are two major exceptions to this general rule.

32. Strict liability

First, the plaintiff may found the claim on the breach of a strict statutory duty. For example, the plaintiff might have injured his hands while working at an unguarded machine in a factory. He might then claim damages for breach of s.14 of the Factories Act. To win the claim he would have to show that the statutory duty had been broken. But as this particular duty is a strict one he would not have to show the defendant's conduct had been negligent in order to prove the breach.

Secondly, where the plaintiff's injury has been caused by the unlawful behaviour of an employee in the course of employment, the plaintiff may elect to sue the wrongdoer's employer rather than, or jointly with, the actual wrongdoer himself. In these circumstances the employer can be held vicariously liable, and have to pay damages to compensate the plaintiff. The principle of vicarious liability enables an accident victim to obtain damages from an employer without proving the employer to be personally at fault.

These themes of strict and fault liability are fundamental to an understanding of the law on health and safety at work. They will be continually referred to, expanded, and applied in this book.

Progress test 2

1. By what law making technique may the European Community bring about improvements in working conditions? **(23** *et seq.***)**

2. What is meant by founding a claim for damages upon a breach of statutory duty? **(10)**

3. What is meant by *mens rea*? **(29)**

4. In which court will most civil actions for damages for personal injuries suffered at the workplace be brought? **(18)**

5. Which court will serve as a court of first instance in criminal cases? **(15)**

6. What is meant by a reference under Article 177? **(27)**

3
History of occupational health and safety law

1. Introduction

English law is, in general, difficult to understand without some insight into its historical development: occupational health and safety law is no exception. This chapter will, therefore, outline the development of occupational health and safety law to explain the context of the present law. Occupational health and safety law had its beginnings in the Industrial Revolution. That is where this outline begins.

Evolution of employment relationships

2. 'Master' and 'servant'

The terms 'master' and 'servant' are very ancient, but originally they applied mainly to the relationships between farmers and farm workers, and householders and domestic workers. Other workers progressed through apprenticeship to be journeymen and then master craftsmen.

The Industrial Revolution led to a different working environment where workers frequently worked with machinery rather than hand tools or animals in manufacturing or transportation. Often the persons who worked in these new tasks had a fairly permanent relationship with their employers, a relationship in which they provided only their labour, which might sometimes be skilled, to operate their employers' plant and equipment. The terms master and servant were extended to cover these new working relationships.

3. Intervention of the courts

In time the master and servant relationship came to be treated as a status relationship. Thereafter courts often had to classify working relationships in order to identify the rules governing them.

The first recorded case is *Yewens* v. *Nokes* (1880), in which Bramwell LJ said:

> A servant is a person subject to the command of his master as to the manner in which he shall do his work.

Before long 'command' was modified to 'control'.

4. 'Employer', 'employee' and the contract of employment

The words 'master' and 'servant' have now given way to 'employer' and 'employee', but the courts still find it necessary to distinguish the contract of employment from other forms of relationship whether or not based on contract. Control over the worker by the employer remains a central feature of the contract of employment.

It was necessary to explain here the contract of employment, and the parties to it, because the nature of the employment relationship has always been an important factor in determining the rights and duties of the persons concerned with both accident compensation and accident prevention. Rights and duties are usually pitched higher where there is a contract of employment.

Compensation for personal injury

5. The doctrine of common employment

Priestley v. *Fowler* (1837) was the first personal injury claim in which importance was attached to the employment relationship. The old law report makes strange reading. However, the facts were broadly that a master butcher employed two servants and had a van in which he carried goods; one servant loaded the van, the other (the plaintiff) suffered injury in the course of a journey in the loaded van. The report fails to make clear whether the accident occurred because the van was defective or because it had been overloaded. At the trial the plaintiff was awarded damages, but that decision was reversed on appeal.

The judgment of the appeal court has been much analysed and severely criticised. Lord Abinger CB made the positive statement that the master '. . . is no doubt, bound to provide for the safety of his servant in the course of his employment . . .', but this was quite overshadowed by the suggestion that: 'If the master be liable to the servant in this action, the principle of that liability will be found to carry us to an alarming extent.' In his Lordship's view finding for the plaintiff would mean that a householder would be liable for accidents caused by faulty goods provided to him by shopkeepers and for injuries suffered by houseguests as a result of the negligence of housemaids. His Lordship apparently failed to recognise that some of his illustrations were unrelated to the employment relationship. More significant, however, was that he attached importance to the lack of evidence that the employer had any knowledge of the events which led to the accident, whereas the victim was able to evaluate the situation. His Lordship concluded:

> . . . to allow this sort of action to prevail would be an encouragement to the servant to omit that diligence and caution which he is in duty bound to exercise on the behalf of his master, to protect him against the misconduct or negligence of others who serve him . . .

To this judgment was attributed the notorious doctrine of common employment under which a master was not liable for injury suffered by a servant as a result of the wrongdoing of another of that master's servants.

6. Application of the doctrine

The development of employers' liability was much restricted by the doctrine of common employment. There may have been justification for the doctrine in cases where there was little social difference between the employing master craftsman and the servant who was injured. Where the undertaking was larger, and more able than the victim to bear the cost of the accident, the rule became clearly unjust. In *Wilson* v. *Merry* (1868) it was used to defeat the claim where a coal miner had been killed by an explosion resulting from a temporary obstruction of air circulation by the employer's manager: the manager was held to be in common employment with the victim. Some of the worst aspects of the doctrine were mitigated by the Employer's Liability

Act 1880 which protected the worker's claim where injury resulted from the negligence of a senior person or one whose orders the workman had to obey.

In the twentieth century the doctrine created difficulties for judges no longer in sympathy with it. In *Wilsons & Clyde Coal Company Ltd* v. *English* [1937] the House of Lords wanted to find for an underground worker injured by a system of work negligently put in place by the qualified manager to whom the employers were required, by the provisions of the Coal Mines Act 1911, to delegate responsibility for running the mine. Their Lordships held that the employers owed a non-delegable duty, which overrode the doctrine of common employment, to provide for the safety of their employees. Lord Wright said:

> The whole course of authority consistently recognises a duty which rests on the employer, and which is personal to the employer, to take reasonable care for the safety of his workmen, whether the employer be an individual, a firm or a company, and whether or not the employer takes any share in the conduct of the operations.

Lord Wright's analysis has survived the demise of common employment and *Wilsons Case* is generally regarded as the foundation of the modern law of employer's liability.

7. Abolition of the doctrine

The doctrine of common employment remained until it was abolished by the Law Reform (Personal Injuries) Act 1948, s.1(1) of which provided:

> It shall not be a defence to an employer who is sued in respect of personal injuries caused by the negligence of a person employed by him, that that person was at the time the injuries were caused in common employment with the person injured.

8. Assumption of risk

One explanation of the doctrine of common employment was that the servant had agreed to accept the risk of injury by another of his master's servants. The concept of acceptance of risk was extended so that the servant was deemed to have accepted the dangers of the workplace. The employer could totally avoid liability by the defence of assumption of risk, known technically as *volenti non fit injuria*. No allowance was made for the fact that workers could not afford to terminate their contracts and lose the source of income on which their survival depended. The House of Lords considered the defence in *Smith* v. *Baker* [1891].

The plaintiff, who was a railway navvy, was working in a cutting while a crane on top of the embankment was removing stones from the cutting. The workman had made several complaints. When stones fell on him he claimed damages. The House found for him; for although he knew of the danger and still continued to do his work, there was no evidence that he had voluntarily undertaken to run the risk of injury.

After this courts have rarely found that an employee has accepted the risk of injury at work.

9. No negligence

The common law of employer's liability was, and still is, fault liability. In order to obtain compensation the plaintiff has to show that the defendant's conduct was negligent and that this negligence caused the plaintiff's injury. The criterion of negligent conduct remains broadly the same now as in the nineteenth century, but courts were then less inclined to find that accidents were caused by an employer's negligence. Society may then have been more cavalier and less safety conscious, but it must also be remembered that there was less technical and scientific knowledge than today, and much less industrial experience, so there was understandably less reason to foresee danger.

10. Negligent system

Today if an accident occurred in circumstances where there was a fault in an organisation's system of work, the courts would find the organisation to be negligent. In the nineteenth century, if the employee knew of the defect in the system and failed to take account of it, then the courts might attribute negligence to the employee rather than the employer. For example, where a railway disaster was primarily attributable to a known inadequate braking system on the train, it might be argued that the real fault lay with the driver for not operating within the capacity of the faulty brakes! The employer might not be liable for injuries suffered by either the driver or the passengers.

11. Fatal accidents

At common law rights to compensation did not survive death. This harsh rule was mitigated by the Fatal Accidents Act 1846 which established a principle which remains part of the law today. It enabled a claim to be made on behalf of a widow and certain other dependent relatives to claim against a person who had unlawfully killed the breadwinner. It had to be established both that it was the defendant's wrongdoing which caused the death and that each claimant was dependant on the deceased for financial support. The court would then award a sum sufficient to provide income maintenance, at the rate the deceased might have provided, given his employment prospects for the remainder of his natural working life.

It is somewhat surprising, given the difficulty of winning an industrial injury claim and that there was little in the way of what has since become legal aid to defray the costs of litigation, that there was any litigation at all.

After *Smith* v. *Baker*, the common law might have developed more favourably to those who suffered injury at work. Whether this would have been so is mere speculation, because the Workmen's Compensation Act 1897 gave employees some entitlement to income maintenance independently of the common law.

12. Workmen's Compensation Act 1897

This legislation imposed upon the employer a duty to provide income maintenance to an employee who suffered injury in an accident 'arising out of and in the course of employment'. The Act was later extended to allow claims to be made where the victim had contracted one of the 'prescribed' industrial diseases. The periodical payments which the employer had to make were modest, being only a proportion of the pre-accident weekly wage of the victim, but they could be claimed without establishing that the injury was caused by the employer's negligence; liability was based entirely on the requirement that the injury arose out of and in the course of employment. The scheme remained in force until after the end of the Second World War and during its operation employee victims had to elect between claiming compensation under the statutory provisions and claiming damages at common law. Between 1896 and 1948 many victims of industrial injury claimed the relatively modest income maintenance which the legislation provided rather than undertake the arduous task of pursuing a common-law claim for negligence.

13. Contract and status

The early rules of liability outlined above were largely applicable to the contract of employment. A parallel relationship, often created independently of contract, was, and continues to be, the relationship between occupier of, and visitor to, premises. After the case of *Indermaur* v. *Dames* (1866) the occupier had a considerable responsibility for the safety of visitors to his premises.

The liability of a person (probably an employer of servants!) having the status of occupier of premises to another (probably a workman) having the status of visitor to the premises were different from those which applied as between master and servant and in many respects favourable to the visitor (for example, the doctrine of common employment would not defeat a visitor's claim where the visitor was injured through the fault of the occupier's servant). On the other hand, the defence of *volenti* could defeat an invitee's claim long after that defence had ceased to be significant in the master and servant relationship. (See *London Graving Dock Co Ltd* v. *Horton* [1951].)

It does not appear to have been usual for injured workers to claim damages for personal injury from defendants who were neither their master nor the occupier of premises at which they were working at the time of the injury. *Heaven* v. *Pender* [1883] was an exception, and created an important precedent.

The plaintiff was employed as a painter. His employer agreed with a shipowner, whose vessel was in the defendant's dock, to paint the outside of the ship. The defendant supplied, under a contract with the shipowner, the staging to be slung alongside the ship so she could be painted. The ropes from which the staging was slung were unsound and the plaintiff was injured when they broke. There was no contract of employment between the injured party and the defendant, nor was the defendant the occupier of the premises where the accident occurred. Nevertheless, in finding for the plaintiff, Brett MR stated:

> Whenever one person is by circumstances placed in such a position with regard to another that every one of ordinary sense who did

think would at once recognise that if he did not use ordinary care and skill in his own conduct with regard to those circumstances he would cause danger of injury to the person or property of the other, a duty arises to use ordinary care and skill to avoid such danger.

14. The tort of negligence

Principles of liability for personal injury had by the 1930s developed so that it was recognised that a defendant would be liable to compensate another if he owed a duty to that other to take care not to cause him injury and broke that duty by negligent conduct. There was, however, a lack of certainty about the situations in which a duty to take care arose. Indeed, apart from occupiers' liability and transport accidents there were few situations in which duty situations were recognised unless the plaintiff and defendant were in a contractual relationship: in contracts, of which the contract of employment was an important, but not the only, example, it could be said that there was an implied duty to take care for the personal safety of the other party to the contract. Thus in employment the master's duty to take reasonable care for the safety of the servant was deemed to be an implied term of the contract of service and one factor which distinguished servants from other persons who had contracts to supply labour. Similarly a seller of goods might well be in breach of contract if the purchaser suffered personal injury from the goods.

In *Donoghue* v. *Stevenson* [1932] the appellant had suffered personal injury when she drank ginger beer in which there were the remains of a snail. The drink had been manufactured by the respondent, and supplied to a retailer from whom it was bought for the appellant by her friend. The plaintiff had not entered into contract with either the manufacturer or the retailer, and could not therefore bring an action for breach of contract. The majority of the House of Lords nevertheless found that the appellant (consumer) was owed a duty of care by the respondent (manufacturer) and would be able to claim damages from him if she could show that it was by his negligent conduct that the snail had contaminated the ginger beer. Lord Atkin built on the words of Brett MR in *Heaven* v. *Pender* to provide a most important statement as to the criterion for liability in negligence:

The rule that you are to love your neighbour becomes, in law, you must not injure your neighbour, and the lawyer's question, Who is my neighbour? receives a restricted reply. You must take reasonable care to avoid acts or omissions which you can reasonably foresee would be likely to injure your neighbour. Who, then in law is my neighbour? The answer seems to be — persons who are so closely and directly affected by my act that I ought reasonably to have them in contemplation as being so affected when I am directing my mind to the acts or omissions which are called in question.

Barely two years later Lord Wright stated in the industrial injury case, *Lochgelly Iron and Coal Co.* v. *M'Mullan* [1934]:

In strict legal analysis, negligence means more than heedless or careless conduct, whether in omission or commission; it properly connotes the complex concept of duty, breach and damage thereby suffered by the person to whom the duty was owing.

The recognition of a tort of negligence, based on a duty of care arising where plaintiff and defendant were in sufficiently close proximity for them to be deemed neighbours, provided a framework within which the existing duty situations could be housed. It also enabled new categories of duty situations to be recognised.

15. The foundations of modern law

Donoghue v. *Stevenson*, by giving recognition to the tort of negligence, and *Wilsons & Clyde Coal Company Ltd* v. *English*, by spelling out the nature of employers' liability, laid the foundations of modern employers' liability law.

The development of this law was assured by postwar legislation. A new income maintenance scheme was introduced in 1948 by the National Insurance (Industrial Injuries) Act 1946, which, in s.89(1), repealed the Workmen's Compensation Acts. While the national insurance scheme retained the principle of income maintenance for the victims of industrial accidents in similar language to the earlier legislation, the new statutory entitlement was not lost by those who claimed damages. Indeed the new statutory scheme was administered by the state and the insured victim claimed through the social security system. However, the Law Reform (Personal Injuries) Act 1948 provided that one half of the value of the new industrial injury benefit should be offset against any common law damages awarded as the result of the same accident (s.2(1)).

The offset of part of the statutory entitlement against a common law claim of which the claim for loss of wages was usually but a small element was no deterrent to a litigant pursuing a substantial claim.

The system of providing compensation for those who accidentally suffered personal injury was subjected to close scrutiny in the 1970s by the Pearson Commission. While the Royal Commission made a number of recommendations for changes within the system, they were of the view that the common law system of fault-based liability should be retained in addition to the social security system. They rejected the suggestion that it would be more satisfactory to make provision for personal injury solely through the social security system.

Prevention of personal injury

16. General historical background

The protection of the workforce from the hazards of an unhealthy working environment and dangerous working practices in order to prevent industrial accidents and diseases has, in the United Kingdom, come to be seen, after nearly two centuries of experience of industrialisation, as a matter for Parliament.

It is possible to trace protective legislation to an Act of 1802 'for the health and morals of apprentices and others'. It covered cotton and woollen mills and factories in which three or more apprentices, or twenty of more other persons, were employed. Such factories were to be limewashed twice a year and provided with sufficient windows and openings to ensure adequate ventilation. It was stipulated that apprentices were to work no more than 12 hours a day. Clergymen and justices were appointed as visitors to inspect mills and to report in writing to the magistrates in quarter sessions. The Act was aimed at the abuses of the parish apprenticeship system under which pauper children were put to work; this system was providing millowners with cheap labour.

It was not only employers who recognised the possibilities of profiting from child labour. Parents were frequently willing to contract to send their children to work in the new factories. This created a dilemma for Parliament — and opened a debate which was to hamper the development of protective legislation throughout the nineteenth century and still continues even today. The problem was of determining the extent to which Parliament should interfere with freedom of contract. In the nineteenth century Parliament intervened only when convinced that statutory protection was necessary to prevent exploitation. At first only the weakest members of society, first children, then women, seemed to warrant protection.

The real advances came in the 1830s and 1840s. In these decades there were a number of official inquiries followed by major statutes to regulate working conditions. The most important of these reports concerned the employment of children in factories, accidents in mines and the working conditions of railway construction workers. The first of these reports led to the further regulation of the hours of labour of children and young persons; the second led to the first major Mines Act and the third led to the first Fatal Accidents Act.

The report on railway labourers differed from the other two reports in that it resulted in statutory provision for accident compensation, whereas the other two led to regulatory legislation, with criminal sanctions, to provide better working conditions. Perhaps this was because the first two inquiries were considering the working conditions of women and children whereas the third was concerned almost exclusively with the employment of men. Indeed the general lack of concern for the safety of men may be inferred from a remark made by a witness to the committee. When asked whether a safer fuse might not have prevented the explosion which killed 26 workmen during the blasting of the Woodhead railway tunnel, he replied that he would not recommend the loss of time which the safer method would involve!

It was nearly the end of the century before the doctrine of *laissez-faire* was contained sufficiently to enable some statutory regulation of employment conditions for men. Even today it is argued that there should not normally be statutory restrictions on the length of the working day, because to impose such restrictions would interfere with freedom of contract.

17. Early factory safety legislation

In 1819 an Act for the regulation of cotton mills and factories prohibited the employment in such places of children under the age of 9 and limited the working hours of those under 16 to 12 hours a day.

In 1833 the second of the inquiries into the employment of children in factories called many witnesses who recounted long hours of work in appalling conditions and presented their deformed bodies as evidence of the outome of long hours of work from an early age in such conditions. The Factories Act 1833 was primarily to control the effects of overlong exposure of the young to such conditions, and limited the length of the working day of persons under the age of 18 to 10 hours. The most innovatory feature of the Act was that it provided for the appointment of four government inspectors to visit factories where children and young persons were employed to ensure that the legislation was observed. This was the origin of the Factories Inspectorate and the model for the more widespread use of government agents to police regulatory legislation.

After this, legislation was passed every few years extending the statutory protection. The Factory Act 1844 regulated the circumstances in which children and young persons might be employed in humid spinning processes and required the guarding of certain machinery. The guarding requirement was subsequently restricted, by the Factory Act 1856, to ensure that it applied only to those parts of the mill gearing with which children, young persons and women were liable to come into contact.

An Act of 1847 restricted the length of the working day for women in textile factories. The Factory Acts Extension Act 1867 extended the scope of protective legislation by bringing premises in which metals were worked within the scope of factory legislation. In 1878 the law was consolidated and extended to men by the Factory and Workshop Act, and in this Act there emerged a pattern which was carried forward through successive Acts to the Factories Act 1961 to provide for the health, safety and welfare of all persons employed in manual labour in factories. Writing at the beginning of the twentieth century, B.L. Hutchins and A. Harrison could fairly suggest:

This century of experiment in factory legislation affords a typical example of English practical empiricism. We begin with no abstract theory of social justice or the rights of man. We seem always to have been incapable even of taking a general view of the subject we were legislating upon. Each successive statute aimed at remedying a single ascertained evil. (*A History of Factory Legislation*)

Until the Health and Safety at Work Act 1974 the Factories Act 1961, and regulations made under it, was the principal regulatory code in respect of occupational health and safety, in that it encompassed a larger proportion of the workforce than any other regulatory code, covering about 8½ million employees. Though much less relevant, after the enactment of the 1974 Act, some of its provisions are still in force.

18. Mines and quarries safety legislation

The Select Committee on Accidents in Mines 1835 investigated the nature and cause of, and suggested means of preventing, accidents in mines. It found that there were 1,000 deaths in mining on the banks of the Tyne and Wear between 1710 and 1810 and (in the same area) 1,125 deaths between 1810 and 1835. It was believed 2,070 persons were killed in mining in 25 years. After considering the question of safety legislation 'on its merits' the Select Committee concluded that the conditions in the mines were too diverse to allow for general rules to be formulated. A further Royal Commission was set up in 1840 to investigate the conditions of children, and was later extended to include women and young persons, working underground in mines.

The first report of the Children's Employment Commission in 1842 was widely regarded as one of the most important social documents in the nineteenth century. The report was graphically illustrated with sketches, demonstrating the appalling working conditions underground. In particular it stressed the conditions in which women and children were working. Women dragged heavy loads of coal and children often spent much of their working days in total darkness. The Mines and Collieries Act 1842 prohibited the employment of women underground, a prohibition which lasted up to, and beyond, the Sex Discrimination Act 1975. Males under the age of 10 were not to be employed; a mines inspectorate was created, and the many penal provisions of the statute provided some evidence of the intention to ensure the Act was observed.

While factory legislation initially showed more concern for hours of work than safety issues, the extremely hazardous nature of underground mining ensured that safety was the primary factor in the development of the legislation after 1842. In 1849 a Select Committee of the House of Lords recommended the appointment of government inspectors charged with responsibility for safety in mines and collieries. The Act for the Inspection of Mines and Collieries 1850 provided for the appointment of four inspectors with minimal powers. Frequent underground disasters ensured that the problem could not be forgotten. A pattern was soon established of disaster, inquiry and preventative legislation, with the emphasis at first on shafts, air circulation, the prevention of fires and explosions, and the support of strata. The law was consolidated in the Coal Mines Regulation Act 1872, which also stipulated the personnel who must be on duty when men were working underground, and imposed a system of qualification for mine management. Subsequent coal mining legislation developed these basic themes, in the light of increasing technical knowledge, rather than adding to their number.

If it is true that the history of factory legislation exemplifies English empiricism, this is equally true of mines legislation. The principal legislation at the beginning of this century was the Coal Mines Act 1911 covering safety in coal mines; in other mines and quarries the legislation was the Metalliferous Mines Regulation Act 1872 and the Quarries Act 1894. In 1909 and again in 1938 Royal Commissions conducted general inquiries into safety in coal mines, as opposed to the specialised post-accident inquiries which had inspired most of the legislative activity for this industry. The principal Act is now the Mines and Quarries Act 1954.

However, the pattern of accident, inquiry, legislation was not to be ended; the Aberfan coal tip catastrophe led to an inquiry and the Mines and Quarries (Tips) Act 1969 to amend the provisions of the principal Act, giving inspectors jurisdiction over coal tips in the interests of public safety. The 1954 Act has survived the Health and Safety at Work Act 1974, but like the Factories Act, is now less significant. The declining importance of the mining industry, the reduction of the underground workforce, and greater mechanisation have also reduced the importance of this legislation. In 1970 the mines and quarries legislation was estimated to protect a workforce of about 345,000.

19. Other regulatory legislation

The empirical approach led to a number of other statutory codes each providing safety standards for a particular group of the workforce. In addition, the principal Acts each supported a number of detailed sets of regulations. By the 1970s there were over 30 statutes and 500 sets of regulations. Apart from factories and mines other areas of employment covered were agriculture, railways, offices shops and railway premises, offshore installations and nuclear installations. The Offices Shops and Railway Premises Act 1963 covered almost as many employees as the Factories Act — 8 million; on the other hand, the Mineral Workings (Offshore Installations) Act 1971 and the Nuclear Installations Act 1965 covered two of the most hazardous operations. It was nevertheless believed that before the Health and Safety at Work Act 1974 there were at least 5 million employees who worked where there were no statutory safety standards; in this group were many employees in premises to which the public were invited such as hospitals, hotels, leisure complexes and educational premises. With hindsight 5 million is believed to be a conservative estimate.

Civil actions for breach of statutory duty

20. Primary purpose of safety legislation

The primary purpose of legislation such as that which has just been discussed is to set standards to remove or reduce the hazards which may result in personal injury. Normally these laws are enforced through the criminal courts. However, in *Groves* v. *Lord Wimborne* [1898] the civil Court of Appeal allowed a plaintiff to rely on the breach of a statutory provision to support a claim for damages.

The defendant employer had failed to comply with a statutory duty to guard certain dangerous machinery where the plaintiff was employed and as a result the plaintiff was seriously injured. The statute provided that in the event of a breach of this duty a fine not in excess of £100 could be imposed and, at the discretion of the Secretary of State, the whole or any part of this could be applied for the benefit of the injured person or his family. The provision clearly envisaged that the compensation award would become payable upon a conviction in the criminal courts. Nevertheless, the

Court of Appeal relied on the statutory provisions to find for the plaintiff in civil litigation and awarded £150. A.L. Smith LJ, in giving judgment, stated:

> ... unless it can be found from the whole purview of the Act that the legislature intended that the only remedy for a breach of the duty created by the Act should be the infliction of a fine upon the master, it seems clear to me that upon proof of such a breach of duty and of injury done to the workman, a cause of action is given to the workman against the master. . .

The Court of Appeal was apparently influenced by the difficulty which common employment created for the employee seeking damages from his employer. The doctrine was not a defence against liability for breach of statutory duty, where the obligation was imposed on the employer personally.

The possibility of using the criminal law in this manner, once admitted, was frequently tested. Judges allowed many of the provisions of the statutory codes to be used in this way, though they were somewhat reluctant to allow health and welfare, as opposed to safety provisions, to be invoked. In the twentieth century regulatory legislation usually states whether civil actions will lie.

Civil litigation on the statutory codes has provided the principal source of statutory interpretation of the words used in the codes.

The Health and Safety at Work Act 1974

21. The Robens Committee

In May 1970 the then Secretary of State for Employment appointed a select committee with the following terms of reference:

> To review the provision made for the safety and health of persons in the course of their employment ... and to consider whether any changes are needed in:
>
> (1) the scope and nature of the major relevant enactments, or
> (2) the nature and extent of voluntary action concerned with these matters . . .

This, the Robens Committee, reported in June 1972. Its succinct report found much wrong with the system and proposed a new approach to the regulatory control of occupational health and safety.

While most of the Report is concerned with making proposals for change, the first chapter, entitled 'What is Wrong with the System?' identified a number of problems which prompted the Committee to consider that the time was ripe for change.

The report noted that every year about 1,000 people were killed at their work in Great Britain and about half a million suffered injuries causing 23 million work days to be lost. Moreover, annual reports from the inspectorates showed that accidents continued to rise. Evidence suggested that new methods of production, including the greater use of chemical substances, might lead to substantial further increases in accidents and ill-health in the relatively near future.

22. Problems in the system of safety legislation

In the Committee's view the most important single reason for accidents at work was apathy. They noted:

> . . . safety is mainly a matter of the day-to-day attitudes and reactions of the individual, . . . if individual experience is not in the normal course conducive to safety awareness, then safety awareness must be deliberately fostered. . .

In looking at the pattern of existing safety legislation, the Committee identified the following matters as militating against safety awareness — many of these defects being caused by the piecemeal development of the system:

(a) *There was too much law*. People thought of safety legislation as detailed provisions imposed by external agencies: they failed to appreciate that the primary responsibility for doing something about work-related accidents and ill-health lay with those who created the risks and those who worked with them.

(b) *The law was defective*. It was badly structured and had an unsatisfactory complexity.

(c) *The law was primarily concerned with physical circumstances*, such as the safeguarding of machinery. It paid too little attention to attitudes and the organisational systems within which people worked.

(d) *The fragmentation of administrative jurisdictions.* Law enforcement was divided between five government departments — in addition there was extensive participation by local authorities.

23. Solutions to the problems

Propositions emerging in the body of the report were:

(a) The criminal process ought to be reserved for cases where there had been a wilful or reckless disregard for safety.
(b) Legislation should impose duties upon employers for the protection of employees and other workers and the general public.
(c) Workers should know of the hazards of their workplace and be consulted about the introduction of and monitoring of safe systems.
(d) The civil action for breach of statutory duty did not assist with accident prevention: fear of civil liability inhibited employers in post-accident investigation and subsequent updating of systems.
(e) Despite its weight and complexity, the law neither gave protection to all employed persons, nor covered all hazardous situations within workplaces which were within the ambit of the regulatory codes.

The committee concluded its survey of what was wrong with the system with the following statement:

> The most fundamental conclusion to which our investigations have led us is this. There are severe practical limits on the extent to which progressively better standards of safety and health at work can be brought about through negative regulation by external agencies. We need a more effectively self-regulating system.

The new approach, of a broad legislative framework of general duties, imposing more positive responsibility on those at the workplace to devise safe systems of work, was to be known as the 'Robens Philosophy'. The publication of the Report was soon followed by the Health and Safety at Work Act 1974, which largely adopted the Robens philosophy.

24. 1974 and beyond

The Health and Safety at Work Act 1974 was intended as framework legislation on which future regulatory control could be based. It now also provides a vehicle through which European Community initiatives are incorporated into UK law.

Progress test 3

1.   Explain the importance of the following cases:

(a) *Smith* v. *Baker*;   (8)
(b) *Wilsons & Clyde Coal Company Ltd* v. *English*;   (6)
(c) *Groves* v. *Wimborne*.   (20)

2.   Why is Parliament sometimes reluctant, even today, to introduce regulatory legislation?   (16)

3.   When, and in what context, were the first government inspectors appointed?   (17)

4.   What Act of Parliament prohibited the employment of women underground in mines?   (18)

5.   Why was the development of health and safety legislation described as 'empirical'?   (17)

6.   What major faults did the Robens Committee find with the regulatory system which had developed by 1970?   (22)

7.   What did the Robens Committee consider to be the major cause of accidents?   (22)

8.   What did the Robens Committee consider to be the solution to the problem?   (23)

Part two

Framework for occupational health and safety

4
Framework legislation for occupational health and safety

1. Introduction

This chapter will describe the purposes of the Health and Safety at Work etc. Act 1974 and outline its provisions. It will also describe the relationship between it and other relevant statutory provisions. Finally it will outline the provisions of the EC's Framework Directive and the UK response to them.

The general duties, regulation making powers and enforcement provisions of the 1974 Act will be dealt with in greater detail in subsequent chapters. These provisions will then also be related to the regulations intended to achieve compliance with the Framework Directive.

2. Background to UK framework legislation

A principal recommendation of the Robens Committee was that:

> There should be a new, comprehensive Act dealing with safety and health at work. The Act should contain a clear statement of the general principles of responsibility for safety and health, but otherwise should be mainly enabling in character.

The Committee reported in June 1972, the Health and Safety at Work Act 1974 (hereafter called the 1974 Act), which received the Royal Assent on 31 July 1974, was passed to implement that recommendation.

The Act was intended, in the Robens philosophy, to be a framework, or enabling Act, i.e. it introduced a broad and general system for the provision of regulatory control of the workplace, while enabling further detailed arrangements to be made as, with the passage of time, changing circumstances might require.

The Health and Safety at Work Act 1974

3.   The purposes of the legislation

In its long title the 1974 Act is described as:

> An Act to make further provision for securing the health, safety and welfare of persons at work, for protecting others against risks to health or safety in connection with the activities of persons at work, for controlling the keeping and use and preventing the unlawful acquisition, possession and use of dangerous substances, and for controlling certain emissions into the atmosphere;. . .

4.   The arrangement of the Act

In order to achieve its purposes the Act is divided into four Parts but this book will mainly be concerned with Part I. Indeed Part III (ss.61–76) which makes provision for building regulations is only marginally related to occupational health and safety and may explain the inclusion of the word 'etc.' in the short title of the Act. Part II (ss.55–60) is entirely concerned with the functions and responsibilities of the Employment Medical Advisory Service and Part IV (ss.77–85) provides for amendment of certain earlier statutes and the extent, application and commencement of the Act itself.

Part I is entitled 'Health, Safety and Welfare in Connection with Work, and Control of Dangerous Substances and Certain Emissions into the Atmosphere'. Within this Part the following matters are covered:

ss.2–9	General duties
ss.10–14	The Health and Safety Commission and the Health and Safety Executive
ss.15–26	Health and safety regulations, approved codes of practice and appointment and powers of inspectors
ss.27–28	Obtaining and disclosure of information
ss 29–32	Special provisions relating to agriculture
ss.33–42	Provisions as to offences
ss.43–54	Financial provisions, application to the Crown and interpretation provisions

The Act contains a number of Schedules some of which relate to matters covered in Part I: of particular importance are Schedule I (Existing Enactments which are Relevant Statutory Provisions) and Schedule 3 (Subject-Matter of Health and Safety Regulations).

5. Objectives of Part I

The first (preliminary) section of the 1974 Act sets out the purposes that Part I is intended to fulfil giving helpful guidance to all those who have to implement the Act — from Secretary of State to employers — as to the meaning of its provisions. Section 1 states:

(1) The provisions of this Part shall have effect with a view to —

    (a) securing the health, safety and welfare of persons at work;

    (b) protecting persons other than persons at work against risks to health or safety arising out of or in connection with the activities of persons at work;

    (c) controlling the keeping and use of explosive or highly flammable or otherwise dangerous substances, and generally preventing the unlawful acquisition, possession and use of such substances; and

    (d) controlling the emission into the atmosphere of noxious or offensive substances from premises of any class prescribed for the purposes of this paragraph.

The Offshore Safety Act 1992, ss. 1 and 2 add to these purposes matters relating to safety on offshore installations and offshore and onshore pipelines.

Thus, while the primary focus of the Act is upon the health and safety of employees, the Act has wider purposes, aiming to protect workers who are not employees and the public.

6. Health, safety and welfare

Rather surprisingly, the concepts, health, safety and welfare, which are central to the purpose of the 1974 Act, are not defined within the Act. Putting the words health and safety in the context of the purposes of the Act the words may reasonably be supposed to mean without risk of personal injury. Since, however, the purpose of the legislation is the prevention of personal injury, a person may well be found liable for creating or permitting a dangerous situation which might foreseeably cause injury, even though injury has not in fact been suffered: the breach of the law is in creating the hazard, or failing to protect against the hazard which has been created, rather than in causing injury.

Welfare is not emphasised in the 1974 Act: it is merely one aspect of the employers' duty to their employees (*see* s.2).

7. The general duties

Sections 2–9 of the 1974 Act impose general duties on persons for the protection of others, as broadly outlined below:

s.2   on employers for the protection of employees;

s.3   on employers for the protection of persons who are not their employees and on the self-employed for the protection of themselves and others;

s.4   on controllers of non-domestic premises for the protection of those who are not their employees but use the premises as a place of work or as a place where they may use plant or substances provided for their use there;

s.5   on the person having control of certain premises to prevent emissions from those premises into the atmosphere;

s.6   on suppliers of articles and substances for use by people at work;

s.7   on employees for their own safety and for the safety of others;

s.8   prohibits any person from interfering with anything provided in the interests of health and safety;

s.9   prohibits an employer from charging an employee for anything done or provided in pursuance of any specific legal requirement concerning safety.

Most of the above duties require the persons upon whom they are imposed to do what is *reasonably practicable* to ensure health and safety. For example, s.2(1) requires an employer:

> . . .to ensure, so far as is *reasonably practicable*, the health, safety and welfare at work of all his employees.

Section 5 — shortly to be repealed — requires the use of the *best practicable means* to secure safety.

Section 40 provides that once it has been shown that a duty or requirement has not been complied with, it is for the defendant to satisfy the court that it was not reasonably practicable, or practicable, as the case may be, to have done more to satisfy the duty or requirement. Section 40 is particularly significant because there are no other defence provisions within the 1974 Act.

8. What categories of persons are protected?

Broadly the Act is intended to provide for the health and safety of all employees, all self-employed persons and the public, but there are exceptions to this general statement. Paragraphs 9–11 below explain this further.

9. Employed and self-employed

The 1974 Act applies to both the employed and the self-employed but individual provisions of the Act may well apply to one category rather than the other. Thus s.2 is concerned with the duties of employers to their employees while s.3 includes the imposition of duties on the self-employed.

10. Other categories of workers

The Act does not necessarily impose duties on, or for the protection of, workers who are neither employees or self-employed persons. For example, charity 'workers' giving voluntary service would not be protected by ss.2 or 6, but might be covered by ss.3 and 4.

11. The general public

The duty which s.3 imposes on an employer 'to conduct his undertaking in such a way as to ensure, so far as is reasonably practicable, that persons not in his employment who may be affected thereby are not exposed to risks to their health or safety' is wide enough to cover public safety, including 'neighbourhood risks', and some regulations made under the Act, such as the Control of Industrial Major Accidents Hazards Regulations 1984, are particularly focused on public safety issues.

Section 4 imposes a duty on controllers of premises to provide for the safety of persons who use those premises as a place where they may use plant or substances provided for their use there. It is essentially an 'occupier's' duty, designed to protect persons who have no legal relationship, other than as visitors, with the 'controller' of the premises. This provision appears broad enough to provide protection to shoppers using supermarket trolleys or customers using washing machines in laundrettes.

The fact that s.2 of the Act applies to many premises to which the public resort, for example hospitals, schools, theatres or sports facilities, gives wide protection to the general public over and above the specific protections given by ss.3 and 4 because these premises will in any event have to be maintained to a high standard by the employer for the protection of persons employed or working in them.

Section 8 of the Act prohibits any person from intentionally or recklessly interfering with or misusing anything provided in the interests of health, safety or welfare 'in pursuance of any of the relevant statutory provisions'. Not only does this provision protect members of the public as well as persons at work but the the public are not exempted from the duty imposed by it.

12. General application of the Act

Section 84(1) of the 1974 Act states that Part I of the Act applies to Great Britain, i.e. England, Wales and Scotland. However, s.84(3) provides that Her Majesty may by Order in Council make provision for the Act (or parts of it) to apply in 'relation to persons, premises, work, articles, substances and other matters outside Great Britain'. An Order in Council has been made to extend the Act to offshore installations in the North Sea (The Health and Safety at Work etc. Act 1974 (Application outside Great Britain) Order) and another to provide for a comparable regulatory system in Northern Ireland (The Health and Safety (Northern Ireland) Order).

The jurisdictional limits to the application of the Act mean that unless there has been an Order in Council made under s.84(3) it will not be possible to invoke the protection of the Act for persons employed to work outside Great Britain, even though such persons may be employed by organisations operating from Great Britain and have contracts of employment made in the UK and governed by UK laws. A major practical reason for the exclusion of such workers from the protection of the Act is that inspectors appointed under the Act have no authority to inspect and institute enforcement proceedings outside the United Kingdom.

Inspectors might visit the employers' operational base in Great Britain and take action there against the employers for operating systems which endangered employees overseas; for example, faults might be found in the employer's systems of training and kitting out personnel to be sent abroad. The circumstances in which this course of action would be available would seem to be fairly limited.

13. Specific situations

Specific situations in which the Act does or does not apply are detailed further below in paragraphs **14–21**.

14. Domestic employment

Section 51 provides that nothing in Part I of the 1974 Act 'shall apply in relation to a person by reason only that he employs another, or is himself employed, as a domestic servant in a private household'.

This section does not prevent inspectors from enforcing the Act in domestic premises. It might be enforced in relation to non-domestic work carried out on such premises, and indeed the Act might be invoked following accidents caused by faulty workmanship connected with provision of public services, such as gas or electricity, to private dwellings.

15. Merchant shipping

Merchant sailors do not enjoy the protection of the 1974 Act. They are given statutory protection through the Merchant Shipping Acts. The 1974 Act will apply to certain operations on or round shipping in harbours, e.g. unloading or loading cargo, and will apply to work undertaken on ships in dry dock.

16. Crown premises

The inspectorate may enter Crown premises where persons are at work, but they cannot bring proceedings to enforce the Act against the Crown (s.48), although the Crown is under an obligation to observe the law. The inspectorate has adopted the practice of serving a 'Crown Notice' on the Crown to record circumstances where the law is not being observed in their premises.

In some situations the activity undertaken in the premises may necessitate a careful balancing of safety against security, e.g. it may be difficult to maintain the security needed in military areas or prisons while providing adequate means of escape in emergency situations. These considerations, though not confined to operations conducted by or on behalf of the Crown, are likely to be particularly relevant to the operations of the Crown.

17. Transport

The Act applies to transport of all descriptions. It will certainly be enforced in relation to transport of articles and substances (*see* s.2(2)(b)) and in premises, such as railway stations, used in connection with the provision of transport services. Passenger transportation (and carriage of goods) by ship or aircraft largely takes place outside the jurisdiction and is in any case specifically covered by other legislation. Similarly there is special legislation dealing with safety on the railways and the roads. Responsibility for enforcement of safety standards in transport by rail has now been transferred to inspectors appointed under the 1974 Act, and the Clapham Junction rail catastrophe resulted in a successful prosecution, leading to the imposition of a very heavy fine on British Rail under that Act. On the other hand, the 1974 Act is not really appropriate for dealing with unsafe driving on the public highway: it has, however, been used to deal with unsafe driving on private premises covered by the 1974 Act (e.g. factory premises) and it might be used in relation to drivers' conditions of employment (e.g. an unsafe system for loading or unloading vehicles). The occupational safety inspectorate has responsiblity for monitoring and enforcing regulations concerned with the carriage of dangerous substances by road (e.g. Dangerous Substances (Conveyance by Road in Road Tankers and Tank Containers) Regulations 1981).

18. Food safety

Food safety is covered by special legislation but the premises where food is manufactured, or where it is supplied to the public, are also covered by the 1974 Act.

19. The police force and other public services

It is questionable whether the 1974 Act applies to protect police constables, since they are neither employees nor self-employed persons. Civilians, who nowadays play an increasingly important role in supporting constables in the operation of police services, are undoubtedly within the protection of the 1974 Act. The Consultative Document on the implementation of the EC Directive on manual handling of loads recognises that to secure full implementation of the Directive special consideration will have to be given to provision of protection for the police.

Similar arguments apply in relation to the armed services: in proposals to implement EC Directives provision is made for the Secretary of State for Defence to exempt military forces from the regulations in the interests of national security.

Other public emergency services, such as those provided by firemen and ambulance crews, are within the ambit of the 1974 Act but the inherently dangerous nature of their work, not least the emphasis on public rather than personal safety, present particular problems in the application of the Act.

20. Agriculture

When the Bill which became the 1974 Act was debated in Parliament there was controversy as to whether agriculture should be included: it is in fact within the Act. It presents its own particular problems not least because of the hazards to which children are exposed on farms both at play and when working with other members of their family.

21. Factories, mines, etc.

There are many workplaces and work related situations, of which factories and mines are but two examples, which were within the ambit of protective legislation before the 1974 Act. This earlier legislation was not immediately repealed by the enactment of the 1974 Act. On the coming into force of that Act it remained in force and the establishments and situations covered became subject to two sets of regulatory legislation, that is both the detailed standards of the old law and the general duties within the new law.

Nearly 20 years later, some of the standards contained in the earlier legislation are still applicable though the penalties and the enforcement procedures are, in respect of both old and new laws, those of the 1974 Act. However, with the passage of time the old laws have become of less significance.

Moreover s.1(2) of the 1974 Act states that it is a specific intention of the new law to enable the older laws to be progressively replaced by a system of regulations and approved codes of practice to operate in association with the provisions of the 1974 Act itself. These new laws must be drafted to maintain or improve the standards established under the earlier Acts. The revision and phasing out of earlier legislation has, since the 1980s, been conducted in the context of UK responses to EC Directives.

The earlier legislation which was to be embraced by the system established by the 1974 Act is identified in Schedule 1 of the Act as 'Existing Enactments which are Relevant Statutory Provisions'. Within this schedule are listed some 30 Acts of Parliament. In the years since 1974 considerable change has in fact occurred, and there have been partial repeals of much of this legislation. The Alkali etc. Works Regulations Act has, for example, been virtually repealed and the situations covered by it are now actually, or about to be, transferred from the jurisdiction of the 1974 Act to an agency with responsibility for environmental protection (HM Inspectorate of Pollution). It is unlikely that much of this legislation will survive the implementation of the Common Market. On the other hand other areas of work not represented in this list, such as employment on railways and offshore installations, have been brought effectively within the jurisdiction of the Health and Safety Executive.

22. Interpretation

Like most contemporary statutes, the 1974 Act contains interpretation sections; in this instance they are mainly located at the end of, and refer to, Part I. They are supplemented by other relevant provisions within other parts of the statute. All of these, together with provisions within other statutes as well as case law, give guidance as to the meaning of the words used within the Act.

Among the more important interpretation provisions are those discussed in paragraphs **23–25** below.

23. 'Work' and 'at work'

Section 52(1), giving meaning to 'work' and 'at work', provides:

(a) 'work' means work as an employee or as a self-employed person;
(b) an employee is at work throughout the time when he is in the course of his employment, but not otherwise; and
(c) a self-employed person is at work throughout such time as he devotes to work as a self-employed person.

Section 52(2) enables the meaning of 'work' and 'at work' to be extended by regulations. However, s.52, like many interpretation sections, leaves questions unanswered. Some further guidance is to be found in other sections of the 1974 Act but the full meaning can only be discovered by reference to case law drawn from general employment law.

24. 'Employee' and 'self-employed'

Section 53, the general interpretation section for Part I of the 1974 Act, provides the important information that:

> 'employee' means an individual who works under a contract of employment, and related expressions shall be construed accordingly;

and:

> 'self-employed person' means an individual who works for gain or reward otherwise than under a contract of employment, whether or not he himself employs others.

These, and other definitions in the interpretation sections and related legislation are particularly important in governing the scope and width of coverage of the 1974 Act. The Health and Safety (Training for Employment) Regulations 1990 have provided that 'employee' includes trainee.

If a contract for work is not a contract of employment, but is with an individual worker, that worker is likely to be a self-employed person, although there are yet other relationships under which work is performed. For example, some persons work under contracts which make them agents for principals. Others, notably policemen, have a special status as 'office holders'.

25. Service contracts

A contract between two employing organisations under which one organisation is to supply labour to, or provide a service for, or work in cooperation with, the other organisation is within the ambit of s.3 of the 1974 Act, which makes provision for one employer to have regard for the health and safety of the other employer's employees. This incidentally is one of the most important sections of the 1974 Act given the importance of ensuring cooperation between employing organisations if safe systems are to be identified, installed and maintained.

26. Administration and inspection

The 1974 Act made radical changes in the arrangements for administration, management, enforcement and development of occupational health and safety law. Section 10 provides for the establishment of two bodies corporate — the Health and Safety Commission (HSC) and the Health and Safety Executive (HSE) — and authorises their powers and functions. The creation of a Commission with responsibility for health and safety, and no other responsibilities, was a major innovation. Previously safety responsibilities had been shared by a number of government departments. Allocating overall responsibility to a specialist commission was calculated to raise the profile of the problem of achieving and maintaining improved working conditions.

The Health and Safety Executive, as its name implies, is the body responsible for putting policy into operation. High in priority among the functions of the Health and Safety Executive are making provision for the appointment of inspectors and monitoring that there is compliance with the provisions of the 1974 Act and other relevant statutory provisions.

27. Regulation-making powers

An important feature of the 1974 Act is the very wide and general powers which it gives to the Secretary of State to make regulations to implement the general duties, or more widely, the general purposes (as set out in s.1(1)) of Part I of the Act (s.15). Schedule 3 of the 1974 Act sets out some of the purposes for which regulations may be made, but s.15(2) in referring to the Schedule makes it clear that it is not an exhaustive list. Section 1(2), expanding on the general purposes of the Act, suggests an intention that in due course the 1974 Act and regulations made subsequent to it should constitute the sole source of occupational health and safety legislation. This intention is rapidly moving towards fulfilment as EC Directives provide the momentum for reviewing the scope and standards of the older UK laws.

It is clear from s.15(3) that, although the general duties may be qualified by the words *reasonably practicable*, regulations may be made to stricter standards, and this is so even if they are expressly related to a particular general duty which is so qualified.

28. Codes of practice and other guidance

Regulations should not be confused with approved codes of practice: the HSC is authorised to issue such codes for the purpose of providing practical guidance with respect to the provisions of the general duties (s.16). In contrast to regulations, compliance with a code is not mandatory so no person may be prosecuted merely for failure to observe a code, but a code may be used in evidence in criminal proceedings for breach of a relevant statutory provision.

The HSE issues guidance on how to comply with the law. Guidance notes do not have any legal significance, but can be of significant practical value and can give insight into the HSE's policy. For example, in connection with their 'Guidance Note: *Training and standards of competence for users of chainsaws in agriculture, aboriculture and forestry*' the HSE expressed the opinion that in order to comply with ss.2 and 3 of the 1974 Act employers and self-employed persons needed to ensure that chainsaw users had adequate training and a certificate of competency. Often regulations are published with both a supporting code of practice and guidance. For example, the Safety Representatives and Safety Committees Regulations 1977 has an accompanying code of practice and two sets of guidance notes.

29. Sanctions and enforcement

The 1974 Act, like earlier occupational health and safety legislation, is rooted in the criminal law. Section 33 provides that it is an offence to break any of the duties imposed by the Act or regulations made under the Act, and that it is also an offence to contravene any requirement imposed by an inspector, or to obstruct an inspector (or indeed other persons) in the performance of the duties imposed upon them by the Act or regulations made under it. The 1974 Act differs from earlier occupational health and safety legislation in two respects: first it creates 'either way' offences under which prosecutions may lead to trial upon indictment in the Crown Court. Secondly, it empowers inspectors to serve notices rather than invoke the criminal law. Notices may be served on persons, who, in the inspector's judgment, are either breaking a duty expressly imposed upon them or are otherwise responsible for a situation entailing a risk of serious personal injury. Notices have proved a useful means by which inspectors can improve workplace health and safety without resorting to prosecution.

30. Worker participation

The Robens Committee was firmly of the view that higher safety standards could only be achieved by cooperation between employers and employees. The legislation authorised the making of regulations to set up a system for the introduction of employee safety representatives with whom the employer would be required to consult on safety matters. The Safety Representatives and Safety Committees Regulations 1977 empowered recognised trade unions to appoint safety representatives.

31. Relationship of the Act with other UK legislation

The 1974 Act from its inception embraced that substantial portion of earlier occupational health and safety legislation which was identified by the Act as 'relevant statutory provisions', and the HSE have more recently been given further responsibilities in relation to industry (e.g. the offshore petroleum industry) and transport (e.g. railways) in situations where the 1974 Act was not originally the principal legislation.

Nevertheless there remain many matters which impinge upon occupational health and safety, such as public health and road safety, where the principal legislation is not within the list of relevant statutory provisions, and the legislation caters for situations where the HSE has no real authority. In some of these situations, for example shops (including those which sell food), the process of inspection and enforcement is simplified because authority has been granted to inspectors, other than those directly employed by the Health and Safety Executive, to enforce both the relevant statutory provisions and other legislation, such as the Public Health Acts. Other legislation, like the Road Traffic Acts, is part of the general criminal law, monitored and enforced by the police, and offences — certainly those committed on the highway — will not be investigated by the HSE.

However, the boundaries between areas of responsibility may sometimes be blurred. The HSE may, for example, have to investigate motor vehicle accidents which occur on factory premises. Similarly the boundaries between environmental protection and occupational health and safety are particularly

unclear in situations where workplace activities may endanger
public health.

EC Framework Directive

32. Relationship between the UK statutory framework and EC requirements

On 12 June 1989 the Council of the European Community
adopted a Framework Directive on the introduction of measures
to encourage improvements in the safety and health of workers at
work. This Directive stipulated implementation of its provisions
in Member States of the Community not later than 31 December
1992.

The provisions of the Directive were broadly similar to the
1974 Act. Indeed it might have been argued that the 1974 Act
implicitly covered the matters dealt with in the Directive.
Nevertheless, in the autumn of 1991, a consultative document was
published proposing the Health and Safety (General Provisions)
Regulations, and an accompanying approved code of practice, to
spell out explicitly the general provisions of the 1974 Act in such
a way that it could not be doubted that the UK was honouring the
Directive.

Since 1974 the UK system has been one in which a very broad
statutory framework is supplemented by detailed regulations to
provide for specific problems, albeit problems common to most
work situations. These general regulations will sit uneasily
between the two familiar levels of provision, giving some flesh to
the general provisions of the Act itself, while falling short of
prescribing standards for control of particular hazards.

33. General provisions of the Framework Directive

The provisions of the Directive concern general principles for
the prevention of occupational risks, the protection of safety and
health, the elimination of risk and accident factors, the informing,
consulting (with balanced participation in accordance with
national laws and/or practices) and training of workers and their
representatives, as well as general guidelines for the implementation of these principles. The Directive is intended to set
minimum standards and is said to be without prejudice to existing

or future national and Community provisions which are more favourable to protection of the safety and health of workers (Article 1). The Directive applies to both public and private sectors of activity (Article 2).

Article 3 defines employer and worker: the latter is any person employed by an employer (thus 'worker' is not necessarily synonymous with UK 'employee').

34. General obligations of the employer under the Framework Directive

The general obligations of the employer are identified as including the prevention of occupational risks and the provision of information and training. The employer's strategy should include avoiding risks wherever possible; evaluating those which cannot be avoided; combating risks at source; adapting the work to the individual; adapting to technical progress; giving collective protective measures priority over individual protection and giving appropriate instructions to workers (Articles 5 and 6). The employer must designate one or more workers to carry out activities related to safety matters; where there are no persons within the organisation competent to do this task, the employer must enlist competent external services (Article 7).

Employers must ensure that workers and/or their representatives are provided with adequate information concerning the safety and health risks at their workplace (Article 10). Employers must consult with workers and/or their representatives on all questions relating to safety, including forward planning (Article 11). Article 12 requires employers to ensure that each worker receives adequate safety and health training.

35. General obligations of the worker under the Framework Directive

Article 13 imposes obligations on workers including the duty to inform their employer immediately of hazards.

36. Comparison between the two frameworks

The EC Directive seeks only to identify minimum standards so it does not invalidate national standards which are higher. With this proviso the following are areas in which there are similarities or differences between the Directive and what is expressly required by the 1974 Act:

(a) Both frameworks are of general application, covering almost every type of employment;

(b) The Directive seemingly makes less distinction between employees and other kinds of workers — the employing organisation has responsibilities to both.

(c) The Directive makes more explicit the employer's duty to train the worker, setting out the occasions when training is needed.

(d) The Directive requires the employer to rate 'collective' safety more highly than the safety of specific employees. If this means providing a safe working environment rather than individual protective clothing etc., it reflects the UK approach.

(e) The Directive requires employers to appoint competent persons to carry out safety management functions.

(f) The Directive envisages a greater degree of worker involvement in consultation with the employer.

(g) The 1974 Act does not expressly require the employer to assess and respond to the assessment of risk. However, regulations made under the Act, e.g. the Control of Substances Hazardous to Health Regulations 1988, do.

It is arguable that any slight mismatch between the 1974 Act and the Directive is not particularly important in view of the practice now adopted by the House of Lords (*see Pickstone* v. *Freemans plc* [1988]) and followed by other lower courts of interpreting UK law purposively, i.e. in such a way as to reflect the intentions of the EC in cases where there is apparent conflict between domestic and EC legislation.

The major mismatch, to which it would be difficult to apply a purposive interpretation, is in relation to worker participation, where the Directive seems to envisage a wider worker involvement than is currently required by UK law where statutory support for worker representation is confined to consultation with appointed representatives of recognised trade unions. The fact that the Directive permits consultation in accordance with national laws and practices may infer recognition of the principle of subsidiarity, which allows Member States to adopt their own practices rather than follow that prescribed in the EC model. On this basis the UK's somewhat narrow approach to worker involvement might lawfully survive the implementation of the Framework Directive, though it is doubtful whether the EC requirement for balanced participation would be met.

37. The UK's position

It has, however, been decided that, for the avoidance of doubt, both the 1974 Act and the UK safety representative arrangements will be supplemented by new regulations which will make explicit that the UK is complying with EC requirements. The general duties will be supplemented by special regulations of general application and separate measures will be taken to give a more general applicability to the safety representatives system than is achieved by the present Safety Representatives and Safety Committees Regulations. Steps which will be taken to widen the system of safety representation will be considered in a later chapter. The more general response to the Framework Directive will be considered below.

UK response to the Framework Directive

38. Health and Safety (General Provisions) Regulations

The Health and Safety Commission's response to the Directive has been to propose the Health and Safety (General Provisions) Regulations, to come into effect on 1 January 1993. The main thrust of these regulations is to impose obligations on employers, supplementary to the general duties in the 1974 Act. They are discussed in more detail in paragraphs **39–48** below.

39. Risk assessment

Every employer and self-employed person is to be required to assess the risks to which employees and other persons are exposed by the conduct of the undertaking. This is the paramount obligation and many of the other requirements of the regulations relate back to the findings of the risk assessment.

40. Health and safety arrangements

Every employer will be required to make, and give effect to, such arrangements as are appropriate for the effective planning, organisation, control, monitoring and review of the protective and preventive measures.

41. Health surveillance

Every employer must ensure that its employees are provided with such health surveillance as is appropriate having regard to the risks which are identified by the assessment.

42. Health and safety assistance

Every employer will be required to appoint competent persons to assist in undertaking the protective and preventive measures.

43. Procedures for serious and imminent danger

Every employer will have to set in place procedures for responding to serious and imminent dangers.

44. Information for employees

Every employer will be required to provide its employees with information about the risks to health and safety identified by the assessment.

45. Cooperation and coordination

Where two or more employers share a workplace these employers must cooperate to produce a safe system.

46. Capabilities and training

Employers must take into account the capabilities of their employees as regards health and safety and also ensure that they are provided with adequate safety training.

47. Employees' duties

Employees must use machinery etc. in accordance with any training or instruction which has been provided, and must inform the employer of any unsafe situation of which he or she is aware.

48. Temporary workers

Temporary workers must be provided with comprehensive safety information.

Progress test 4

1.   What is 'enabling legislation'?   **(2)**

2.   On whom are the general duties of the 1974 Act imposed?   **(7)**

3.   What sections of the 1974 Act protect:

(a) the self-employed;
(b) the general public?   **(9–11)**

4.   Are there any employees not covered by s.2?   **(14, 15)**

5.   What are the principal functions of:

(a) the Health and Safety Commission;
(b) the Health and Safety Executive?   **(26)**

6.   What is meant by 'relevant statutory provisions'?   **(4, 21)**

7.   What are the principal employer obligations identified by the Framework Directive?   **(34)**

8.   How does the UK propose to comply with the Framework Directive?   **(38** *et seq.***)**

5
The general duties and general principles of liability

1. Introduction

The Health and Safety at Work Act appears to contain little substantive law: this impression is deceptive. The Act was novel in that it contained no detailed regulatory standards: instead it contained very broad and general duties, which covered virtually every contingency relating to health and safety at the workplace. There was in 1974 no British precedent for this broad approach to regulation, and many doubted whether the Act could succeed in its objectives. It is interesting, however, that this regulatory technique has now been followed in other legislation e.g. the Consumer Protection Act.

This chapter will describe the general duties and analyse the general principles of liability under the 1974 Act. It will also suggest how the Health and Safety (General Provisions) Regulations, which are intended to ensure compliance with the Framework Directive, are likely to relate to particular general duties. In the two subsequent chapters the individual duties will be considered in greater depth. There is little case law interpreting these duties. This is not unusual, for regulatory legislation which is largely enforced in magistrates courts and (apart from the Road Traffic Acts!) is rarely the subject of appeal.

The general duties

2. Under the 1974 Act

The general duties in the 1974 Act, in accordance with the

purposes of the Act (s.1(1)), relate to all persons at work and the protection of others who might be injured by the activities of persons at work. They also aim to ensure that all persons, whatever their status, who are associated with the workplace, and the activities carried out and the articles and substances used there, bear some responsibility for health and safety in relation to that workplace. It is as if the legislature regarded the workplace as a stage and ensured that each person who walked on stage had some role to perform. Alternatively, perhaps the legislature modelled these duties on the civil law of negligence in which a general duty to take reasonable care rests on persons who are in sufficient proximity to each other for them to be deemed to be 'neighbours'.

3. Comparison with the EC Framework Directive

The EC Directive is narrower than the 1974 Act; it is concerned only with the safety and health of workers. Thus it focuses on the relationship between employer and worker but defines the employment relationship widely (Article 3). It is not concerned with the other roles which the employing organisation may fulfil, such as occupier of premises or manufacturer of articles and substances.

4. The duty of employers to employees

The 1974 Act emphasises that employers have great responsibilities for establishing and maintaining the safety of workplaces. Thus s.2(1) of the Act imposes a general duty on the employer:

> to ensure, so far as is reasonably practicable, the health, safety and welfare at work of all his employees.

This is the core provision of the Act, placed early in the order of arrangement of the duties, and spelt out in considerably more detail than any of the other duties. The priority given to the employers' duty to protect their employees is in the traditional pattern of occupational health and safety legislation. It also reflects the legislature's statement of intent in s.1(1)(a) of the Act, where the first and foremost of the intentions of the Act is said to be 'securing the health, safety and welfare of persons at work'.

The breadth and generality of the duty distinguishes it from earlier statutes with their narrow standards. Moreover, in contrast to earlier legislation, this duty, as spelled out in s.2(2), is at least as much concerned with human behaviour as with the physical environment in which persons are employed.

5. Duties of the employer to non-employees

Section 3 of the Act also imposes a general duty on employers, but in this case the duty is imposed in respect of the conduct of their undertakings for the protection of persons other than their employees. The general duty in s.3(1) requires the employer:

> to conduct his undertaking in such a way as to ensure so far as is reasonably practicable, that persons not in his employment who may be affected thereby are not thereby exposed to risks to their health or safety.

This duty aims to protect at least two categories of persons. First, it serves to protect workers, such as the employees of another employer, or the self-employed; the duty is particularly significant where two or more organisations are working in proximity on the same or related projects, e.g. on a construction site. Secondly, it requires the employer to have regard for the safety of members of the public.

6. Duty of the employer not to charge for safety measures

Section 9 is barely a general duty, but is contained in that part of the Act which sets out the general duties. It prohibits the employer from:

> levying or permitting to be levied on any employee of his any charge in respect of anything done or provided in pursuance of any specific requirement of the relevant statutory provisions.

This clearly prohibits any charge being made, for example for personal protective equipment, such as safety boots, glasses or hard hat which is specifically required by statute. It is not self-evident that it actually prohibits making a charge for any other safety measure which the employer regards as a practical requirement if a safe system of work is to be achieved; for example, the employer might wish to make it a work rule that safety glasses must be worn not only by persons working on the production process but also by any person passing through the production area. Whatever the extent of s.9, if the employer's assessment that the protection is necessary to the operation of a safe system is correct, it seems unlikely that an employer would be deemed to have done all that was reasonably practicable to achieve that system if he issued a ruling about the use of protective equipment expecting individual employees to provide it for themselves.

7.   Regulations in response to EC Directive

The principal obligations which the Framework Directive seeks to impose upon employers, namely to evaluate and combat risks (Article 6), to inform workers of the risks to which they are exposed (Article 10) and to provide safety training to workers (Article 12), bridge ss.2 and 3 of the UK Act. The proposed UK Regulations (i.e. Health and Safety (General Provisions) Regulations) reflect the particular obligations the Directive seeks to impose on employers, but for the most part impose obligations on employers only in respect of their own employees (e.g. Regulation 5, health surveillance; Regulation 8, provision of information; Regulation 10, training). However, Regulation 3, introduced in order to comply with the EC requirement for risk assessment, is so worded as to cover the relationships envisaged by both ss.2 and 3 of the 1974 Act. The draft Regulation 3(1) proposes:

(1) Every employer shall adequately assess —

   (a)   the risks to the health and safety of his employees to which they are exposed whilst they are at work; and

   (b)   the risks to the health and safety of persons not in his employment arising out of or in connection with the conduct by him of his undertaking...

By including public safety it goes beyond the Directive's requirements.

Regulation 9, which requires cooperation and coordination when two or more employers share a workplace, builds on s.3 of the 1974 Act by requiring the employer to:

inform the other employers concerned of the risks to their employees' health and safety arising out of or in connection with the conduct by him of his undertaking.

Regulation 12 relates to temporary workers and is, strictly speaking, intended to implement the Directive on temporary workers rather than the Framework Directive. It imposes obligations on employers to provide information to temporary workers and to ensure they are trained for the tasks required of them. It is intended to ensure that workers who are not full-time employees receive the protection which is provided by the regulations. The combined effects of Regulations 9 and 12 should ensure (given a purposive interpretation) that the narrow concept of employment with which UK law is familiar, does not prevent the Directive applying, as it is intended, to the entire workforce.

8. Duties of those in control of premises

Section 4 imposes duties upon the controller (in effect the occupier) of premises. Since the duty does not apply to domestic premises, it is in practice often imposed on a corporate body. The section recognises that control of premises may be shared and provides that any one controller is only to be liable in relation to those matters which are within his control. This duty, while primarily an occupiers' duty, may well fall upon a body which is also an employer. The duty is a complex one. It is a duty to do 'what it is *reasonable* for a person in his position to do to ensure, so far as is *reasonably practicable* that the premises, all means of access thereto or egress therefrom and any plant or substance in the premises, or provided for use there, is safe and without risks to health'.

The duty is owed to persons who are not employed by the controller but who go to the premises as a place of work or to use plant or substances provided for their use there. The duty applies equally to persons other than employers, for example a landlord, who has some right of control over the premises without employing anyone there, e.g. the occupiers of an exhibition hall, let out to exhibitors with cleaning and catering services provided by sub-contractors.

9. Duties with regard to emissions into the atmosphere

Section 5 imposes a general duty on persons in control of certain premises in relation to harmful emissions into the atmosphere. This section straddles the boundary between occupational safety and environmental protection: the Environmental Protection Act 1990 acknowledges this and makes arrangements for it to be repealed and its substance put more firmly into legislation whose primary purpose is protection of the environment. The duty in s.5 requires the controller of premises to use the best practicable means to prevent emissions into the atmosphere of harmful substances.

10. Duties of those supplying goods

Section 6 imposes duties on those supplying goods to the workplace. Section 6 predated, but now marches with, consumer safety legislation: it imposes duties upon designers, manufacturers, importers or suppliers of articles for use at work and is matched by similar duties on persons manufacturing, importing or supplying substances. Broadly it is the duty of these persons to ensure, so far as is reasonably practicable, that the articles or substances supplied are as safe as is reasonably practicable for use at the workplace. The Consumer Protection Act aimed to place a similar duty on sellers of dangerous goods, and, on the enactment of the latter legislation, the opportunity was taken to amend s.6, in order to bring consumer safety and this aspect of occupational safety broadly into line, while updating occupational safety law in the light of experience.

Personal duties

11. General

While the main thrust of the 1974 Act is against the corporate entity in one or other of its capacities (i.e. employer, occupier of premises, manufacturer and/or trader) it also imposes duties upon individuals. These are discussed in more detail in paragraphs 12–18.

12. Duty to take reasonable care

Section 7 of the 1974 Act imposes duties upon each individual employee to take reasonable care while at work for the health and safety of himself and other persons. This is a much wider duty on employed persons than any found in earlier legislation which has either proscribed wilful wrongdoing or imposed relatively narrow duties on certain persons with particular qualifications and/or responsibilities. Regulation 11 of the General Provisions Regulations supplements s.7 by spelling out that employees must not use things such as machinery or dangerous substances other than in accordance with any instruction and training respecting their use which has been provided by the employer. Nor must employees interfere with any things which their employers have provided. Regulation 11(2) requires employees to inform their employer, or the employer's safety specialist, where there is a dangerous situation, or a shortcoming in the employers' safety arrangements, which affects them personally.

Most managers will be employees and so also subject to these duties.

13. Duties of the self-employed

While s.3 is a duty imposed primarily upon employers it recognises that there are some business organisations which consist only of the self-employed proprietor. It therefore imposes on the self-employed person the same duty to ensure the safety of others, so far as is reasonably practicable, as is imposed on the employer (s.3(2)). The self-employed are also required by s.3 to take care for themselves.

Regulation 3(2) of the General Provisions Regulations imposes on the self-employed virtually the same duty to assess risks as regulation 3(1) places on employers.

14. Personal and corporate liability

Thus the 1974 Act, like certain other regulatory legislation (e.g. seat-belt provisions of road traffic legislation), does not allow a person to escape the burden of compliance where no other person is at risk. In the case of the 1974 Act, however, it is comparatively rare for the individual worker to be solely liable: it is likely, though not inevitable, that if an individual worker is creating a hazard, there will be an organisation — either an employer or a contractor — who is at fault for tolerating the presence of this hazard. If this is so, that organisation may also face prosecution. For example, if a worker is not using plant and equipment according to proper safety routines, then the organisation is likely to be at fault for permitting this misuse.

15. Duty not to interfere with safety precautions

Section 8 imposes a duty on all persons not intentionally or recklessly to interfere with or misuse anything provided in the interests of health, safety or welfare in pursuance of any of the relevant statutory provisions. This duty could be invoked against members of the public as well as persons at work, e.g. against a student who took a guard off a machine in a training workshop, a hospital patient who interfered with some electrical equipment, or a customer in a department store who removed an emergency exit sign. The limitation on the scope of the provision is not on the classes of person who might be liable but on the conduct which is proscribed, i.e. liability is only for reckless or intentional interference. This leaves questions as to whether there could be liability for well-motivated but dangerous interference, e.g. switching off a fire alarm believed to be too sensitive to be reliable.

Liability is only for interference with something which has been provided specifically to comply with safety legislation. Thus not every dangerous practical joke (e.g. putting a mouse trap in the drawer of an office desk) or theft of valuable equipment (e.g. a word processor) would necessarily create liability under this section.

16. The actual offender

The 1974 Act contains complex provisions such as are commonly found in regulatory legislation to enable an actual wrongdoer to be brought to justice where a duty has been placed upon one person, but the breach in law has been caused by another. Paragraphs **17** and **18** below give further details.

17. Offences caused by others

Section 36 provides that where the commission by any person of an offence under any of the relevant statutory provisions is due to the act or default of another person that other person may be charged with and convicted of the offence whether or not proceedings are taken against the other person. For example, if an employee (or the student in the example given above in relation to s.8) took a guard off a machine, the presence of the unguarded machine could render the employer in breach of s.2 and/or s.3 of the 1974 Act. The person who had removed the guard might be personally prosecuted by virtue of s.36, but this prosecution would not preclude the employer from being prosecuted also, and

convictions might be secured against both person and organisation
if the circumstances were such as to show they were both at fault
— the individual for doing the wrongful act, the organisation for
failing to identify and rectify the situation.

18. Directors' liability

Section 37, a 'directors' liability' provision, enables liability to
be imposed upon board-level managers where the corporate body
is in breach of its duties. The section may only be invoked against
the most senior management, persons who, as it were, represent
the *alter ego* (the very brain) of the corporation. Whereas s.36 is
aimed primarily at the person who by *positive action* brings about
an unsafe situation, s.37 is particularly appropriate for situations
where senior managers have *omitted* to set up a safe system or to
curb unlawful behaviour — allowing wrongs to go unchecked
through connivance or ignorance based on neglect.

Section 37(1) provides:

> Where an offence under any of the relevant statutory provisions
> committed by a body corporate is proved to have been committed
> with the consent or connivance of, or to have been attributable to
> any neglect on the part of, any director, manager, secretary or other
> similar officer of the body corporate or a person who was purporting
> to act in any such capacity, he as well as the body corporate shall be
> guilty of that offence and shall be liable to be proceeded against and
> punished accordingly.

A person may be liable under this section even though he does not
in fact have the management position he holds himself out as
having. Also the section assumes a conviction under this section
will be in addition to, rather than an alternative to, a conviction
against the corporation.

Section 37(2) provides that if the affairs of a corporation are
managed by its members such members may be prosecuted as if
they were directors.

Liability under both ss.36 and 37 lies in relation not only to
breaches of the general duties under the 1974 Act itself but also in
relation to breaches of duties in other relevant statutory
provisions.

Application of the law

19. Criteria for prosecution

It is now necessary to consider what the prosecution has to prove to establish that the accused is guilty of an offence, and what the defendant has to establish in order to escape liability. This is partly a matter of determining the relevance of the defendant's attitude (or state of mind — see paragraphs **21–28** below), and partly a question of identifying the standard of performance the law requires.

20. Standard of performance required

The majority of the duties under the 1974 Act — i.e. ss.2, 3, 4, 6 — require the person upon whom they are imposed to ensure health and safety at the workplace to the extent that is *reasonably practicable*. However, s.4 is complicated by the further qualification that a controller of premises has to take such measures as is *reasonable for a person in his position* to ensure the premises are as safe as is *reasonably practicable*. Section 5 requires *the best practicable means* to be taken by the controller of premises to prevent emission into the atmosphere of noxious or offensive substances. Section 7 requires the employee to take *reasonable care*. Section 8 imposes liability only on the person who *intentionally or recklessly* interferes. Section 9 imposes on the employer an *absolute prohibition* on raising levies to pay for safety measures. The duties imposed by the Health and Safety (General Provisions) Regulations are strict.

These standards are considered further in paragraphs **29–34** below.

Defendant's state of mind

21. Common law rules

The common law rule is *actus non facit reum nisi mens sit rea*, i.e. a wrongful act does not make a person guilty unless their mind is also blameworthy. Thus the common law imposes on the prosecution the burden of proving both *the wrongful state of affairs (actus reus)* and the state of mind in which the wrong was committed (*mens rea*) in order to establish that a defendant has committed an offence. If both elements of the offence cannot be proved then the prosecution has not made out a case. The following paragraphs explore this aspect further.

22. *Mens rea* in statutes

Section 8 of the 1974 Act, which states that liability depends on proof that the accused had intentionally or recklessly interfered with something provided in the interests of health, safety or welfare, is, at least as far as the word intentionally is concerned, in the tradition of the common law *mens rea* offences, requiring the prosecution to establish that the accused actually intended to interfere. The courts have interpreted 'intention' as being synonomous with 'aim'. In *R* v. *Mohan* [1976], the Court of Appeal defined intention as:

> a decision to bring about, insofar as it lies within the accused's power, [a particular consequence], no matter whether the accused desired that consequence of his act or not.

23. Reckless

The meaning of the word reckless is more problematic. It has been considered by the courts on a number of occasions in the context of a number of statutes, and it is not easy to reconcile the various judicial statements. It is clear that a person is reckless when taking an unjustifiable risk. The doubt is whether the test of what is unjustifiable is an objective or a subjective test. That is to say, is it unjustifiable because reasonable people would think it unjustifiable (the objective test), or is it unjustifiable because the defendant personally foresaw that he was taking a risk (the subjective test). For example, applying the subjective test might exonerate someone of limited intelligence who took what to normal people might appear an unjustifiable risk.

To some extent the case law varies according to the statute under consideration. It is arguable that s.8 of the 1974 Act has much the same purpose as s.1 of the Criminal Damage Act 1971 which makes it a criminal offence for someone intentionally or recklessly to destroy property belonging to another. In relation to this section the courts have in recent years applied the subjective test, using what is now known as the *Caldwell* test.

In *R* v. *Caldwell* [1982] Caldwell set fire to a hotel, when he was drunk, in pursuit of a grievance he had against the owner. Caldwell claimed that he was so drunk that he did not know what he was doing. While disallowing a defence of being drunk, the House of Lords nevertheless chose to give an explanation of the meaning of recklessness as used in s.1(1) of that Act. Lord Diplock, with whom two other of their Lordships agreed, said:

> In my opinion, a person charged with an offence under s.1(1) of the 1971 Act is 'reckless as to whether or not property would be destroyed or damaged' if (1) he does an act which in fact creates an obvious risk that property will be destroyed or damaged and (2) when he does the act he either has not given any thought to the possibility of there being any such risk or has recognised that there was some risk involved and has none the less gone on to do it.

In *R* v. *Savage* (1991), the House of Lords considered *Caldwell* in the context of s.20 of the Offences Against the Person Act 1861. They held that under s.20 the prosecution had to prove either the defendant intended, or that he actually foresaw, his act would cause harm.

24. Ambiguity in statutory provisions

Where the legislature's intentions are less clearly stated, it is necessary to refer to the rule that statutes should be interpreted as narrowly as possible, on the presumption that they do not intend to change the common law. Applying this rule in *Sweet* v. *Parsley* [1969] (a case concerning unlawful possession of drugs) the House of Lords took the view that, even if a statutory provision is silent as to whether the prosecution has to establish the defendant's *mens rea*, the normal rules of statutory interpretation imply the necessity for the defendant to be shown to have had a guilty mind, if the offence is an indictable one with a heavy penalty. It is arguable that the *Sweet* v. *Parsley* ruling should be applied to offences under the 1974 Act when they are tried upon indictment, but it may be that proof of *mens rea* is only required if the offence is one which carries imprisonment.

25. Strict liability

Traditionally, regulatory legislation dealing with matters such as occupational health and safety has deviated from the common law rules by imposing strict liability, i.e. the prosecution has been required only to show that the accused's act or omission was wrongful in order to discharge the burden of proving an offence has been committed.

The Factories Act 1961 had within it a number of duties which were of strict liability, the best known of which, s.14 (1), provided: 'Every dangerous part of any machinery . . . shall be securely fenced . . .'.

Courts to some extent reduced the duty by finding that the machinery was not dangerous and therefore did not require a fence. Cases like *Hindle* v. *Birtwhistle* [1897] established that for the purposes of s.14(1) machinery was only to be regarded as dangerous if it were a reasonably foreseeable cause of injury to anybody acting in a way in which a human being may be reasonably expected to act in circumstances which may be reasonably expected to occur. Thus what might otherwise have been regarded as an offence of little less than absolute liability was reduced to one of strict liability, by making reasonable foresight of danger a criterion of liability.

26. Absolute liability
Offences of absolute liability are rarely found in English law. An offence is of absolute liability if it is one in which the defence has no answer once the prosecution has made out a prime facie case.

Arguably s.9 of the 1974 Act is in this category.

27. Defences
Sometimes the legislation expressly gives certain defences to offences of strict liability: these can be invoked by a defendant to answer the prosecution case. For example, s.161 of the Factories Act 1961 enabled a person charged with an offence to lay information alleging that someone else was the actual offender; then, if the offence was established against the person charged, that person might escape liability if he could prove to the satisfaction of the court:

(a) that he has used all due diligence to enforce the execution of this Act . . . ; and

(b) that the said other person had committed the offence in question without his consent, connivance, or wilful default.

Defence sections containing the phrases 'used all due diligence' and 'without his consent, connivance, or wilful default' were often written into regulatory statutes, and are still found in regulations. There is no such defence provision in the 1974 Act.

However, the General Provisions Regulations introduce strict liability offences without a 'due diligence' defence. It will therefore be interesting to learn whether courts will mitigate them by introducing concepts like reasonable foresight as a prerequisite of liability. For example, Regulation 3(1), the risk assessment provision, requires an employer adequately to assess risks: possibly foreseeability and adequacy might be related concepts, i.e. to be adequate an assessment would need only to identify foreseeable risks.

28. Reasonably practicable and state of mind

The fact that all the general duties are qualified by expressions such as *reasonably practicable* suggests they are not pitched at a standard of strict liability. But it has been held that these duties are strict, subject only to the s.40 defence that it was not reasonably practicable to achieve absolute safety (*see Mailer*, below). It must follow that the prosecution can make out a case without reference to the defendant's state of mind, but, possibly the defendant could rebut a prima facie case of liability by showing a lack of intent — the reverse of the normal rule of criminal law. Moreover, a defendant would not succeed by establishing lack of intent if, in the view of the court, his conduct had, objectively considered, been negligent or lacking in foresight. There is no such uncertainty concerning the General Provisions Regulations whose duties are strict.

Standard of defendant's conduct

29. Reasonably practicable

This expression, which is used so frequently to qualify the standard of performance required by the duties under the 1974 Act, was previously used to qualify some of the duties in the Factories Acts and Mines and Quarries Acts. Judicial statements as to the meaning of the expression were given in civil cases for damages for breach of statutory duty. Thus in *Nimmo* v. *Alexander*

Cowan & Sons Ltd [1968], a case on the interpretation of s.29(1) of the Factories Act 1961 (safe means of access to, and safe place of, employment), the House of Lords held that, once the hazard had been established, the onus of proving that it was not *reasonably practicable* to remove it in order to comply with a statutory obligation lay on the defendant. This judicial interpretation of the onus of proof, given in a civil court, has now been placed firmly in the criminal law by s.40 of the 1974 Act. Section 40, which also applies to duties where the qualifying words are *practicable* or a duty requires the use of *the best practical* means, provides:

> In any proceedings for an offence under any of the relevant statutory provisions consisting of a failure to comply with a duty or requirement to do something so far as is practicable or so far as is reasonably practicable, or to use the best practicable means to do something, it shall be for the accused to prove (as the case may be) that it was not practicable or not reasonably practicable to do more than was in fact done to satisfy the duty or requirement, or that there was no better practicable means than was in fact used to satisfy the duty or requirement.

The Act is unclear as to what the prosecution has to establish before the burden of proof passes to the defendant. At first sight the duties are strict duties comparable to the strict duties of the earlier legislation such as the Factories Act 1961 — the comparison seems the more appropriate because the defence of 'reasonably practicable' appeared in that legislation also. The matter was considered by Lord Goff in *Mailer* v. *Austin Rover Group plc* [1989], a case concerned with the liability of controllers of premises under s.4 of the 1974 Act. In considering the meaning of 'safe and without risks to health' as used in s.4(2), Lord Goff stated:

> Counsel for the respondents submitted that, for present purposes, premises should be regarded as 'safe and without risks to health' if they are in such condition as to be unlikely to be the cause of injury, harm or risk to health to persons who are, or who may reasonably be expected to be, in them . . .
>
> This proposition I am, however, unable to accept. To me the words 'safe and without risks to health' mean prima facie, what they say, though no doubt they have to be related to the use for which the relevant premises are made available. Take the example of premises which, owing to an unknown and indeed unforeseeable defect, are in fact unsafe for such use . . . I do not for my part see how the

unforeseeable nature of the defect... can nevertheless mean that the premises . . . are safe . . . It may be that if the danger in question is not foreseeable, the defendant will not be held to be in breach of his duty; but if so, that will not be because, in the examples I have given, the premises ... are to be regarded as safe, but because the qualified nature of the duty may not give rise to any liability in the particular circumstances.

Thus his Lordship was arguing that the duties are absolute rather than strict duties, and unforseeability relates to the defence of reasonably practicable rather than to the standard of the initial duty.

Lord Goff's analysis was not expressly adopted by the remainder of the House.

30. What the defendant has to establish

Lord Goff's proposal that the defendant could escape liability by pleading that the risk was not foreseeable — presumably that it was not objectively foreseeable, rather than that the defendant personally did not foresee it — raised a previously unconsidered interpretation of the defence allowed by s.40. The usual interpretation is that the task of evaluating what is *reasonably practicable* is a cost-benefit exercise, a matter of weighing the cost of removing or controlling the hazard against the probability of injury and the likely severity of that injury. The words of Asquith LJ in *Edwards* v. *National Coal Board* [1949], spoken in the context of a civil action for breach of the duty imposed by s.102 of the Coal Mines Act 1911, are usually adopted as expressing the criteria of liability:

> 'Reasonably practicable' is a narrower term than 'physically possible', and implies that a computation must be made in which the *quantum* of risk is placed in one scale and the sacrifice involved in the measures necessary for averting the risk (whether in money, time or trouble) is placed in the other, and that, if it be shown that there is a gross disproportion between them — the risk being insignificant in relation to the sacrifice — the defendants discharge the onus upon them. Moreover, this computation falls to be made by the owner (i.e. defendant) at a point of time anterior to the accident.

The question of what was *reasonably practicable* was considered in *West Bromwich Building Society Ltd* v. *Townsend* [1983] in which the building society had an improvement notice served on it requiring it to instal bandit screens. The case was of considerable importance because it had implications for all banking premises. On appeal the High Court allowed the appeal of the building society making the point that the risk had to be weighed against the cost, which would be onerous, and suggested that the industrial tribunal had considered only whether it was physically and financially possible to erect the screens, rather than whether it was reasonably practicable to do so.

Recently in an unreported appeal, heard in an industrial tribunal against a prohibition notice, the tribunal again had to consider the cost in relation to the risk. A prohibition notice was served upon a hotel proprietor requiring certain improvements to a swimming pool. The owner complied with all but one term of the notice — a term which required that there be constant lifeguard supervision while there were bathers in the pool. The proprietor stated that the cost of full-time supervision would be in the region of £30,000 p.a. and alleged that this type of expenditure was not *reasonably practicable* in view of the small number of local users who would continue to use the pool in the off-peak season. The tribunal agreed that, when a computation was made between the degree of risk and the amount of money which would have to be spent, the term was not a reasonable one and should be removed from the notice.

31. No defence of limited means
An organisation is not able to argue that its own limited means make it impracticable for it to comply with the terms of either an improvement or a prohibition notice: the cost-benefit analysis is in relation to the risk, not the profitability, or indeed the viability, of the enterprise (*Belhaven Brewery Company Ltd* v. *McLean* [1975]).

32. Cost-benefit vs. foresight?
The cost-benefit and the foresight tests are not necessarily mutually exclusive. It is not inconceivable that a relatively cheap safety measure might be ignored because the need for it was not foreseen. For example, a poisonous fluid can easily be coloured at

small cost: it would not appear necessary to do this if it is not foreseeable that the fluid might otherwise create a hazard.

33. Best practicable means

This standard is used only in s.5 of the 1974 Act but has been used from time to time in earlier statutory provisions, such as s.157 (impracticable) of the Mines and Quarries Act 1954. While it is agreed that the defendant who is required to do what is *practicable* has to do more than one who merely has to do what is *reasonably practicable*, there is no clear judicial statement of the meaning of the expression *best practicable means*.

It is agreed that *practicable* means something other than physically possible: to be *practicable* a measure must be possible in the light of current knowledge and invention (per Parker J in *Adsett* v. *K & L Steelfounders and Engineers Ltd* [1953]). In *Jayne* v. *National Coal Board* [1963] Veale J held that 'impracticability' was a concept different from that of 'impossibility'. He said:

> . . . the latter is absolute, the former introduces at all events some degree of reason and involves at all events some regard for practice.

34. Reasonable care

The employee is required to take reasonable care for the safety of himself and of other persons while at work. The concept of *reasonable care* is more commonly associated with the civil law of negligence than with the criminal law. In civil law the term is applied to evaluate the defendant's conduct objectively: it is a matter of what other reasonable people think about the defendant's behaviour and it is immaterial what the defendant himself believed or intended. It seems that when used in the context of s.7 of the 1974 Act it is used as a yardstick of the defendant's conduct rather than in relation to the guilty intention of the defendant.

Competent persons

35. General

The general duties under the 1974 Act do not expressly require the appointment of competent persons, though it is arguable that if the employer is to set up the safe systems which the Act undoubtedly requires, then competent persons must be appointed.

36. Concept of competence

The concept of competence has been given particular significance recently because Article 7 of the EC Framework Directive requires employers to appoint competent persons 'to carry out activities related to the protection and prevention of occupational risks for the undertaking.' Furthermore, if there are not competent persons within the organisation the employer is required to 'enlist' competent external services. The Directive explains that the persons designated 'must have the necessary capabilities and the necessary means'. This Article has raised some concern among employers in the UK exactly because there is no comparable requirement expressly spelled out in the 1974 Act. The problem is addressed by the General Provisions Regulations: Regulation 6(1) requires an employer to appoint 'competent persons to assist him in undertaking the protective and preventive measures'. Regulation 6(5) envisages the possibility that persons appointed may be persons who are not employees of the organisation using their services.

There is some learning on the meaning of competency because it has been included in earlier legislation. Indeed, it has been used fairly frequently in the Factories Acts and the Mines and Quarries Acts, and associated subordinate legislation, to describe the qualifications of a person entitled to carry out periodic statutory examinations on pressure vessels, lifting machinery and the like, or, in some circumstances, to supervise safe working conditions. It is also to be found in regulations made under the 1974 Act (e.g. the Electricity at Work Regulations 1989 and the Control of Substances Hazardous to Health Regulations 1988).

37. Lack of legislative definition

The term has not hitherto been interpreted in legislation, though a Home Secretary expressed the opinion that in relation to the examination of machinery or plant the person should have such practical and theoretical knowledge and actual experience of the type of machinery or plant which he had to examine as would enable him to detect defects or weaknesses which it was the purpose of the examination to discover.

Winn J considered the concept in *Brazier* v. *Skipton Rock Company* [1962] a case arising under the Quarries (General) Regulations, 1956, Regulation 41 of which required the manager '. . . to make and ensure the efficient carrying out of arrangements to secure that every inspection . . . to be carried out or done by a competent person appointed by him is assigned to a competent person so appointed.' His Lordship expressed the opinion that experience might be as important as academic qualifications. The case was a compensation claim in which the plaintiff (appointed as the competent person), a one-eyed man, had failed to observe a hazard and had in consequence suffered personal injury. His Lordship stated, dismissing the claim:

> It sometimes seems to me that when, in courts of law, we consider the practical workings of industrial and other organisations, we tend to become somewhat academic and overlook the fact, the truth, that experience is so often of much greater value than book learning or certificates, and that a man who has been at the job for the best part of 25 years day by day watching the indications of peril to himself and his mates is at least as likely to be competent as a young man who has just come from a mining technical college.

In effect the organisation which has to appoint a competent person must exercise its judgment as to whether a particular person is suitable for the appointment. In the event that an obvious hazard is discovered, or an accident occurs which is related to the appointment, then the appointing organisation will be put on enquiry to as whether they have discharged their duty.

38. Statutory definition

Regulation 6(6) of the General Provisions Regulations will for the future provide a definition of competence. It states:

> A person shall be regarded as competent for the purposes [of the Regulation] where he has sufficient training, experience, knowledge or other qualifications to enable him properly to assist in undertaking the protective and preventive measures or, as the case may be, to undertake the protective and preventive measures without any assistance.

The identification of standards for national vocational

qualifications for personnel with safety responsibilities may clarify the meaning of 'competence' and indeed identify what is required in specific situations.

The significance of the general duties

39. Common attributes

The following attributes are shared by all the general duties:

(a) They are enforceable in their own right. The contrary argument was made, and rejected, in the Court of Appeal, criminal division, in relation to s.3(1) in *R* v. *Swan Hunter Shipbuilders Ltd* [1981].

(b) The general duties may be used to support regulations, but regulations may be made under s.15 for the general purposes of the Act without relying on a general duty.

(c) Regulations may stipulate minimum standards in relation to general duties.

(d) Regulations, and indeed particularisation of duties within the Act itself, will not exhaust the general duty. For example, s.2(2) following on from the statement made in s.2(1) of the employers' general duty to his employees, begins:

> Without prejudice to the generality of the employer's duty under the preceding subsection . . .

and then proceeds to list matters to which the general duty extends — but the preamble clearly intends that the following paragraphs (a) to (e) do not exhaust the duty in s.2(1).

(e) The duties are enforceable to ensure the control of hazards; thus liability can arise even though there has been no incident, accident or injury.

(f) The duties carry criminal sanctions, but their interpretation frequently falls to be made in appeals arising out of improvement or prohibition notices, proceedings which are not, in themselves, criminal.

(g) The duties are not intended to secure environmental protection though they may incidentally assist this in that some environmental pollution is hazardous to health.

(h) The general duties may not be used to support a civil action for compensation (s.47(1)(a)).

(i) The provisions of the Act, including the general duties, are not enforceable against the Crown (s.48), though Crown premises are not generally exempt from inspection.

(j) The similarity between the general duties and the civil law invites reference to compensation claims based on negligence to provide guidance in their interpretation. This invitation was accepted by Dunn LJ in giving judgment in the *Swan Hunter* case:

> Mr Potts, for the Crown, submitted that there was nothing revolutionary or novel in the duties imposed by ss.2 and 3 of the 1974 Act. He pointed out that before 1974 there was a duty on the main contractor to co-ordinate the operations at a place of work so as to ensure the safety not only of his own employees, but also the employees of sub-contractors. He referred us to *McArdle* v. *Andmac Roofing Co and Others* [1967] . . .
>
> His Lordship then went on to quote at some length from the judgment of Edmund Davies LJ in the civil case.

Progress test 5

1. Name the categories of persons on whom general duties are imposed. **(4–15)**

2. Which of the duties are not at the standard of what is 'reasonably practicable'? **(20)**

3. Outline the meanings which judges have given to the expression 'reasonably practicable'. **(29, 30)**

4. What provision is there in the 1974 Act for ensuring that actual wrongdoers do not escape liability? **(16–18)**

5. What is meant in this context by 'directors' liability?' **(18)**

6. What is meant by:

(a) strict liability; **(25)**

(b) absolute liability; **(26)**

(c) *mens rea*? **(21–24)**

7. Are the general duties enforceable:

(a) in their own right;   **(38)**
(b) against the Crown?   **(39)**

6
Responsibilities of employers and employees

1. Introduction

This chapter will provide more detail about the general duties which, under the 1974 Act, regulate the relationship between employers and their own employees (s.2) and their relationships with other workers (s.3 and s.4). The duties which employees owe to themselves and to others will also be analysed (s.7). The likely impact on these general duties of the Health and Safety (General Provisions) Regulations will be discussed.

2. Duties owed in respect of employees

The paramount duty of employers under the 1974 Act, as under earlier statutory provisions, is to provide safe working conditions for their own employees. Section 2 of the Act, which sets out this duty, covers the following matters:

(a) the general duty (s.2(1));
(b) particular matters related to the general duty (s.2(2));
(c) safety policy (s.2(3));
(d) worker participation (s.2(4)(6) and (7)).

The following paragraphs generally follow this analysis.

The employers' general duty

3. Summary of s.2(1)

The general duty set out in s.2(1) has already been identified in the previous chapters. It is therefore only necessary now to make a few brief points:

(a) The duty is owed by the employer in respect of his employees, so it cannot be imposed upon an enterprise in situations where it has no employees.

(b) Persons other than employees may incidentally benefit or suffer according to whether the duty is observed or not, e.g. visitors to a safe workplace will not be placed at undue risk.

(c) The duty is in respect of health, safety and *welfare*. The concept of welfare is rarely invoked in the 1974 Act. Most of the matters which would formerly have been classified as welfare issues are now likely to be considered as health matters.

(d) The duty has hitherto applied only so long as the employee is 'at work'. The General Provisions Regulations extend the meaning of 'at work' both for the purposes of the regulations and of the Act itself. Employees will be at work whenever they are present at the premises to which the regulations apply, even while they are not 'in the course of their employment'.

(e) The duty is owed in respect of employees, rather than to employees: it is not enforceable by employees but by the Health and Safety Executive or their agents.

(f) There is some doubt as to the circumstances in which enforcement can be based on breaches of s.2(1). On the one hand an improvement notice based on a breach of s.2, standing alone, was upheld in *Chrysler UK Ltd* v. *McCarthy* [1978]; on the other hand McNeill J in the *West Bromwich Building Society* case said:

> It is not easy to visualise the factual situation in which a breach of s.2(1) could be charged and my impression is that it is really a parliamentary 'safety net' designed to catch any, if there be any, alleged breaches of obligations other than the obligations in s.2(2) to (7) inclusive . . .

Nevertheless the Court of Appeal upheld a conviction under both s.2(1), and the comparable s.3(1), in the leading case of *Swan Hunter*.

4. Section 2(1) and the General Provisions Regulations

Regulation 3 of the General Provisions Regulations, which requires every employer 'to adequately assess' . . .

> the risks to the health and safety of his employees to which they are exposed whilst they are at work,

gives specificity to s.2(1) of the 1974 Act. The Regulation embraces, but goes further than, the requirements of certain other regulations, particularly the Control of Substances Hazardous to Health Regulations, which require employers to identify and evaluate particular hazards. While it is arguable that the import of Regulation 3 was already present in s.2(1) the new provision emphasises the onerous nature of the employers duties under the 1974 Act. Regulation 3(5) requires employers who have five or more employees to make a written record of the assessment and record any group of employees identified by the assessment as being especially at risk.

Regulation 4 builds on Regulation 3, requiring employers to have a system of safety arrangements, presumably such as to indicate a proper response to the findings of the risk assessment exercise. Regulation 4(1) stipulates:

> Every employer shall make and give effect to such arrangements as are appropriate, having regard to the nature of his activities and the size of his undertaking, for the effective planning, organisation, control, monitoring and review of the protective and preventive measures.

Regulation 4(2) requires the employer who employs five or more employees to record these arrangements in writing. Regulation 5 requires every employer to ensure that his employees are provided with such health surveillance as is appropriate for the identified risks.

Particular matters related to the general duty

5. General

Section 2(2)(a) to (e) itemises particular aspects of the employers' duty to their employees in very general terms. The emphasis is throughout on *systems* rather than *standards* and in every paragraph the requirements are qualified by the words *reasonably practicable*. It is not easy to relate s.2(2)(a) to (e) to the newer duties just described to assess and respond to risks. It can only be posited that, since Regulation 3(1) is qualified by 'adequate' and Regulation 4 by 'appropriate', compliance with paragraphs (a) to (e), i.e. doing what is reasonably practicable, would be a discharge of the regulations in relation to these specific matters.

While s.2(2), paragraphs (a) to (e), are very general, they apply to every workplace within Great Britain whereas earlier legislation and regulations made under it applied only to specified categories of premises or situations and the 1974 Act in no way extended the ambit of these earlier laws. Nevertheless earlier regulatory standards accepted by industry in the particular situations to which they applied might, since 1974, have been evidence of what it was reasonably practicable for all employers to do in compliance with the more general requirements of s.2(2)(a) to (e). For example, the standards set for the heating and lighting of factories under ss. 3 and 5 of the 1961 Factories Act might well have been indicative of the standards which it was reasonably practicable to achieve in workplaces which are not covered by detailed regulatory standards.

The value of these older regulatory standards has decreased, because the standards themselves have been overtaken by advancing technical knowledge and also because many of them have been replaced by regulatory standards often for general application to persons 'at work'. When the EC Directives on standards for workplaces and work equipment have been incorporated into UK law, relevant standards will apply directly to all workplaces rather than by analogy to the old laws.

6. Section 2(2)(a): machinery

Section 2(2)(a) requires:

> the provision and maintenance of plant and systems of work that are, so far as is reasonably practicable safe and without risks to health.

Giving first priority to safety of machinery at the workplace follows in the tradition of earlier legislation which laid considerable emphasis on this aspect of workplace safety. There are, however, a number of ways in which s.2(2)(a) enables progress beyond the point of the detailed provisions of the earlier legislation and the regulations made under it:

(a) It requires not only the installation of safe plant, it also requires it to be maintained and used according to a safe system, e.g. not overloaded or used for purposes other than that for which it was intended.

(b) It requires the plant and systems to be such as not to endanger health, e.g. plant in itself safe, in that it was securely guarded might nevertheless be in contravention of this provision if it were set at such a speed as to cause the user to suffer repetitive strain injury.

7.   Section 2(2)(b): handling, storage and transport
Section 2(2)(b) requires:

> arrangements for ensuring, so far as is reasonably practicable, safety and absence of risks to health in connection with the use, handling, storage and transport of articles and substances.

This paragraph takes the 1974 Act beyond the Robens Report for transport which was expressly excluded from that Committee's terms of reference. However, s.2(2)(b) relates only to transport of goods, not to the transport of persons.

Transport and handling of goods at the workplace is clearly an important aspect of workplace safety. Hoists and lifts and lifting tackle have long been subject to regulatory control (*see* ss. 23–27 of the Factories Act 1961).

Section 2(2)(b), imposing duties on employers in respect of the handling of goods, relates to s.6, and regulations such as the Classification, Packaging and Labelling of Dangerous Substances Regulations 1984, as amended, made under it. The duties under s.6 are imposed primarily on persons such as the supplier of these substances, but clearly s.2(2)(b) imposes a duty on the employer to ensure that the information supplied by the supplier is taken into account at the workplace.

In the same manner the requirements of the Control of Substances Hazardous to Health Regulations 1988 and the duties they impose on the employer to assess substances before they are used at the work place and ensure that they are used safely, serve to discharge the obligations imposed by s.2(2)(b).

The Health and Safety Executive have introduced training systems for fork-lift truck drivers.

8. Section 2(2)(c): information, instruction, training, supervision

Section 2(2)(c) requires:

> the provision of such information, instruction, training and supervision as is necessary to ensure, so far as is reasonably practicable, the health and safety at work of his employees.

This paragraph is at the very core of the legislation. It provides the element which distinguishes it from earlier statutes which placed their emphasis on the working environment rather than on the behaviour of people at the workplace.

Section 2(2)(c) is now strengthened by the duty imposed on the inspector under s.28(8) to communicate to employees factual information obtained by him during an inspection of premises about matters which affect their health, safety or welfare. The employer is additionally under a duty to consult with appointed safety representatives (s.2(6)). The duty under s.2(2)(c) is, however, owed to each employee individually, not to safety representatives.

The requirement for the provision of instruction, training and supervision stresses the need for employers to introduce and maintain systems of work. Before new systems are introduced those whom they will affect should be instructed as to their purposes, trained as to their implementation and thereafter monitored to ensure that the systems put in place are actually employed in practice.

9. Meaning of 'instruction'

There is judicial authority for the proposition that 'instruction' has two meanings: it means both to teach and to order (*Boyle* v. *Kodak Ltd* [1969]), and the employer who is to discharge his duties must be prepared in the last instance to invoke disciplinary measures against an employee who does not follow the systems put in place for reasons of safety. In practice it is unlikely that an inspector will prosecute a worker who is not following the employers' system of work without also bringing a parallel prosecution against the employers for failure to do all that is reasonably practicable to ensure that the system is actually implemented and maintained.

10. Wider implications of s.2(2)(c)

The discussion about s.2(2)(c) has, to this point, focused on its operation in the context of the contract of employment, and there is no doubt that a duty imposed for the protection of employees will not be complied with if it is not implemented in the relationship between the employer and his own employees. However, a careful reading of s.2(2)(c) reveals that it does not merely require the employer to provide information, instruction, training and supervision to employees so that they may protect themselves. It also requires the dissemination of information, the provision of instruction and training to, and the supervision of whomsoever might otherwise by their conduct endanger employees. This was confirmed by the Court of Appeal in:

> *R* v. *Swan Hunter Shipbuilders Ltd* [1981]: There was a fire on HMS *Glasgow* which was under construction in Swan Hunter's yard: eight men were killed. The fire started during welding operations by contractors. The fire, which started in a confined space in the well of the ship, was particularly intense because the atmosphere was oxygen enriched. The dangers of using oxygen in poorly ventilated spaces were well known to Swan Hunter and their Safety Officer had drawn up a 'Blue Book' of instructions for users of fuel and oxygen. Copies of this book were distributed to Swan Hunter's own employees but not to employees of other companies working alongside Swan Hunter's own men. At the trial Swan Hunter were found guilty of failing to provide information to Telemeter employees. They appealed against this conviction.
>
> The Court considered the application of s.2(2)(c) to these facts. Swan Hunter had, at trial, submitted that no duty lay on them under s.2(2)(c) to provide information or instruction to any workers other than their own employees. The trial judge had ruled against this submission and the main ground of the appeal was that, as a matter of law, the judge was wrong. It was submitted for Swan Hunter that an employer had no right to instruct the workers of others and that therefore the duty to provide information, instruction and training could not extend to employees of other undertakings. The Court of Appeal nevertheless upheld the

ruling of the trial judge that there was a strict duty to provide a safe system of work for an employers' own employees, and if fulfilling that duty involved information and instruction being given to persons other than the employer's own employees, then the employer was under a duty to provide such information and instruction. The employers's protection was contained in the words 'so far as is reasonably practicable': the onus of proving, on a balance of probabilities, that it was not reasonably practicable in the particular circumstances of the case lay on the employer. If another employer obstructed the giving of the necessary information and instruction, then that employer would himself be guilty of an offence under s.36 of the Act.

11. Section 2(2)(c) and EC Directives

Section 2(2)(c) must in future be interpreted in relation to provisions introduced to implement EC Directives. Thus Regulation 8 of the General Provisions Regulations implementing the Framework Directive require every employer to give comprehensive and relevant information to their employees on:

(a) risks to their health and safety identified by the employers' risk assessment;
(b) protective and preventive measures;
(c) procedures for dealing with emergency situations;
(d) identity of those persons nominated to implement emergency procedures;
(e) risks notified to the employer by other employers with whom he is cooperating in work activities.

Regulation 10 of these regulations requires the employer to ensure that his employees are provided with adequate health and safety training.

Regulation 12 requires employers to provide information to those who work for them as temporary workers about the risks of the work and the qualifications needed for its safe performance.

12. Section 2(2)(d): place of work

Section 2(2)(d) requires:

so far as is reasonably practicable as regards any place of work under the employer's control, the maintenance of it in a condition that is safe and without risks to health and the provision and maintenance of means of access to and egress from it that are safe and without risks.

This provision virtually replicated s.29 of the Factories Act 1961, but unlike s.29, it applies to all workplaces. This difference is compensated by the qualification in s.2(2)(d) that the employer's duty extends only to any place of work which is under the employer's control.

13. Section 2(2)(e): working environment

Section 2(2)(e) requires from the employer:

the provision and maintenance of a working environment for his employees that is, so far as is reasonably practicable, safe, without risks to health, and adequate as regards facilities and arrangements for their welfare at work.

This provision does not seem necessary in relation to the physical working environment which is provided for in earlier paragraphs, especially in s.2(2)(d). It is arguable that it applies to job satisfaction, and in particular to stress engendered by poor working arrangements.

Possibly this paragraph could in future be related to the requirements of Article 6 (2)(d) of the Framework Directive which requires:

adapting the work to the individual, especially as regards the design of work places, the choice of work equipment and the choice of working and production methods, with a view, in particular, to alleviating monotonous work and work at a predetermined work-rate and to reducing their effect on health.

14. Impact of individual EC Directives on s.2(2)

The five individual Directives subordinate to the EC Framework Directive require organisations to set standards and/or lay down systems for the matters covered by s.2(2) of the 1974 Act. These Directives have to be incorporated into UK law by the end of 1992 and will govern new premises and equipment brought into use after 1 January 1993 and apply generally to all workplaces after 1996. Their introduction will necessitate a good deal of revision and rationalisation of existing regulations. For example, it is proposed to repeal s.29 of the Factories Act when regulations implement the workplace Directive.

Safety policy

15. Requirements of s.2(3)

A novel and important feature of the 1974 Act was the requirement in s.2(3) that an employer write a safety policy. Section 2(3) is not particularly well phrased and needs careful analysis in order to understand its full import. It reads:

> Except in such cases as may be prescribed, it shall be the duty of every employer to prepare and as often as may be appropriate revise a written statement of his general policy with respect to the health and safety at work of his employees and the organisation and arrange-ments for the time being in force for carrying out that policy, and to bring the statement and any revision of it to the notice of all of his employees.

The subsection in fact requires three matters to be addressed:

(a) the organisation's statement of policy;
(b) an identification of personnel with safety responsibilities;
(c) a statement of arrangements for dealing with particular hazards.

Organisations have found it difficult to determine what s.2(3) requires and have been puzzled why the Health and Safety Commission does not provide more detailed guidance. For the Commission to have provided a model document would have completely defeated the purpose of the section. The intention is that the organisation shall spend time identifying the relationship between the actual management structure and system of operation and its safety needs. The requirements of s.2(3) will be considered in more detail in a subsequent chapter.

16. Application of s.2(3)

All but the smallest organisations have to have safety policies: the Employers Health and Safety Policy Statements (Exceptions) Regulations 1975 exempted organisations where less than five people were employed in the undertaking. This is in line with the

General Provisions Regulations which require a written record of the outcome of risk assessment and of resulting safety arrangements in organisations where more than five are employed.

In *Osborne* v. *Bill Taylor of Huyton Ltd* [1982], the defendant company were served with an improvement notice under s.2(3) requiring them to prepare a written safety policy. Subsequently when they were charged with the criminal offence of ignoring the notice, they argued that they were within the exception regulations. The company owned and controlled 31 betting shops but at the shop which was the subject of the notice they employed only two full-time, and one part-time, member of staff. The justices accepted that the betting shop was a distinct place of work; it was the undertaking for the purposes of the Regulation and the exception regulations applied. On appeal by the prosecution by way of case stated it was held by the Divisional Court that the justices had correctly interpreted the regulations in that the test was not how many employees were on the 'payroll' but how many were at work at any one time; provided no more than five worked at one time an undertaking was exempt.

In *J Armour* v. *Skeen* [1977] there was a controversial conviction of the director of roads for Strathclyde under s.37 of the 1974 Act following a fatal accident in which a workman had fallen to his death. Mr Armour's prosecution under s.37(1) was in relation to his 'neglect' in fulfilling the responsibilities for health and safety placed on him by the council, including having a sound safety policy for his department, informing employees of the implications and requirements of the Act, and training and instructing them in safe working practices. Mr Armour appealed against the decision of the Sheriff Court on the grounds that he personally was not under a statutory duty to provide a safe system of work and therefore the accident could not be attributable to any neglect of such a duty. In addition, he claimed that he could not be personally prosecuted as he did not fall within the ambit of s.37(1).

The High Court of Judiciary upheld the conviction. The

neglect on the part of a person charged under s.37(1) need not be a neglect only in relation to a duty which the legislation had placed on that person; s.37 referred to *any* neglect. In the present case the council's Safety Policy placed responsibility for ensuring safe conditions of work on directors and the appellant's duty was to prepare a written general safety policy in relation to the work of his department. His failure to do so constituted neglect within the meaning of s.37(1). Moreover, while the appellant was not a 'director' as that word was used in s.37(1), having regard to his position in the organisation of the council, and the duty which was imposed on him in connection with the safety policy, he was within the class of person referred to in s.37.

Worker participation

17. Section 2

The remaining provisions of s.2, while imposing duties on employers, are somewhat different in emphasis from the earlier subsections of s.2, being concerned with procedures for worker involvement in safety at the workplace. These provisions were a response to the Robens Committee's concern that accidents were caused by apathy arising from workers' failure to associate themselves with maintaining safe systems at the workplace. The detail and implications of these provisions will be discussed in the chapter on worker involvement.

Employers' duties to workers not their employees

18. General

Section 3 of the 1974 Act imposes upon employers duties in respect of persons who are not their employees. Section 4, while imposing its obligations upon controllers of premises, in practice may often be imposing duties on employers in respect of workers visiting their premises: such certainly was the situation in the *Austin Rover* case. Neither s.3 nor s.4 is exclusively concerned with the protection of employed persons; indeed, both sections are wide enough to provide protection for persons other than workers. It has been held that an organisation may owe duties under s.4 even though there are no persons employed to work at the premises concerned (*Westminster City Council* v. *Select Managements Ltd* [1985]). In this chapter ss.3 and 4 will only be considered in the context of the protection of workers.

19. Duties imposed by s.3(1)

Section 3(1) imposes a general duty in the following words:

> It shall be the duty of every employer to conduct his undertaking in such a way as to ensure, so far as is reasonably practicable, that persons not in his employment who may be affected thereby are not thereby exposed to risks to their health or safety.

This duty has proved to be most important, making a very substantial contribution to the establishing and maintaining of safe systems of work where two or more undertakings are working in close proximity. Section 3(1) is particularly suited to the situation, such as commonly occurs on building sites, where a head contractor (who may possibly have his own employees on site) subcontracts to one or more other organisations to carry out specialist work on site. There is, in these circumstances, a need for each group of workers to have regard for the other group(s) when planning their work and there may on occasion be a need for the head contractor to inform the subcontractors of hazards, e.g. asbestos, which may be encountered in the course of the work. The importance of the section has increased because of the tendency in permanent workplaces to reduce the size of the directly employed work units, whereby employers contract-out services such as catering and cleaning. At mobile work sites, as are found in construction work, there has been a considerable growth of small specialised employers.

The requirements of s.3(1) were considered by the Appeal Court in the *Swan Hunter* case (*see also* 10 above). Swan Hunter argued that s.3(1), though directed to the protection of persons like the visiting employees of the subcontractors, imposed no duty on them because it required nothing specific. They pointed out that s.3(3) enabled regulations to be made identifying circumstances in which employers had to provide information to persons not in their employment and argued that the only cases in which there would be a duty on employers like themselves would be if there had been regulations made under s.3(3) specifying that particular information had to be imparted. The trial judge dismissed this contention and the Court of Appeal had no hesitation in adopting the words in which he did so as being a correct statement:

> ... subsection (3) does not impinge upon nor does it limit in any way subsection (1) of s.3. Subsection (3) is dealing with a very limited class and a very limited number, namely the prescribed cases where only prescribed information is to be given. If subsection (1) were to be subject to subsection (3), why then I should expect it to say so, but the words in my judgment in subsection (1) are wide enough to include the giving of information and instruction to employees other than one's own employees ...

The Court of Appeal therefore held that s.3(1) required the giving of information to the visitors for their own protection.

20. Satisfying the duties imposed by s.3(1)

The principal way in which employers may provide for safe systems when making arrangements for two or more groups of workers to work in proximity is through contractual arrangements. Where there is a contract between two organisations for the performance of work that contract should almost certainly contain details as to the system to operate for the purposes of ensuring safety. The occupier of premises bringing another employer's workforce on to the premises may well wish to stipulate that the visitors follow the established site procedures. This contractual provision will only be effective if the occupier can be confident that both the visiting employers and their workers are conversant with these procedures. Merely enclosing a copy of the safety policy amongst other contractual documents may not achieve this. It may well be necessary to instruct and supervise the visiting workers directly.

The giving of information contractually to employers of other workers is only relevant in cases where there is a contract between the two employers. It would not be relevant where both employers were subcontractors of the head contractor. In cases such as this the subcontractors are each dependent on their separate contracts with the head contractor.

Where a subcontracting organisation considers its employees are endangered by the working conditions under the contract, that employer owes a duty to its own employees either to ensure that the working arrangements are made safe or the contract is terminated. Putting pressure on the head contractor is likely to be the only practical way in which a subcontractor can respond to hazards created by another subcontractor. The obverse of this proposition is that there is a duty on the head contractor in such circumstances to make certain that the work of the subcontractors is coordinated so that the undertaking, of which their separate undertakings are but part, is in total a safe operation. The Court of Appeal noted this in *Swan Hunter*, quoting from the judgment of Edmund Davies LJ in *McArdle* v. *Andmac Roofing Co. & Others* [1967], a compensation case arising out of personal injury suffered by a contractor's (Andmac) employee when working together with the employees of another subcontractor (Newton), at a site occupied by the head contractors (Pontins). Of the latter's contract manager his Lordship said:

> He not only engaged the subcontractors but directed all the work that they were to do and when they were to do it, and in some instances gave orders how it was to be done. He conceded that he was the coordinating authority to bring together the various subcontractors at the right time and the right place . . . Safety precautions were never discussed with any subcontractor . . . He simply expected them to make such safety arrangements as they thought fit.

Pontins' failure to set up a safe system rendered them liable to contribute to the compensation of the accident victim. They shared liability with the two subcontractors whose systems were at fault in that they ought also to have foreseen the hazards created by the uncoordinated system of work. Under the 1974 Act all three employers might expect to be found criminally liable under s.3(1) in a situation such as this.

In *R* v. *Mara* [1987] the Court of Appeal considered the meaning of the phrase *conduct his undertaking* as used in s.3(1). Mr Mara was the director of a cleaning company under contract with a high-street store. The cleaning work involved the use of certain electrical cleaning machinery, including a polisher/scrubber. To overcome problems of interfering with the clients' work, it was agreed that cleaning of the loading bay should be done by the clients themselves but using the contractor's equipment. The prosecution arose because one of the client's employees was electrocuted by the contractor's defective polisher/scrubber. Mara was convicted under s.3(1). The question raised on appeal was whether the use of the defective equipment by the employee at the store in the particular circumstances could be said to relate to the conduct of Mara's undertaking, since the accident occurred on a day when Mara had no contractual duty to clean the premises. The Court of Appeal nevertheless upheld the conviction. In their view the employees at the shop were persons who might be affected by the conduct of Mara's undertaking and the court could not accept the argument that the duty in s.3(1) was only applicable when the undertaking was in the process of actively being carried on.

21. Section 3(2): duties imposed on the self-employed
Section 3(2) treats the self-employed person as if he were an employer and places exactly the same obligation upon him in regard to the conduct of his undertaking as s.3(1) places on the employer. In *Jones* v. *Fishwick* (1989) an industrial tribunal upheld an improvement notice served on a master butcher under s.3(2), requiring him to wear a chainmail apron to prevent him stabbing himself when boning out meat.

22. Section 3(1) and EC Directives
These interpretations of the obligations imposed by s.3(1) match the obligations envisaged by Article 6 of the Framework Directive:

> . . . where several undertakings share a work place, the employers shall cooperate in implementing the safety, health and occupational hygiene provisions and, taking into account the nature of the activities, shall coordinate their actions in matters of the protection and prevention of occupational risks, and shall inform one another and their respective workers and/or workers' representatives of these risks.

23. Duties imposed by s.4

The duties which s.4(1) imposes upon a controller of premises are owed in relation to persons who are not the controller's employees, but who use those (non-domestic) premises as a place of work or as a place where they may use plant or substances provided for their use there. The duty is imposed by virtue of s.4(2) on each person who has, to any extent, control of premises to which the section applies. It is a duty to take such measures as it is reasonable for a person in the controller's position to take to ensure so far as is *reasonably practicable*, that the premises are safe and without risks to health. The section suggests that the duty may be confined to making the premises safe for the purpose for which the controller makes them available, but this is not entirely clear; it may be that the controller, having granted access to the premises, is liable for their condition, even if used beyond the purposes for which he intended access. However, the liability in respect of plant or substances is expressly limited to liability for plant and substances provided for the use of the visitors.

> The House of Lords considered the implications of this section in relation to visiting workers in *Mailer* v. *Austin Rover Group plc* [1989]. Austin Rover (the respondents) had premises containing a spray painting booth beneath which was a large sump used to collect excess paint and thinners during painting operations. The booth contained a piped supply of highly flammable thinners for use in painting. The respondents employed a contractor to clean the booth at times when there was no production. The contract for the work required that nobody should be in the sump when anyone was working in the booth above, that the contractor's employees should not use the piped supply of thinners but should use their own supplies, that thinners used in the cleaning should not be sent into the sump, and that only a flameproof electric lamp should be taken into the sump. These safety provisions were ignored. There was a flash fire and a man in the sump was killed. The respondents were prosecuted under s.4(2) for failure to take such measures as were reasonable for them to take to ensure so far as was reasonably practicable that the sump and piped thinners were safe and without risks to health.

The House of Lords held that once it was proved in a
prosecution under s.4(2) that premises which had been
made available by a controller were unsafe and constituted
a risk to health the onus lay on the respondent to show that,
weighing the risk to health against the means, including
cost, of eliminating the risk, it was not reasonably
practicable for him to take these measures. However, if the
premises were not a reasonably foreseeable cause of danger
to persons using the premises in a manner or in
circumstances which might reasonably be expected to occur,
it was not reasonable to require any further measures to be
taken to guard against unknown and unexpected events
which might imperil their safety.

Since it was not reasonable for the respondents to take
measures to make the spray painting booth and sump safe
against the unanticipated misuses of those premises by the
contractor's employees the magistrates had been wrong to
convict the respondents.

The reasoning of their Lordships was interesting. They
took the view that the starting point was that the premises
should be absolutely safe so that if they proved to be unsafe,
regardless of the way in which they had been used, the
burden shifted to the controller, who might then escape
liability by establishing that it was not foreseeable that the
premises would be used in the manner in which they had
been used and/or it was not incumbent on him to have done
more to make the premises safe. In deciding the extent of
the duty the court had to bear in mind the double
qualification on the controller's duty: s.4(2) required the
controller to do only what was reasonable for someone in
his position to do to ensure so far as was reasonably
practicable that the premises were safe.

Duties on the employee

24. Duty to take reasonable care
Section 7(a) imposes on the employee while at work a duty to
take reasonable care for the health and safety of himself and of
other persons who may be affected by his acts or omissions at work.

While the duty is to take reasonable care, it is owed not merely by ordinary employees, but also by management up to board-room level. What is required for the discharge of the duty may well vary according to the status of the employee, and the terms of the contract of employment. The unskilled worker is unlikely to be liable for anything short of dangerous horseplay; the senior manager may be liable for failure in professional judgment, if that failure amounted to negligence. Even at management level, however, the employee's conduct will be judged in relation to the training he has been given, the authority he has, and the resources he has been allocated for the performance of his task. There has been a reluctance to invoke s.7 when the true responsibility lies with the employer. Indeed, even in those cases in which there is actionable conduct on the part of the employee, the organisation may well be prosecuted for tolerating this conduct within its system.

25. Duty to cooperate with employer
Section 7(b) of the 1974 Act imposes on the employee a duty:

> as regards any duty or requirement imposed on his employer or any other person by or under any of the relevant statutory provisions, to cooperate with him so far as is necessary to enable that duty or requirement to be performed or complied with.

This provision may overlap with s.8 which renders an employee (as any other persons) liable for wilful or reckless interference with anything provided for safety. It may also overlap with s.36 which enables the actual wrongdoer to be prosecuted rather than the person upon whom the duty is imposed. However, there may be circumstances which neither of these other provisions cover, e.g. where an employee did not interfere with anything and did not actually cause his employer to break a duty imposed on him but merely made it more difficult for that duty to be performed, as by failing to provide the employer with information needed for the performance of his duty. In this connection it is obvious that the more senior the employee in an organisation, the wider will be the area within which his failure to 'cooperate' may render him criminally liable under s.7(b).

26. Duties under the General Provisions Regulations

Regulation 11 of the General Provisions Regulations is likely to impose further and more specific duties upon employees. Regulation 11(1) provides that no employee shall:

(a) use any machinery, equipment, dangerous substance, transport equipment, means of production or safety device provided to him by his employer other than in accordance with any instruction and training respecting such use which has been provided to him by that employer in compliance with his duties under the relevant statutory provisions; or

(b) interfere with any of the items so provided.

While it is arguable that this provision merely reiterates s.7 of the 1974 Act, Regulation 11(2) goes further. It imposes responsibilities on the employee to inform his employer 'or any other employee of that employer with specific responsibility for the health and safety of his fellow employees':

(a) of any work situation which may reasonably be considered to represent a serious and immediate danger to health and safety; and

(b) of any matter which may reasonably be considered to represent a shortcoming in the employer's protection arrangements for health and safety.

Progress test 6

1. How did the *Swan Hunter* case link the employers' duty to his own employees with that owed to visiting workers? **(10)**

2. How may employers ensure that safe systems exist where several workforces are working in close proximity? **(10, 20)**

3. Can an employer be conducting his undertaking though his own employees are not at work? **(20)**

4. What organisations are excepted from the requirement to have a written safety policy? **(16)**

5. What matters ought a safety policy to cover? **(15)**

6.   What provisions of the 1974 Act require information to be given to employees or their representatives?   **(8)**

7.   What meaning have the courts given to the word 'instruction'?   **(9)**

7
Other general duties: safe industrial activity

1. Introduction

In this chapter the general duties will be considered in relation to the safety of goods marketed for the workplace and also in relation to public safety. These are matters which the EC has not addressed in its occupational health and safety Directives since these have been made under Article 118A of the Treaty of Rome which is concerned only with the health and safety of workers. Therefore this chapter is solely concerned with the way in which the 1974 Act approaches these issues.

Some consideration must also be given to the behaviour of the public. Can members of the public be liable if workers are endangered by their activities? Could employers be liable if members of the public placed their employees in danger?

Protection for all

2. Protection of the public

The 1974 Act gave statutory recognition to the dangers to which the public can be exposed as a result of work activity. The general purposes of the 1974 Act set out in s.1(1) include not only the safety of people at work but also:

> protecting persons other than persons at work against risks... arising out of or in connection with the activities of persons at work (s.1(1)(b)).

The incident that endangers employees may also endanger other workers, the self-employed and the public. For example, a group of workers treating wood with toxic chemicals may endanger themselves if they are not wearing suitable masks and other protective clothing; for this their employers may be liable under s.2 and the workers might bear some personal responsibility under s.7. If the spraying activity endangers other workers engaged nearby in, say, putting in window frames, then the woodtreaters' employers might be in breach of s.3, using that section in the way that it was discussed in the previous chapter in relation to the protection of workers not in the employment of the employer upon whom the duty is placed. Those put at risk might include residents in a neighbouring flat or workers employed by another employer who, at the time (as was actually the position in an unreported case) were taking a meal break, sitting eating their sandwiches in the vicinity of the spraying!

In these examples s.3 and s.7 would be wide enough to cover the factual situations, for neither the employer's duty under s.3, nor the employee's duty under s.7, is confined to circumstances in which those at risk are persons at work; both sections can also be invoked where the persons at risk are members of the general public.

3. Duties of the self-employed

The duties would be the same if the workers using the wood treatment were self-employed; s.3 would impose on them duties for the protection of other persons (both other workers and members of the public) and themselves. However, by virtue of Regulation 14(2) of the proposed General Purposes Regulations, the workers enjoying their lunch break will in future be deemed to be 'at work'.

4. Duties of controllers of premises

Similarly s.4 imposes duties on controllers of premises for the protection of the general public as well as for the protection of workers.

5. Duties with respect to the environment

Section 5 has hitherto enabled the placing of duties on persons in respect of the protection of the environment against pollution that has a potential either for causing injury to health or offence to the senses.

6. Duties on manufacturers and distributors

Section 6 imposes duties on persons engaged in the production and distribution of articles and substances for use by persons at work.

7. Scope of the 1974 Act

Sections 3, 4 and 5 are the sections most relevant for protection of persons other than persons at work, though s.7 might well be invoked against an employee who, through lack of care, endangered the public, e.g. was extremely negligent in maintenance work carried out in domestic premises. Section 6, while closely related to consumer protection legislation, is in fact directly concerned with the safety of persons at work, albeit not in the employment of, or working in any geographical proximity to, any person upon whom the s.6 obligations are imposed, i.e. the duty under this section is imposed for the protection of the 'ultimate consumers' of the article or substance, rather than the protection of those engaged in the manufacture or supply of that article or substance.

It does not appear that the 1974 Act is intended to protect the public from hazards other than those created by people at work.

Relationship between the 1974 Act and other legislation

8. General

Many of the problems raised in this chapter are problems which were beyond the scope of earlier occupational safety legislation which focused narrowly on the employers' responsibilities to his own employees; some problems of public safety and health were formerly only dealt with in separate legislation such as environmental protection or transport safety legislation. Experience, since the implementation of the 1974 Act, has been that the boundaries between occupational safety, public safety and environmental protection are extremely difficult to maintain, though environmental protection is a wider concept, covering preservation of amenity as well as safety.

9. Leisure and sports facilities

The 1974 Act brought premises where leisure activities are

enjoyed, like theatres and sports arenas, within the ambit of occupational health and safety legislation for the first time. This also blurred the boundaries between public and employee safety. For example, there was a suggestion that the HSE should bear some responsibility for the tragic fire causing the death of spectators at the Bradford football stadium, when it emerged that HSE inspectors had failed to take action which might have prevented the fire when they had noted the debris which had accumulated under the spectator seating — debris which was, with hindsight, found to be a substantial cause of this fire.

10. Transport

The general duties in s.2 clearly extend to protect transport workers, and s.3 extends to passengers and others who might be affected by the transport undertaking, but the extent to which the 1974 Act ought to be relied on in transport cases remains controversial when more specialised legislation, and, in some cases a more specialist inspectorate, is involved. However, the tendency is to bring transport within the province of the HSE: the HSE is responsible for enforcing the Dangerous Substances (Conveyance by Road in Road Tankers and Tank Containers) Regulations 1981 (revised 1992) and the Road Traffic (Carriage of Dangerous Substances in Packages etc.) Regulations 1986 (revised 1992).

Similarly the HSE has recently assumed responsibility for rail transport, using both the 1974 Act and (acting under an agency agreement with the Department of Transport) the older, specialised railway safety legislation; this special legislation is largely concerned with the safety of railway passengers.

The 1974 Act and public safety

11. Basic duties

The basic duties in s.3(1) (on the employer) and s.3(2) (on the self-employed) are sufficiently wide to require those upon whom they are imposed to consider the safety of the general public as well as of workers who are not in their direct employment. Both duties are phrased in the very widest possible terms requiring from the employer the 'conduct of his undertaking in such a way as to ensure so far as is reasonably practicable that persons not in his employment who may be affected thereby' are not endangered.

12. Situations in which the Act applies

Now that cases such as *Swan Hunter* have established that s.3(1) is enforceable in its own right, it is apparent that there are innumerable situations in which an employer needs to consider, if s.3 is to be complied with, whether his undertaking is endangering the public. For example, construction work undertaken near to the highway must be arranged in such a way as to ensure that building materials do not fall on to pedestrians. In 1991 a construction company were convicted under s.3(1), and fined £15,000, when falsework fell from the seventh floor of a building under construction and killed a young woman in the street below. Similarly, an employer operating a storage and distribution unit may need to consider whether the movement of his heavy lorries to and from the highway endangers neighbouring residents and road users, and an employer may need to consider whether contaminated work clothing taken home for laundering might endanger those with whom his employees share living accommodation.

13. Provision of safety information

Section 3(3) envisages that certain situations might be identified in which regulations might impose detailed requirements on employers and self-employed persons to give information to others. The provision refers throughout to 'prescribed circumstances':

> In such cases as may be prescribed, it shall be the duty of every employer and every self-employed persons, in the prescribed circumstances and in the prescribed manner, to give to persons (not being his employees . . . the prescribed information.

The statutory language is somewhat vague in that it does not indicate how these situations may be 'prescribed'; any doubt is removed by the interpretation section which states that prescribed means prescribed by regulations (s.53).

14. Subordinate legislation

The Control of Industrial Major Hazards Regulations 1984

provide an example of exactly the sort of subordinate legislation which s.3(3) seems to expect. These regulations require that the manufacturer operating a site which constitutes a major hazard should provide information to people living or working in the vicinity of the site. In fact these regulations were made under the general regulatory power given by s.15 of the 1974 Act without reference to s.3(3).

The regulation power under the Act is so wide that it is not necessary, as was the case with older legislation, for particular sections of the Act to expressly empower the making of regulations in relation to matters dealt with in that section. It is interesting, therefore, that specific power is given in relation to this general duty — possibly for clarification given the novelty of the duty itself. Certainly it is noteworthy that the Act is similarly specific in relation to regulation-making powers in the two other areas in which duties, which were at that time novel, were created or proposed, namely safety policy and safety representatives.

15. Employers' duties with regard to the public

In *Swan Hunter* s.3(1) was read in conjunction with s.2(2)(c) to require an employer to provide information, instruction and supervision to workers, other than his own employees, in order to protect his own employees from hazards which might otherwise be created by the other workforce. There seems no reason, in principle, why in certain circumstances, employers might not have the same obligations placed upon them to inform and even supervise the conduct of members of the public, even though no specific regulations have been made under s.3(3) or otherwise. For example, it is common practice for public utilities to place warning notices, such as 'Danger, Keep Away' or 'No Smoking' when their employees are working in or near manholes or excavations on the highway. It is arguable that this warning to the public is needed for employers to comply with both their s.2 duties to their employees and their s.3 duty to the public.

If, as seems probable, the employers' duty does require some control of the public in such situations, both for their own safety and for the safety of the workforce, it may be questioned whether merely placing a warning notice, without taking further 'policing' measures to ensure that the notice is obeyed, is doing all that is reasonably practicable to ensure the safety of either the workers or the public.

Safety of premises

16. Safety of premises open to the public

A feature of the 1974 Act was that it brought within occupational health and safety legislation for the first time many premises which were open to the public generally, or in consequence of contractual arrangements between the occupier of the premises and individual members of the public, such as educational establishments, leisure premises from theatres to sports centres, hospitals and hotels.

17. Compliance with ss.3 and 4

In many cases compliance with s.3 duties may make adequate provision for the safety of persons visiting such premises; it would certainly be arguable that the employers were not conducting their undertaking to the standard required by s.3 if their premises were not as safe as it was reasonably practicable for them to be for the persons they invited to come on to them. Section 4 makes special provision for situations in which persons are lawfully on non-domestic premises otherwise than in the course of employment by the occupier of those premises in circumstances in which the controller may not be an employer conducting an undertaking. Thus while there are large areas of overlap between ss.3 and 4 the two sections are not necessarily coterminous.

18. Safety of non-domestic premises

The s.4 duty is imposed by s.4(1) on persons controlling non-domestic premises in relation to those (excluding the employees of those on whom the duty is imposed) who use premises:

> made available to them as a place of work or as a place where they may use plant or substances provided for their use there (s.4(1)(b)).

It has already been noted that this provision was invoked in *Mailer* v. *Austin Rover Group plc* for the protection of visiting workers using premises and plant and equipment on the premises to carry out

maintenance work at a time when the controller's own employees
were not on the premises.

19. 'Place of work'

Indeed, in so far as the persons protected are required by the
first limb of the subsection to be using the premises as a 'place of
work' the s.4(1)(b) duty envisages exactly, and little more than, the
circumstances of the *Austin Rover* case. 'Work' in the expression
'place of work' is subject to the interpretation given in s.52, i.e.
work as an employee or a self-employed person. This limb of s.4(1)
therefore would grant no protection to, for example, under-
graduates using a reference library in the course of their studies,
albeit they themselves would consider they were 'working' in the
library!

20. Other premises

While the student in the example in **19** might not be within
the ambit of the first limb of the subsection there are nevertheless
situations in which members of the public might be within the
ambit of the second limb of s.4(1)(b) as persons who use
non-domestic premises as a place where they may use plant or
substances provided for their use there. When the 1974 Act was
first enacted it was noted that the Robens Report had expressed
some concern at the hazards faced by members of the public using
machinery such as washing machines in laundrettes, a situation
which is not necessarily within the protection of the Offices, Shops
and Railway Premises Act 1963. It was therefore suggested that s.4
was intended to provide safety standards in premises such as
laundrettes. Certainly the word 'plant' interpreted in s.53 to mean
'machinery, equipment or appliance' would seem to include
washing machines in laundrettes, facilities in public conveniences,
supermarket trolleys, petrol pumps and other garage forecourt
equipment, and perhaps furniture in hospital wards or hotel
bedrooms, to mention but a few examples.

21. Scope of the provision

Since the duty is only owed in relation to non-domestic
premises, there is some doubt whether the provision would apply
to blocks of flats. It is true that s.4 was utilised successfully in
relation to a block of flats in *Westminster City Council* v. *Select*

Managements Ltd [1985] but the application was somewhat special, and the Court of Appeal was not unanimous. The case arose because inspectors had required a property management company to carry out work to improve the lift at a block of flats. Although the company did do the repair work, they challenged whether s.4 of the 1974 Act could be used to require them to do so, since they alleged that the flats were domestic property. In the principal judgment Parker LJ referred to s.53 and found that it provided that 'domestic premises means premises occupied as a private dwelling'. In his Lordship's view the lifts and other common parts of the premises were not within the definition of domestic property. He also found that the definition of premises included an 'installation' and he considered the lifts to be installations within the definition of premises. The majority held that s.4 did apply even though there was no evidence that the property company actually employed any person to work on the premises: the purposes of the Act were wide enough to protect the public even where no worker was at risk. Eveleigh LJ dissented, because there was no evidence that any person at work, such as a milkman visiting the premises, would be at risk. In his view s.4 was only intended to protect persons at work.

None of their Lordships noted that the purposes in s.1 of the Act are limited to protecting persons other than persons at work from risks arising out of or in connection with the activities of persons at work. If this provision were narrowly interpreted it is doubtful whether the above case would be considered good law, and indeed many of the hypothetical examples listed above might prove to be beyond the scope of the provision, including the laundrettes identified by Lord Robens, unless the washing machines therein had been rendered unsafe by poor maintenance carried out by persons at work!

22. Significance of the benefit

The significance of any benefit given to the public in any case depends entirely on the extent to which the section can be enforced since no civil action for breach of statutory duty may be brought by any person who suffers personal injury because this duty (or indeed any other general duty) has not been observed. Possibly there are fewer opportunities for inspectors to identify risks to the public in breach of s.4, than there are for identification of hazards in industrial premises.

The controller of premises

23. Meaning of 'controller of premises'
Section 4(2) imposes the duties under s.4 on:

> each person who has, to any extent, control of premises . . . or of the means of access thereto or egress therefrom or of any plant or substance in such premises . . .

The provision thus contemplates that more than one person may have some control of any given premises at any given time, and that every person with control has some responsibility under s.4. It is rather surprising that the statute uses the word 'controller' since both civil and criminal law are more inclined to use the word 'occupier'. However, the argument is circular: the Occupiers' Liability Act 1957 fails to define 'occupier' but states that for the purposes of the civil liability under that Act the 'persons who are to be treated as an occupier . . . are the same as the persons who would at common law be treated as an occupier . . .' (s.1(2)). The civil case of *Wheat* v. *Lacon & Co Ltd* [1966] (though not necessarily a binding precedent when determining issues of criminal liability under s.4 of the 1974 Act) may usefully be considered in the present context.

> *Wheat* v. *Lacon & Co. Ltd* [1966]: The case concerned premises which were owned by a brewery. The ground floor was run as a public house by a manager employed by the brewery. The manager occupied the upper part as his private dwelling and, in the summer, his wife took in boarding guests for her private profit. Mr Wheat (a guest) fell to his death down the back staircase in the private part of the premises. The trial judge found that there were two causes of the accident: (a) that the handrail was too short; and (b) that there was no bulb in the light fitting on the stairs. Their Lordships had to determine whether the brewers or their manager were occupiers. Lord Denning deduced:

In order to be an 'occupier' it is not necessary for a person to have entire control over the premises. He need not have exclusive occupation. Suffice it that he has some degree of control. He may share the control with others. Two or more may be 'occupiers'. And whenever this happens, each is under a duty to use care towards persons coming on to the premises, dependent on his degree of control.

Their Lordships found that both the brewery and the manager were occupiers of the premises. The manager had responsibility for the day-to-day management, including ensuring the presence of a light bulb; the brewery had responsibility for structural matters such as the handrail.

24. Duties when more than one controller

Not only does the criminal law, as set out in s.4 of the 1974 Act, now recognise the possibility of dual control of premises, but it similarly spells out that responsibilities may be shared between controllers according to the extent of their control: s.4(2) provides that it is the duty of each person who has to any extent control of premises to which the section applies 'to take such measures as it is reasonable for a person in his position to take'.

25. Scope of the duty

The duty is complicated because it is not a duty to ensure that the premises are absolutely safe, but only to make them as safe as is reasonably practicable. Thus the duty of individual controllers is to do what is reasonable to achieve what is reasonably practicable! In *Mailer* v. *Austin Rover* it was held that a controller had a duty to ensure that the premises were safe for those to whom he had given the right of entry and would be prima facie liable if the premises proved unsafe, even if the defect was unforeseeable, or the visitor put them to some unexpected use. The controller in such circumstances would, in the view of Lord Goff, only escape liability if it were not reasonably practicable for him to foresee the risk. By stressing that the duty is an absolute one subject to the defence of reasonable practicability his Lordship leaves open the question of the relevance of the word 'reasonable' in relation to the duty.

26. On whom might the duty be imposed?

The duty is imposed on any person who, by reason of a contract or tenancy in relation to premises, has responsibility for maintenance or repair of the premises or for the safety (or absence of risk to health) of plant or substances at the premises (s.4(3)). The duty under s.4 applies only to a person who has control of premises in connection with the carrying on by him of a trade, business or other undertaking (whether for profit or not) (s.4(4)). Arguably, therefore, — depending on the interpretation of 'undertaking' — the s.4 duties might apply to church premises or premises occupied by a charity for a fund-raising event, provided always, however, that there was sufficient association between the hazard and the activities of persons at work for the situation to be within the purposes of s.1(1)(b) of the Act.

27. Effect on the general public

It is not impossible that in order to comply with s.4 controllers of premises might have to exercise some control over members of the public, such as crowd or vehicle control, if, without such control, the premises would not be safe.

Neighbourhood risks

28. Emission of noxious or offensive substances

It has been noted that s.3 requires the undertaking to have regard for neighbourhood risks. Section 5 relates to a particular neighbourhood risk: the emission into the environment from the work premises of noxious or offensive substances. The section was expressly related to the purposes of the Act set out in s.1(1)(d):

> controlling the emission into the atmosphere of noxious or offensive substances from premises of any class prescribed for the purposes of this paragraph.

29. Scope of the provision

Section 5 relates only to premises, and the emission therefrom of noxious and offensive substances where the premises and the proscribed substances have been identified by regulations. The section clearly had in view the situations covered by the earlier Alkali etc. Works Regulation Act 1906, which was a relevant statutory provision. The Health and Safety (Emission into the Atmosphere) Regulations 1983 prescribed certain classes of premises for the purposes of s.5 and further provided that premises which the 1906 Act treated as scheduled premises should be deemed to be 'prescribed premises' under the 1974 Act and that the same substances should be deemed to be noxious and offensive for the purposes of both Acts.

For present purposes further discussion of these issues is no longer appropriate for the Environmental Protection Act 1990 made provision for the repeal of both s.1(1)(d) and s.5 and in the foreseeable future therefore these matters will cease to be within the ambit of the 1974 Act, although the 1990 Act makes complex arrangements for the involvement of the HSE in the identification and resolution of environmental matters which would formerly have been within Part I of the 1974 Act.

The worker as a consumer

30. General

Section 6 of the 1974 Act contained provisions for the worker, as a user of articles and substances, in terms which have since been largely adopted for the protection of consumers generally by virtue of the Consumer Protection Act 1987, Part II. In addition, on the enactment of the 1987 Act, s.6 of the 1974 Act was revised both to clarify certain phrases originally used within s.6 and also to bring fairground equipment within the ambit of s.6 (Consumer Protection Act 1987, s.36 and Schedule 3). Section 6 is, however, except for the provisions concerning fairground equipment, intended solely for the protection of persons at work.

31. Persons under duty

Section 6 imposes its duties on persons who design, manufacture, import and supply articles for use at work (s.6(1)) or any article of fairground equipment (s.6(1A)), and on persons who manufacture, import or supply any substance for use at work (s.6(4)). Surprisingly, in the revised wording, the duty in regard to articles apparently applies only when goods are intended, i.e. manufactured etc., for use at work, whereas the duty in respect of substances applies when substances are used at work, seemingly

whether or not this was the intention of the manufacturer etc.
Section 6(3) places duties on persons who erect or install articles
for use at work, or who erect or install fairground equipment.

32. Nature of duty

The duties in s.6 are to do what is *reasonably practicable* to ensure
so far as is *reasonably practicable* that the articles, fairground
equipment and substances are safe and without risks to health in
the circumstances to which the duties relate. The difference in
wording between s.6(1) and s.6(4) identified in the previous
paragraph may not therefore be very significant: a supplier etc.
who does not intend that substances are for use at work may be
able to establish that it was not *reasonably practicable* for him to
identify the risk of their being so used.

33. Activities to be protected

(a) An article is required to be safe and without risks to health, so
far as reasonably practicable, 'at all times when it is being set, used,
cleaned or maintained by a person at work', and that (see below
in relation to provision of information) it is safe etc. 'when it is
being dismantled or disposed of'.
(b) The obligation in respect of fairground equipment is to ensure
its safety 'at all times when it is being used for or in connection
with the entertainment of members of the public'.
(c) The obligation in respect of a substance is to ensure its safety
'at all times when it is being used, handled, processed, stored or
transported by a person at work or in premises to which s.4
applies', and that (see below in relation to provision of
information) it is safe etc. 'when being disposed of'.

34. Application of the provisions

Broadly the obligations apply to the use of the articles,
equipment and substances at work, but it has been deemed
necessary to spell out activities in association with their use to
ensure that the duty is not evaded by arguing that the activity being
conducted was not use at work. For example, if the words 'stored',
'transported', 'cleaned' and 'maintained' had not been expressly
included it might be argued that any of these activities, even
though possibly associated with use at work, was distinct from that

activity and without the scope of a duty which was stated merely to apply to 'use'.

Nevertheless in *McKay* v. *Unwin Pyrotechnics* (1991) the Divisional Court held that there had been no contravention of the duty under s.6(1)(a) when a person was injured while carrying out the first trial and demonstrations of a dummy mine. It could not be said that the mine was designed for use at work. Thus there was no breach of the provision even though the victim had been injured while at work.

35. Fairground equipment

In the case of fairground equipment the requirement relates to its condition when it is being used for, or in connection with, the entertainment of members of the public. Bringing this provision within the 1974 Act illustrates the concern which has been felt in recent years for matters of public safety.

36. Specific requirements regarding articles

Those bearing duties in respect of articles and fairground equipment are required to ensure that these commodities are safe (and without risks to health) in design and construction. Further to this requirement they are required to carry out, or arrange for the carrying out, of such testing and examination as may be necessary to ensure their safety. However, persons are not required to repeat any testing or examination if the circumstances are such that they may reasonably rely on the results of work which has been undertaken by others.

37. Provision of information

There is a duty, expressed in similar, but not identical terms, in relation to the provision of adequate information about articles and fairground equipment:

> to take such steps as are necessary to secure that persons supplied by that person with the article are provided with adequate information about the use for which the article is designed, or has been tested and about any conditions necessary to ensure that it will be safe and without risks to health.

The duty in respect of articles applies when they are being set, used, cleaned or maintained by a person at work and when they are being dismantled or disposed of. The duty in respect of fairground equipment applies only when it is being used for, or in connection with, the entertainment of members of the public. This raises the question whether there is any statutory protection for those who are cleaning, maintaining, dismantling, etc., fairground equipment. Presumably it would be argued that when these activities are being carried out by persons at work, and the public is not involved, the general provisions concerning articles would apply to the equipment in question, i.e. that the special provisions in relation to fairground equipment are in addition to, not an alternative to, the general provisions relating to articles.

38. Revision of information provided

In respect of both articles and fairground equipment there is a duty to secure, so far as is reasonably practicable, that persons who have been supplied with information are also provided with any revisions of information which are necessary by reason of it becoming known that anything gives rise to a serious risk to health or safety.

39. Specific requirements regarding substances

The specific duties in respect of substances are very similar to those outlined in respect of articles, though, to take account of the different inherent problems in relation to substances, the duty in respect of provision of information is somewhat differently worded (s.6(4)(c)):

> to take such steps as are necessary to secure that persons supplied by that person with the substance are provided with adequate information about any risks to health or safety to which the inherent properties of the substance may give rise, about the results of any relevant tests which have been carried out on or in connection with the substance and about any conditions necessary to ensure that the substance will be safe and without risks to health . . .

The duty to carry out tests and research in relation to substances before they are marketed for use at work (s.6(5)) is especially important given the large number of new chemical substances being brought into use in industry at the present time. The onerous nature of the duties means that it will be unlikely that a manufacturer or supplier of something which emerges as a dangerous substance is able to plead that the risk to persons at work from the use of that substance was not foreseeable.

These duties are only imposed in respect of things done in the course of a trade, business or other undertaking, but they apply whether or not the activity is carried on for profit.

40. Scope of duty imposed

A person's duty extends only to matters which are within that person's control. This suggests that the ambit of the manufacturer's duty might be different from that of, say, the supplier. In this respect s.6 may be contrasted with the Consumer Protection Act 1987: under that Act the strict civil liability to compensate for injuries caused by unsafe goods is placed primarily upon the producer (i.e. the manufacturer), whereas the criminal liability rests primarily upon the supplier (i.e. generally the shopkeeper). However, under both consumer and occupational safety legislation the primary objective must be to identify unsafe goods before they have been supplied for use, and serve a prohibition or similar, notice to prevent their onward supply. Consumer protection legislation has focused on seizure of unsafe goods at the point of entry into the jurisdiction and has given customs officers power to seize and detain imported goods to facilitate the work of enforcement officers. The 1987 Act inserts s.25A into the 1974 Act to give customs and excise officers similar powers in respect of articles intended for use at work.

41. EC safety standards

It is not normally possible to invoke s.6 against goods which comply with EC safety standards.

42. Written undertakings

Section 6(8) gives limited powers to persons who design, manufacturer, import or supply articles to reduce their obligations: it enables them to get a written undertaking from the person with whom they are dealing that that other person will take specific steps sufficient to ensure that the article will be used in compliance with the requirements of s.6. This subsection cannot be interpreted as a general invitation to manufacturers and suppliers to enter into contracts transferring their statutory responsibilities to their customers. It is clear that the subsection is intended only to apply to limited circumstances where the nature and extent of the transfer of obligations is clearly spelled out; it seems likely that there would need to be established that there was some particular purpose for the arrangement other than lightening the obligations of the person taking the benefit of the undertaking. Possibly the special reason might be that the article was supplied for incorporation in some larger article the purchaser was constructing to a special specification, e.g. a guard might not be needed for a part of a machine where the whole, of which it was to be a part, would be covered by a protective device.

43. Risk not foreseeable

Section 6 originally contained a proviso exonerating manufacturers etc. from liability in cases where it could be shown that the article or substance in question had been rendered unsafe by being other than 'properly used'. The application of this proviso proved problematic and since the 1987 Act the expression is no longer used. Instead the exemption from liability is given in relation to what is reasonably foreseeable. Section 6(10) now provides:

> For the purposes of this section an absence of safety or a risk to health shall be disregarded in so far as the case in or in relation to which it would arise is shown to be one the occurrence of which could not reasonably be foreseen . . .

The addition of this proviso does not appear to add anything to the interpretation of *reasonably practicable* (which is the standard in s.6) which was given in the *Austin Rover* case; it will be recalled that in that case it was stated in the House of Lords that the defence of reasonable practicability would be established by showing that the risk was not foreseeable. Moreover, the wording of s.6(10) suggests that the burden would be on the defendant to establish under that subsection that the risk was not foreseeable.

44. Articles and substances

Section 6 relates to articles and substances, whereas the Consumer Protection Act, in the tradition of consumer protection, relates to goods. It is probable that largely the same commodities are covered by both safety statutes. Certainly the EC's Directive on classification, packaging and labelling of dangerous substances has resulted in similar regulatory provisions under both pieces of legislation (subject to provisions to accommodate the fact that substances are often supplied to industry in bulk). However, the 1974 Act envisages also equipment which would have no place in the supermarket and it contains its own definitions:

'article for use at work' means —
   (a) any plant designed for use or operation (whether exclusively or not) by persons at work, and
   (b) any article designed for use as a component in any such plant;
'substance' means any natural or artificial substance (including micro-organisms), whether in solid or liquid form or in the form of a gas or vapour (s.53).

45. Relationship between s.6 and employers' duties

It has always been apparent that s.6 and s.2 were related: s.6 imposes upon suppliers etc. obligations to ensure that safe goods are supplied to the workplace accompanied by proper instructions as to their use, while s.2 imposes upon the employer the duty to ensure that the articles and substances brought into the workplace are safe and used in accordance with any manufacturer's instructions. In particular employers need to ensure that information supplied with invoices, or on bulk packages, actually reaches the worker using them. They also need to ensure that the worker is trained, monitored and, if necessary, disciplined to ensure safety instructions are observed. The employers' general duty has now been strengthened by the duty to assess the safety of products which is imposed upon them by the Control of Substances Hazardous to Health Regulations 1988.

Other duties which involve the public

46. Duty of employees

The duty imposed on the employee under s.7 is wide enough to require employees to have regard for public safety when they are at work, since they are required to take reasonable care for the health and safety of other persons (without any qualification) who may be affected by their acts or omissions at work.

47. Duty of the general public

Similarly s.8 imposes duties on the general public, since without qualification it places a prohibition on interference with anything provided in compliance with any of the relevant statutory provisions. However, there is only liability under this section for behaviour which is an intentional or reckless interference.

48. Limitation of the provisions

Section 8 (as indeed s.7 or the other general duties) cannot be invoked by enterprises against any persons who, by their behaviour, create hazards. Such organisation will have to rely on any powers they may have by reason of contract or licence to control persons whose conduct is creating hazards. Organisations may need to exercise these powers if they are to avoid being in breach of ss.2, 3 and even 4 of the 1974 Act. If those who are creating hazards will not respond to requests it may be necessary to call the police in order to restrain them. Any hazardous situation which has been created will have to be remedied by the organisation as speedily as possible, whatever the long-term possibilities of obtaining an indemnity from the wrongdoer.

Progress test 7

1. Within what parameters does the 1974 Act provide protection for the public? **(2)**

2. In what circumstances does s.4 provide protection for the public? **(20)**

3. What statute made provision for the repeal of s.5 of the 1974 Act? **(29)**

4. To what extent is foresight relevant to liability under ss. 4 and 6? **(25, 43)**

5. What aspects of environmental protection are clearly beyond the ambit of the 1974 Act? **(8)**

6. In what circumstances does s.6 require articles and substances to be safe? **(33)**

7. What responsibilities does s.6 impose in respect of testing and research? **(36)**

8. In what circumstances may a person on whom the s.6 duties are imposed reduce their obligations? **(42)**

8
Other relevant statutory provisions

1. Introduction
Section 53, in Part I of the 1974 Act, defines 'relevant statutory provisions':

(a) the provisions of this Part and of any health and safety regulations; and
(b) the existing statutory provisions.

The 'existing statutory provisions' were a number of earlier pieces of legislation identified in Schedule I of the 1974 Act and placed within the jurisdiction of the HSC and HSE.

Since 1974 the jurisdiction of HSC and HSE has been further extended to a number of additional situations, such as railways, offshore installations and carriage of dangerous substances by road. At the same time the existing statutory provisions have been largely repealed, in furtherance of the intention expressed in s.1(2) of the 1974 Act that the enactments identified in Schedule 1 and regulations made under them should be:

> progressively replaced by a system of regulations and approved codes of practice . . . designed to maintain or improve the standards of health, safety and welfare established by or under those enactments.

2. Scope of this chapter
This chapter will consider the more important of the remaining provisions of the 'existing statutory provisions' and then consider legislation which has been brought into the system since 1974.

Many of the statutes covered in this chapter only apply to particular workplaces, particular classes of workers, or particular work activities, and they, or regulations made under them, contain detailed regulatory standards which now apply in addition to the general duties within Part I of the 1974 Act itself. The relevant legislation itself interprets the scope and application of its provisions, but nevertheless there has been much case law further interpreting the intention of the legislature.

3. The existing statutory provisions

Schedule 1 of the 1974 Act lists over 30 statutes, the whole or part of each of which were in 1974 both existing statutory provisions and, for the purposes of the Act, 'relevant statutory provisions'. Of these the following are sufficiently important to warrant consideration here:

> The Mines and Quarries Act 1954
> The Agriculture (Safety Health and Welfare Provisions) Act 1956
> The Factories Act 1961
> The Offices, Shops and Railway Premises Act 1963
> The Mines and Quarries (Tips) Act 1969

The Factories Act 1961

4. General

This legislation is the most significant of the Schedule 1 statutes; even in the present 'post-industrial' society, it applies to more workplaces than any other occupational health and safety statute except the 1974 Act itself. The standards in the Act (and its supporting regulations) have often provided useful guidelines as to what is 'reasonably practicable' for many other workplaces.

Much of the Factories Act has been repealed; administrative, legislative, enforcement and penal provisions have all been assimilated in the general system under the 1974 Act (*see* the Factories Act 1961 (Repeals) Regulations 1975 and 1976, and the Factories Act 1961 (Repeals and Modifications) Regulations 1974). Additionally, many of the new regulations made under the 1974 Act, with the object of bringing together and simplifying numbers of statutory duties, have repealed parts of the 1961 Act (*see*, for example, the Health and Safety (First Aid) Regulations 1981).

Some of the new regulations have brought to factories entirely new protection, e.g. the Control of Lead at Work Regulations 1980. More of the 1961 Act, and a number of regulations made under it, will be repealed and phased out with the implementation of regulations to comply with EC Directives, particularly the Workplace (Health, Safety and Welfare) Regulations which will implement the Workplace Directive.

5. Application of the Act

The 1961 Act applies to a number of premises and processes, together with a list of specific activities which it has been decided on policy grounds to treat as factories. The present statutory interpretation of 'factory' is contained in s.175. The most significant elements of s.175 are:

> ... any premises in which, or within the close or curtilage or precincts of which, persons are employed in manual labour in any process for or incidental to any of the following purposes, namely —
> (a) the making of an article or part of any article, or
> (b) the altering, repairing, ornamenting, finishing, cleaning or washing, or the breaking up or demolition of any article; or
> (c) the adapting for sale of any article . . .
> . . . being premises in which, or within the close or curtilage or precincts of which, the work is carried on by way of trade or for purposes of gain, and to or over which the employer of the persons employed therein has the right of access or control.

Section 175(2) extends the definition to a number of other premises in which persons are employed in manual labour in specified processes, e.g. construction, reconstruction or repair of locomotives (s.175(2)(g)) and printing by letterpress, lithography, photogravure (s.175(2)(h)).

It has proved impossible to frame a definition to include all the necessary matters, namely geographically defined premises, manual labour employed by the controller of the premises, production of an article by a process, and a commercial objective. Thus building and work of engineering construction required specific treatment 'bypassing' the s.175 definition (s.127).

The major provisions of the Act are discussed further in paragraphs **6–12** below.

6. Part I: health

(a) *Cleanliness.* Every factory must be kept in a clean state, in accordance with regulatory standards (s.1 and the Factories (Cleanliness of Walls and Ceilings) Order 1960).

(b) *Overcrowding.* No factory shall be so overcrowded as to cause risk of injury to the health of the persons employed in it. Each worker must have a minimum of 11 cubic metres of space (s.2).

(c) *Temperature.* Effective provision must be made for securing and maintaining a reasonable temperature; the temperature must, if the work is sedentary, be at least 16°C after the first hour of work (s.3).

(d) *Ventilation.* Effective and suitable provision must be made for securing and maintaining the circulation of fresh air in each workroom (s.4).

(e) *Lighting.* Effective and suitable provision must be made for securing and maintaining sufficient and suitable lighting, whether natural or artifical (s.5).

(f) *Drainage of floors.* Where any process is carried on which renders the floor liable to be wet, effective means shall be provided and maintained for draining off the wet.

(g) *Sanitary conveniences.* Sufficient and suitable conveniences must be provided, maintained and kept clean (s.7 and the Sanitary Accommodation Regulations 1938).

7. Part II: general safety provisions

(a) *Machinery.* The arrangements for the safeguarding of machinery are dated, being framed for the nineteenth-century factory with a substantial steam or water-driven 'prime mover' (s.12) driving quantities of shafting or belting (transmission machinery, s.13) which carried power to the individual loom or other machine (other machinery, s.14). All machinery must be securely 'fenced' (guarded). Section 14(1) remains of great importance. It requires that:

> every dangerous part of any machinery, other than prime movers and transmission machinery, shall be securely fenced, unless it is in such a position or of such construction as to be as safe to every person employed or working on the premises as it would be if securely fenced.

Section 14(1) covers *inter alia* lathes, looms, presses. Since it is only required that 'dangerous parts' be fenced, there has been much litigation on this phrase (especially in the civil courts), but, once the duty to fence is held to arise, the obligation is treated as an absolute one — the fact of injury to an individual is evidence that the duty has not been discharged (*see John Summers & Sons Ltd* v. *Frost* [1955]). Regulations may be made reducing the strict nature of this duty, making compliance with the regulations sufficient for compliance with the Act, e.g. the Abrasive Wheels Regulations 1970.

(b) *The supplier*. Under s.17 elementary safety duties are imposed upon the supplier of certain machines.

It is proposed that regulations to implement the EC Directive on Work Equipment will repeal ss.12–17, but s.14(1) will be replaced by a similar duty for application to workplaces generally.

(c) *Young persons*. Similarly s.21 (and the Dangerous Machines (Training of Young Persons) Order 1954) provides that young persons must not work at prescribed machines without instruction as to the dangers, and either training or adequate supervision.

(d) *Hoists and lifting tackle*. Detailed provisions govern the construction, maintenance and examination of hoists and lifts. There are additional mechanical safeguards required for those used for carrying persons (ss.22–25). Such equipment must be periodically examined and certificates of the examination must be made and kept available. In the case of electrically operated lifts, the certificates must comply with EC norms (*see* Electrically Operated Lifts (EC Requirements) Regulations 1986).

(e) *Chains, ropes and other lifting tackle*. These are strictly regulated as regards strength of material, construction and regularity of testing (s.26). Cranes and other lifting machines must be of good construction, sound material, adequate strength and free from patent defect, and proper precautions must be taken against overloading (s.27).

The courts have interpreted the statutory duties in relation to hoists and lifting tackle as imposing a very strict obligation upon the occupier.

(f) *Floors, steps, passages and gangways*. These must be of sound construction and properly maintained, and, as far as reasonably practicable, be kept free from any obstruction and from substances likely to cause persons to slip.

(g) *Safe means of access.* This must be provided and maintained to every place at which a persons has to work, and the place of work itself must, likewise, be made and kept safe (s.29).

(h) *Steam boilers and pressure vessels.* Sections 32–34 make detailed provisions for steam boilers. Section 35 makes similar provision for steam receivers (i.e. a vessel in which steam is stored, not generated), while s.36 provides, on the same basis, for air receivers used for compressed air. While air and steam receivers are met with in present-day industry, steam boilers are rarely encountered.

(i) *Protection of eyes.* A power to require the use of eye protection was formerly contained in s.65. This power has now been subsumed under s.15 of the 1974 Act, but the Factories Act regulations, i.e. the Protection of Eyes Regulations 1974, remain in force for the time being.

8. Part III: welfare

(a) *Drinking water* (s.57). There must be an adequate supply of drinking water.

(b) *Washing facilities* (s.58). There must be adequate and suitable facilities for washing, including a supply of clean running hot and cold water, and soap and drying facilities.

(c) *Accommodation for clothing* (s.59). There must be adequate and suitable accommodation for clothing not worn during working hours.

(d) *Seating facilities* (s.60). There must be suitable facilities for sitting where employees may have the opportunity to sit without detriment to their work. Where a substantial proportion of the work can properly be done sitting, the seats must meet the standards of s.60(2), i.e. be of a suitable design, construction and dimension for the worker and the work.

9. Interpretation the 1961 Act

The safety provisions contained in the 1961 Act have been in force for many years, many having been carried forward from even earlier legislation; furthermore, many of them are supported by detailed regulations which are also now of some age. The tendency has been to retain phrases that have been examined in litigation, and thus attracted a considerable legal learning, in

successive legislation provisions, e.g. 'securely fenced' in relation
to machinery (ss. 12,13,14); 'dangerous part of any machinery'
(s.14); 'maintained', 'properly maintained' in relation to machine
guarding, hoists and lifts, floors steps and stairs, and steam boilers
(ss.16,22, 28,33).

10. Standard of care required

Most of the offences are of strict liability. Many of the cases in
which they have been interpreted have been civil claims for
compensation, but the interpretations of the civil courts have been
used in criminal enforcement, often creating more onerous duties
than usually found in criminal law. For example, in *Galashiels Gas
Co.* v. *O'Donnell* [1949] the House of Lords held, in a civil claim,
that the duty in s.22, that every hoist or lift should be properly
maintained, imported an absolute obligation, and it was no
defence to establish that a reasonable system of routine inspection
and repair was in force.

In contrast the comprehensive obligations under ss.28 and 29
(safe floors etc., and safe means of access), are not absolute duties:
they are duties to do what is reasonably practicable. The
qualification to these duties means that a claim, for example that
a spillage had rendered a passageway an 'unsafe means of access',
might be met by evidence of the frequency with which the
passageway was swept or otherwise cleaned (e.g. *Braham* v. *J Lyons
& Co. Ltd* [1962]).

11. Duties

Where there is failure to comply with the statutory obligations
the 'occupier' of the factory is guilty of an offence (s.155(1)).
'Occupier' is not defined in the Act, but the courts have identified
that the occupier is the person or business organisation by whom
the business is carried on. The occupier need not be the owner of
the premises, but must be the employer of some at least of the
workers at risk. Exceptionally, certain provisions impose duties
directly upon the owner of the premises, e.g. the owner of a
tenement factory; similarly, where a machine or equipment used
in a factory is the property of some other person than the occupier,
that other person is liable in respect of that particular machine
(s.163).

12. Defences

Now that the penalties and enforcement provisions of the 1961 Act have been replaced by those of the 1974 Act the special defences made available against contraventions of the latter Act (*see* ss.36 and 37 of the 1974 Act) may also be invoked for breaches of the 1961 Act.

13. Proposals for repeal

It is proposed to repeal provisions relating to health (ss.1–7), hoists (s.24), safe means of access (s.29) and welfare (s.57–60) when the Health Safety and Welfare Regulations are introduced in January 1993, but these provisions will largely continue to apply to existing workplaces until 1996 and may, in this interim period, influence the interpretation of the new regulations and accompanying code of practice in their application to new workplaces.

The Offices, Shops and Railway Premises Act 1963

14. General

The long title of this Act describes it an as Act to make fresh provision for securing the health, safety and welfare of persons employed to work in office or shop premises and provision for securing the health, safety and welfare of persons employed to work in certain railway premises. It was the first statutory protection for office workers; on the other hand the hours of work of shop workers had for long been, and after 1963 continued to be, governed by Shops Acts. The coverage of railway premises is limited, this Act being intended only to deal with premises not already covered by other legislative provisions.

15. Differences and similarities to the Factories Act 1961

The 1963 Act largely follows the format of the Factories Act 1961; the differences being partly that the 1963 Act does not adopt the more outdated provisions of the Factories Act and also, as it relates to less dangerous employment, it does not incorporate those provisions of the 1961 Act which apply to hazards peculiar to factories. While its provisions are similar to the Factories Act, the 1963 Act is not supported by a great number of detailed regulations, though it did contain a regulation making power (s.20). Nevertheless the similarities are sufficient for the 1963 Act to be treated only briefly here. As with the Factories Act, provisions relating to administration, enforcement and regulation-making power have been repealed and replaced by the general scheme contained in, or by regulations made under, the 1974 Act. Again, as with the Factories Act, it is likely to be further repealed by regulations to implement EC Directives.

16. Scope of the Act

Section 1 defines the premises to which the Act is intended to apply. In outline these are:

Office premises means a building or part of a building being a building or part the sole or principal use of which is as an office or for office purposes.

Shop premises means —
(i) a shop;
(ii) a building or part of a building, . . . which is not a shop but of which the sole or principal use is the carrying on there of retail trade or business;
(iii) a building occupied by a wholesale dealer or merchant where goods are kept for sale wholesale . . .
(iv) a building to which members of the public are invited to resort for the purpose of delivering there goods for repair or other treatment . . .
(v). . . fuel storage premises . . . occupied for the purpose of a trade or business which consists of, or includes, the sale of solid fuel . . . (s.1(3)).

Railway premises means a building occupied by railway undertakers for the purposes of the railway undertaking carried on by them and situate in the immediate vicinity of the permanent way . . . but does not include —
(a) office or shop premises;
(b) premises used for the provision of living accommodation for persons employed in the undertaking, or hotels; or
(c) premises where are carried on such processes or operations as are mentioned in s.123(1) (electrical stations) of the Factories Act 1961 . . .

The 1963 Act, in the pattern of the pre-1974 statutory provisions, is only intended to protect employed persons, so s.2

expressly excludes from its ambit premises in which only family members are employed; it also excludes 'homeworkers' even if employed by other than a relative. Nor does it apply to premises which are used by employed persons for less than 21 hours a week.

17. Health, safety and welfare of employees
The Act makes provision for the following, in terms similar to the Factories Act:

(a) *cleanliness* (s.4);
(b) *overcrowding* (s.5);
(c) *temperature* (s.6);
(d) *ventilation* (s.7);
(e) *lighting* (s.8);
(f) *sanitary conveniences* (s.9);
(g) *washing facilities* (s.10);
(h) *supply of drinking water* (s.11);
(i) *accommodation for clothing* (s.12);
(j) *sitting facilities* (ss.13 and 14);
(k) *eating facilities* (s.15): where persons employed to work in shop premises eat meals there, suitable and sufficient facilities for eating them shall be provided;
(l) *safety of floors, stairs, steps, passages and gangways* (s.16): a hand-rail must be provided to staircases, on the open side(s) if applicable. Where there is an open side(s) this must be guarded so as to prevent persons from falling through the space between the handrail and the stairs;
(m) *dangerous parts of machinery must be securely fenced* (s.17).

18. Proposals for repeal
It is proposed that ss. 4–16 will be repealed in January 1993 by the Health, Safety and Welfare Regulations and will therefore not apply to premises brought into use after that date; their standards will continue to apply to other premises until 1996.

The Mines and Quarries Act 1954

19. General
Of all the enactments in Schedule 1 of the 1974 Act, the Mines

and Quarries Act (the 1954 Act) seems the least likely to be absorbed by the 1974 Act although the technical requirements as set out in the 1954 Act may well need to be updated from time to time, by regulations made under the 1974 Act.

The 1954 Act was perhaps the most effective of the pre-1974 occupational safety codes; it resulted in a significant reduction in mine accidents and fatalities in the 1955–1975 period. Nevertheless, the introduction of the 1974 Act has meant that much of it has been replaced by the provisions of the 1974 Act, particularly in relation to administration, regulation-making, inspection and enforcement. However, the 1954 Act and its surviving codes of regulations remain a vital source of technical safety standards and practices peculiar to mining conditions.

Although the 1954 Act deals with all mines and all quarries in Britain, it deals separately with (a) coal mines and mines presenting similar problems; (b) non-coal mines (miscellaneous mines); and (c) quarries — representing, as they do, a descending order of danger. Thus the most rigorous standards apply to underground coal mines.

20. Coal mine regulation

The term 'coal' covers, for the purposes of the 1954 Act, mines of coal, stratified ironstone, shale and fireclay. Part I of the 1954 Act, which deals with the powers, duties and responsibilities of all levels of mine managers, technicians and officials, applies in its full rigour only to 'coal' mines, but the legislative requirements relating to management in other mines and quarries are broadly the same.

21. Management and control

The owner of every coal mine has duties to ensure both that the mine is managed and worked in compliance with the 1954 Act, and that all provisions of the Act and regulations are complied with by all persons concerned (s.1). These duties will normally (and in the case of mines must) be discharged through the agency of a competent manager, possessing the prescribed qualifications, appropriate to the size and complexity of the particular mine. In the case of any coal mine employing more than 30 people underground, no manager is qualified unless he possesses a statutory first-class certificate of competency obtained by formal written examination (s.4).

22. The manager-employer relationship

An important feature of the 1954 Act is the power to disqualify the holder of a statutory certificate of competency. Disqualification may be effected either by order of a court following conviction of an offence under the Act, or by the decision of a special administrative tribunal upon evidence of 'misconduct, incompetence, or gross negligence' (s.150). Further, the relationships between mine owners and managers of coal mines are hedged with detailed statutory provisions that are peculiar to the mining industry. The manager's primary duty is to have 'management and control' of the mine, and to secure the discharge by all others of their statutory duties with regard to the mine (s.2(2)), thus he bears a heavy personal responsibility in the event of accident or disaster. Nevertheless, he still remains subject to the command of his employer but commands, which are not in writing, must be so reduced by the employer at the manager's request (s.3(1)). Additionally, the owner of a coal mine may not, except in an emergency, or with the consent of the manager, give instructions directly to subordinates of his: where the owner exercises his right to give such orders he must be prepared to confirm them in writing to the manager (s.3(2)).

Section 3(3) entitles the manager to decline to obey orders from his employer concerning the safety and health of the employees for whom he is responsible, until they have been confirmed in writing by a person who holds statutory qualifications to manage a coal mine, and is necessarily subject to the same legal and professional discipline as the manager is himself subject.

23. Delegation of duties

Some of the manager's duties may be delegated to a manager's assistant, providing he holds the necessary qualifications (the Mines (Management) Act 1971). An undermanager (or undermanagers) must be appointed in all but the smallest mines; the appointee must hold the specified qualifications, and be subject to the same special professional discipline. Surveyors, officials and technicians must also be appointed for the mine from those possessing the qualifications specified for such persons in the legislation (ss.9–14).

24. Mine safety standards

Owners and managers of coal mines must comply with the detailed requirements — known as 'good mining practice' — set out in the surviving provisions of Part III of the 1954 Act, and the large number of regulations applicable to mining activity, in addition to the provisions of the 1974 Act and certain general regulations such as the Electricity at Work Regulations 1989.

The special mining requirements include safe means of egress and ingress requirements — including a 'two means of egress' requirement (the Mines (Safety of Exit) Regulations 1988) and safety precautions in connection with shafts and entrances (ss.30–32, 36–37, 39–47).

25. Statutory duties

(a) A vital management duty is to ensure the support of the strata of every road and working place (ss.48–54).

(b) The duty to secure the ventilation of the mine, both to protect the health of mineworkers, and to dilute the flammable gases present in the air of the mine, is imposed in the first instance upon the manager (ss.55–60). A duty also exists to remove all potential sources of ignition against fire or explosion arising from lighting sources, electrical apparatus, blasting materials, or otherwise. The strictness of this duty naturally varies according to the severity of the explosion risks in particular mines (ss.55–60, ss.62–64 (as amended)). The duty is most stringent in the most gaseous mines — known as 'safety lamp mines' (defined s.182(1)), in which only tested flameproof electrical apparatus or safety lamps may be used, and in which smoking is prohibited. There is a strict duty to take precautions against dust in mines, as a precaution against both respiratory disease and explosive hazards (s.74).

(c) Stringent precautions in the use of explosives in mines are contained in the Coal Mines (Explosives) Regulations 1961.

(d) Special arrangements must be made and maintained for fire precautions in mines, and for the organisation of central rescue stations where specially trained rescue personnel and equipment are available to assist following mine disasters (ss.70 and 72).

(e) A most important provision requires the securing of the safety of employees against the dangers from underground water, mud or similar hazards, or from incursions from the sea or other surface water (ss.81–87).

(f) Provisions relating to the safety of machinery, plant, apparatus and structures are similar to those in the Factories Act 1961.

26. Standard of duties

Duties are generally to 'secure' or to 'take such steps as may be necessary to secure' (e.g. ventilation standards, roof support, lighting, protection against water) or to 'ensure' (e.g. dust precautions). This may be contrasted with the 'reasonably practicable' qualification governing the general duties under the 1974 Act. However, s.157 of the 1954 Act offers a defence of proof that it was 'impracticable' to avoid or prevent a contravention. This defence is available in either civil or criminal proceedings.

27. Workmens' inspectors

There is a right of inspection of all parts of the mine by appointed employee representatives (s.123). This system is similar to that set up by regulations made under the 1974 Act for other workplaces.

28. Employment of women

The prohibition of employment of women underground, introduced in 1842, was repealed by s.9 of the Employment Act 1989.

29. Miscellaneous mines

This category of mine includes all mines other than 'coal mines'. Broadly they represent fewer hazards to those employed in them. In general, the management of such mines must comply with most of the safety provisions of the Act, including the appointment of a qualified manager. Noteworthy differences are omission of the 'two means of egress' requirement, a modified mechanical winding apparatus requirement, and a modified support of strata requirement. The Miscellaneous Mines

Regulations 1956 contain detailed provisions for such mines. The use of explosives in these mines is regulated by the Miscellaneous Mines (Explosives) Regulations 1959.

30. Quarries
The 1954 Act (principally Parts IV and V) regulates all quarries in Britain. A quarry is defined as a place where there is natural light at the workings, although a miner working in a quarry in which the mineral is followed underground does not convert the whole operation into a mine (s.180(1)).

31. Management responsibilities
No quarry may be worked unless it is under the control of an appointed manager (s.98), but this manager needs no formal qualifications. His duty is to manage and control the quarry, and to secure the discharge by all others of their statutory responsibilities, subject only to the instructions of the owner. As in the case of mines, the manager may insist upon written confirmation of orders, and is similarly protected against being 'bypassed' by the owner. The Act calls for the manager (or in his absence his substitute) to exercise 'close and effective supervision' over all operations in the quarry (s.103).

There are stringent obligations for the safe operation of the quarry. The manager's duty is to secure that all quarry operations are carried out so as to avoid danger from falls (s.108); to provide safe means of access to every working place (s.109); to provide suitable and sufficient artificial lighting (s.111); and, together with the owner, to secure the safe condition of machinery and apparatus (s.115). Quarries near to a highway, or otherwise representing a danger to the public, must be fenced.

32. Supplementary legislation
The Act is supplemented by the Quarries (General) Regulations 1956. Danger from mechanical transport is addressed by the Quarry (Vehicles) Regulations 1970.

33. Shotfiring
The Quarries (Explosives) Regulations 1988 cover shotfiring, one of the major sources of accidents in quarries. The shotfiring regulations deal with storage, handling, issue and return of

explosives. Shotfiring must be carried out by 'authorised persons', using equipment provided by the quarry owner, following the procedures set out in the regulations, and generally in accordance with good practice. The shotfirer must delimit a 'safety zone' before firing, ensure that all persons are withdrawn to management-provided shelters, and observe the procedures for dealing with misfires. Shotfiring must only be carried out during daylight hours.

The Mines and Quarries (Tips) Act 1969

34. Safety of tips

The 1969 Act imposes upon mine management a duty to ensure that every tip to which the Act applies is 'made and kept secure'. This duty applies to active or disused tips connected with a still active mine or quarry. Management must also have specified information concerning such tips, must formulate and enforce 'tipping rules', and, on the abandonment of the mine, must send plans and sections of all the associated tips to the inspectorate. After abandonment, primary responsibility for tip safety passes to the relevant local authority, but subject to the ultimate liability of the tip owner. The duty to report accidents in connection with mine and quarry tips has, since 1986, been governed by the general Reporting of Injuries etc., Regulations 1985.

35. EC proposals

EC proposals, under the Social Charter, for the extractive industries are likely to impact on UK legislation for mines and quarries.

The Agriculture (Safety, Health and Welfare Provisions) Act 1956

36. General

This is now the only one of the pre-1974 statutory provisions relating to agriculture which is still enforced. Much of it will be repealed and phased out after 1 January 1993 with the introduction of the Health, Safety and Welfare Regulations. The Agriculture (Poisonous Substances) Act 1952 was repealed and the regulations which had been made under it were replaced by the Control of Substances Hazardous to Health Regulations 1988.

37. Purpose and scope of the Act

The 1956 Act enabled making of regulations for the protection of workers employed in agriculture against the risk of bodily injury or injury to health from the use of machinery, plant, equipment or appliances, the carrying on of an operation, or the management of animals (s.1). Such regulations could impose duties on employers, farmworkers and other persons, the importance of this latter provision being that only a minority of persons engaged in agriculture could be described as employees. Very many farmers at risk work without employees and rely on the services of contractors, but they are nevertheless obliged to comply with the statutory safety standards.

38. Regulations in force

While the Act is now largely assimilated into the 1974 Act's structure (the Agriculture, etc. (Repeals and Modifications) Regulations 1975 and the Enforcing Authority Regulations 1977) regulations made under it remain in force, though new ones are made under the 1974 Act. Regulations in force which were made under the 1956 Act are:

   The Agriculture (Ladders) Regulations 1957
 * The Agriculture (Power Take Off) Regulations 1957
   The Agriculture (Tractor Cabs) Regulations 1974
   The Agriculture (Safeguarding of Workplaces)
   Regulations 1959
 ** The Agriculture (Circular Saws) Regulations 1959
 * The Agriculture (Stationary Machinery) Regulations 1959
 ** The Agriculture (Threshers and Bailers) Regulations 1960
 * The Agriculture (Field Machinery) Regulations 1962.

It is proposed to repeal the whole of regulations marked * and part of regulations marked ** when UK regulations are introduced to implement the EC work equipment Directive.

Jurisdiction acquired after 1974

39. General

Since 1980 the HSC has acquired responsibilities for nine new areas of work, including carriage by road of dangerous substances, mains gas safety, asbestos licensing, control of pesticides and nuclear safety research. Most of this new work is accounted for in regulations, but there are three areas in which transfer of departmental responsibilities has brought additional statutes into a position analogous to the original relevant statutory provisions. These areas are railway safety, the offshore oil industry and fire precautions.

40. The Mineral Workings (Offshore Installations) Act 1971

The Mineral Workings (Offshore Installations) Act 1971, the first UK statute to provide expressly for the health and safety of those engaged in this industry, recognised the similarities with merchant shipping. Regulations made under this Act built on shipping law while introducing construction and production systems comparable to those devised to regulate similar situations onshore. The Act required that every manned installation have a competent installation manager on board at all times and placed on this manager responsibilities similar to those held by the captain of a ship, including authority over all persons on board the installation (s.4), and activities within the 500 metre safety zone surrounding the installation. The legislation imposes duties, the breach of which may result in criminal sanctions. In addition to the installation manager, responsibilities are placed upon the operator (i.e. the licensee conducting the activity — s.5) and the owner of the installation who is primarily responsible for the structure and equipment of the installation.

41. Regulations under the 1971 Act

Regulations made under the Act cover such matters as the structure of the installation (the Offshore Installations (Construction and Survey) Regulations 1974); the systems of work on the installation (the Offshore Installations (Operational Safety, Health and Welfare) Regulations 1976); offshore emergencies, whether caused by weather or oil-related activities (the Offshore Installations (Emergency Procedures) Regulations 1976); and the provision of equipment for emergency situations (the Offshore Installations (Life-saving Appliances) Regulations 1977 and the Offshore Installations (Fire-fighting Equipment) Regulations 1978). The regulatory system has, nevertheless, left much to the discretion of the operators — for example, there are no regulatory standards for manning, either in terms of numbers or (or for the most part) qualifications of personnel employed.

42. Enforcement of the 1971 Act

Enforcement of the 1971 Act lay with the Department of Energy. In 1977 an Order in Council (the Health and Safety at Work Act (Application Outside Great Britain) Order 1977) extended the 1974 Act offshore, but did not so extend those regulations which had by then been made under it. Some of the regulations subsequently made under the 1974 Act have been extended offshore (e.g. the Diving at Work Regulations 1981 and the Control of Lead at Work Regulations 1980). The inspectorate of the Department of Energy were empowered, by an agency agreement made by the HSE with the Department,to enforce so much of the 1974 Act as was applicable offshore.

Since 1 April 1991 all enforcement offshore, of both the 1971 Act and its supporting regulations, and the 1974 Act and those of its regulations that have been specifically assigned offshore, has been carried out by the HSE inspectorate, exercising the powers of inspection and enforcement — including improvement and prohibition notices — granted by the 1974 Act. The Offshore Safety Act 1992 makes the 1971 Act a relevant statutory provision; thus fully relating it to the 1974 Act and facilitating the task of HSC in revoking old and making new regulations for application off shore.

43. Railway safety legislation

Rail transport, like road transport, was already the subject of safety legislation when the 1974 Act was passed. Nevertheless, the statutes relating to safety of passengers and railway employees were not made relevant statutory provisions under the 1974 Act. However, the general duties in s.2 clearly protect railway workers, while s.3 duties protect passengers and criminal charges brought against British Rail following the Clapham railway disaster were formulated in terms of ss.2 and 3 of the 1974 Act. Moreover, many activities related to the operation of the railway system had been within the ambit of the Factories Act. Following a number of accidents and incidents on railways the railway inspectorate was transferred from the Department of Transport to the HSE in the autumn of 1990. HSE inspectors now enforce the 1974 Act in respect of rail transport, and enforce the earlier transport legislation as agents for the Department of Transport.

44. Duty to report incidents

The Railway Employment (Prevention of Accidents) Act 1900 applies to all railways used for public traffic including either goods or passengers. This Act imposes a duty upon railway management to report incidents in which persons have been killed or injured on the railway to the Department of Transport (*see* Railways (Notice of Accidents) Order 1986). This system has not been replaced by the reporting of accident regulations made under the 1974 Act.

45. Regulations under the 1900 Act

Regulations (which are the responsibility of the Department of Transport) have been made under the 1900 Act in a number of specific situations involving danger to persons from railway operations, e.g. Railway (Prevention of Accidents) Rules 1902.

46. Railways in factories and mines

Railways forming part of a factory or a mine are subject to regulations made under the Factories Acts or the mines legislation (currently Locomotives and Waggons on Lines and Sidings Regulations 1906 and Coal and other Mines (Sidings) Regulations 1956). Quarry sidings are regulated under the Quarries (General) Regulations 1956. These regulations are framed for the protection of persons against the risks inherent in the movement of wagons and locomotives on mine and factory premises; their impact is much reduced at the present time due to the decline in the use of railway haulage in so many industries.

47. Sheds used for repairs to railway stock

Sheds used for the repair of locomotives and other rolling stock are factories within the Factories Act 1961, and so are 'running sheds', where running repairs are undertaken.

48. Fire Precautions Act 1971

By s.1(2)(f) of this Act a fire certificate is required from the fire authority for premises put into use as a place of work. Paragraph (f) was added to the 1971 Act by s.78 of the Health and Safety at Work Act.

49. Application for a fire certificate

Section 5 requires that an application for a fire certificate must be made to the fire authority in the prescribed form. The application:

(a)   must specify the particular use or uses of the premises which it is desired to have covered by the certificate; and

(b)   must give such information as may be prescribed about the premises and any prescribed rules connected with them; and

(c)   if the premises consist of part of a building, must, in so far as it is available to the applicant, give such information as may be prescribed about the rest of the building and any prescribed matters connected with it.

50. Inspection of premises

The fire authority may require plans of the premises and must inspect the premises and satisfy itself as to:

(a)   the means of escape . . .

(b)   the means for securing the means of escape . . .

(c)   the means for fighting fire . . .

(d)   the means for giving warning . . . (s.5(3)).

51. Issue of a certificate

If the authority is satisfied it must issue a fire certificate. Details of the matters outlined in (a) to (d) will be specified in the certificate. The fire authority may require that alterations be made to a building before a fire certificate is granted. Operating without a fire certificate (except between application to and approval by the fire authority) is an either way offence which carries, on conviction on indictment, a maximum penalty of two years imprisonment.

52. Regulations under the 1971 Act

Regulations may be made under the Act for the following purposes (s.12(3)):

(a) the provision, maintenance and keeping free from obstruction of means of escape in case of fire;

(b) the provision and maintenance of means for securing any means of escape can be safely and effectively used at all material times;

(c) as to the provision and maintenance of means of fighting fire and means of giving warning in case of fire;

(d) as to the internal construction of the premises and the materials used in that construction;

(e) for prohibiting altogether the presence or use in the premises of furniture or equipment of any specified description or prohibiting its presence or use unless specified standards or conditions are complied with;

(f) for securing that persons employed to work in the premises receive appropriate instruction or training in what to do in case of fire;

(g) as to the keeping of records of instruction or training given, or other things done, in pursuance of the regulations.

53. Enforcement

In the case of workplaces, the functions of the fire authority in enforcing the provisions of the fire certificate are normally performed by the inspectors with responsibility for enforcing the 1974 Act in those premises (s.18). Moreover, if the fire authority proposes to require alterations to be made to work premises before granting a fire certificate, it will consult with the relevant health and safety inspectorate.

54. Compliance with EC legislation

While the EC Framework Directive makes provision for fire precautions it has not been considered necessary, given the existing UK system, to make special provision for this in the General Provisions Regulations which aim to effect compliance with the Directive.

Progress test 8

1. What meaning did the 1974 Act give to the expression 'relevant statutory provisions'? **(1)**

2. What statutes were 'existing statutory provisions'? **(1, 3)**

3.   What are the principal elements of the interpretation given to the word 'factory' by s.175 of the Factories Act 1961?   **(5)**

4.   What is the obligation imposed by s.14(1) of the Act?   **(7, 9)**

5.   What is the principal legislation for mines and quarries?   **(19)**

6.   How does this legislation classify mines and quarries?   **(19)**

7.   In what ways does mining legislation make the position of mine manager quite different from other manager positions in Great Britain?   **(21–23)**

8.   What areas of responsibility have HSC and HSE acquired since 1974?   **(39)**

9.   What (apart from the 1974 Act) is the principal legislation for offshore installations?   **(40)**

10. Which body grants a fire certificate?   **(49)**

11. On what matters must the authority be satisfied before a certificate is granted?   **(50)**

9
Regulations

1. Introduction

This chapter will outline such of the major sets of regulations made since 1974 (using the regulation-making power in s.15 and Schedule 3 of the 1974 Act) as have not been dealt with in other chapters of this book, namely:

(a) Notification of New Substances Regulations 1982
(b) Classification, Packaging and Labelling of Dangerous Substances Regulations 1984
(c) Control of Industrial Major Accident Hazard Regulations 1984
(d) Control of Asbestos at Work Regulations 1987
(e) Control of Substances Hazardous to Health Regulations 1988
(f) Electricity at Work Regulations 1989
(g) Noise at Work Regulations 1989
(h) Dangerous Substances (Notification and Marking of Sites) Regulations 1990.

In recent years regulations have often been made in response to EC Directives. Currently there are five individual directives, made further to the Framework Directive, to which the UK must respond before 1 January 1993. The requirements of these Directives and, where known, the proposals for dealing with them are set out at the end of the chapter.

2. Pre-1974 regulations

The chapter will not include regulations made before 1974. The Robens Committee identified over 500 sets of regulations in existence in 1970 and the sheer weight of this subordinate legislation was one of their criticisms of the system then in existence. Many of the pre-1974 regulations have now been revoked.

3.   Post-1974 regulations

The post-1974 regulations are systematic in their approach, often intended for application to workplaces generally and frequently requiring organisations to identify and respond to hazardous situations. They are usually accompanied by approved codes of practice, and sometimes guidance has also been published by HSC.

4.   Breaches of regulations

Breaches of regulations are presumed to give rise to civil liability (s.47(2)). Many of the regulations discussed below relate to issues which may give rise to civil claims.

Post-1974 regulatory codes

5.   Notification of New Substances Regulations 1982

These regulations impose a duty on any manufacturer, importer or supplier of a new substance (within the meaning of the regulations) to notify the HSE of the particulars of the substance, as laid down in Schedule 1 of the regulations, before that person supplies that substance in a quantity of one tonne or more in any period of 12 months.

As part of that notification, the results of standard toxicity tests on that substance, carried out in accordance with the principles of good laboratory practice, must be given to HSE.

The regulations flesh out s.6 of the 1974 Act. They also implement the EC Directive on the notification of substances.

6.   Classification, Packaging and Labelling of Dangerous Substances Regulations 1984 (as amended)

These regulations are made jointly under the 1974 Act and the European Communities Act 1972, and cover all the listed substances, including mixtures, classified within the regulations as 'dangerous for supply' or 'dangerous for conveyance by road'. Their aim is to regulate the use of these substances, both at work and as consumer products.

The main requirements concerning substances for supply or conveyance are:

(a) safe packaging;
(b) proper labelling.

The regulations are designed to protect not only the ultimate user of substances, but those transportation workers who might be put at risk by substances in transit, and also emergency service workers, such as police, firemen or rescue workers.

The regulations rationalise, update and extend the existing piecemeal legislation relating to supply and conveyance of substances. They have been subject to frequent amendment.

7. Control of Industrial Major Accident Hazards Regulations 1984 (as amended)

These regulations were formulated, in part in response to the disaster at Flixborough in 1974, and in part in response to the EC 'Seveso' Directive. They apply where hazardous or ultra-hazardous activities might present a danger to employees or to the public. The regulations introduced into UK law the concept of the documented 'safety case'; they require manufacturers controlling certain industrial processes to:

(a) assess and document the hazards of their operations;
(b) organise and document an adequate accident prevention system;
(c) report major accidents to the HSE according to a special dossier;
(d) prepare and update a detailed safety analysis of the more high-risk of their activities;
(e) make provision (including disclosure of information to the public) for limiting the effects of major accidents.

These requirements are in a 'two-tier' classification of hazards. In the 'lower tier' — in specified, less dangerous situations — manufacturers must have available the evidence, including documentation, to demonstrate that they have identified the major hazards, taken the necessary steps to control them, and to limit their consequences should they take place. They must also notify the HSE of any major accidents, and the results of their internal investigation, together with the steps proposed to alleviate their effects and to prevent their recurrence.

The 'upper-tier' duties, which apply only where substantial quantities of listed hazardous substances are involved, require manufacturers to notify the HSE three months prior to beginning the activity which falls under the regulations, submitting the specified 'safety case' relating to the activity, including details of the dangerous substances involved, the proposed management system for hazard control, the potential major accidents, and the laid-down emergency procedures. This 'safety case' must be updated every three years to take account of developments in safety and hazard assessment. The manufacturers' duty, as part of the upper-tier safety precautions, to formulate on-site and off-site emergency plans to deal with the consequences of a major accident, has already been referred to.

8.   Control of Asbestos at Work Regulations 1987

These regulations, together with the Asbestos (Licensing) Regulations 1983 and the Asbestos (Prohibitions) Regulations 1985, form the regulatory code for the protection of persons against the risks associated with use of asbestos at work. They implement EC Directives.

They impose duties on employers for the protection of employees who may be exposed to asbestos at work, and for the protection of other persons who are liable to be affected by work involving asbestos. The first duty of employers is to identify the type of asbestos utilised in their work, and to assess the nature and degree of exposure to this asbestos, and the steps to be taken to reduce that exposure. They must then respond positively to the problem as identified by that assessment, by preventing the exposure at work of employees or other persons, or by reducing that exposure to the lowest level reasonably practicable. If exposure is not reduced to below the specified control limits, employees must be provided with respiratory protective equipment that will reduce their exposure below those limits.

The effectiveness of the employees' protection against exposure must be monitored, and, in the case of employees who are liable to be 'significantly exposed', the monitoring must be reinforced by regular medical surveillance.

Certain activities involving the use of asbsestos, such as

spraying, are prohibited by the regulatory code. All work involving the use of asbestos must be notified to the enforcing authority.

9. Control of Substances Hazardous to Health Regulations 1988

These regulations require all employers to carry out a thorough assessment of the risks to their employees arising from the use in their work of a wide range of hazardous substances as identified by the regulations, as well as other substances creating hazards comparable to those identified within the regulations. Employers are under a similar duty towards persons not in their employment who may be affected in like manner by those substances.

Employers must respond positively to the risks identified by the assessment, by controlling the exposure through their system of working. Wherever possible employers should adopt a system of control which does not involve the use of personal protective equipment by the persons at risk (i.e. 'engineering controls'). Only in the situation where no other system of protection is effective must personal protective equipment be provided by employers and used by employees. Employers are under a duty to 'take all reasonable steps' to ensure that this equipment is properly used.

Where the nature of the hazard requires it, employers must, in addition, monitor the performance of the system both generally, and, in appropriate cases, through health surveillance of employees.

The regulations are supported by codes of practice and guidance. Since they came fully into force on 31 December 1989, one of their most striking effects has been the demand they have created for trained and competent persons to carry out their complex requirements.

The principal requirements are of strict liability.

10. Electricity at Work Regulations 1989

These replace 75 outmoded codes of regulations dealing with particular applications of electricity in the work situation. They apply to all aspects of work, including mining, involving the use of electricity. They require 'safe systems' of working. They place responsibilities upon, *inter alia*, employers and self-employed persons, managers of mines and quarries, and employees while at work, for the protection of employees, as well as third persons, against electrical dangers. The essence of these regulations is in their simplicity and flexibility. Typical of this approach is regulation 16, which stipulates:

> No person shall be engaged in any work activity where technical knowledge or experience is necessary to prevent danger, or where appropriate, injury, unless he possesses such knowledge or experience, or is under such degree of supervision as may be appropriate having regard to the nature of the work.

The regulations are supported by three sets of guidance.

11. Noise at Work Regulations 1989

These regulations implement the EC Directive on noise. They apply to all workplaces within the UK, other than ships and aircraft, and impose duties upon employers, the self-employed, employees, and machine designers and suppliers. The primary duty they impose is to reduce the risk of hearing damage at work to the lowest level reasonably practicable.

Additionally, further duties, of increasing orders of stringency, are imposed upon employers at the 'first and second action levels', which are defined as 85 DBA and 90 DBA respectively. At these higher levels the employers' obligations are based upon the concept of 'assessment and response' made familiar by the Control of Substances Hazardous to Health Regulations (*see* 9).

At these levels, it is the duty of employers to ensure that a noise assessment is carried out by a competent person, and that workers who are found by that assessment to be at risk above the lower action level are provided with suitable and efficient personal hearing protection. At the higher action level, it is, additionally, the employers' duty to reduce, so far as is reasonably practicable, this exposure to noise by means other than personal hearing protection.

It is also the duty of the employers, at first or second level of exposure, to provide all employees exposed with all relevant information relating to the noise hazard.

The obligations to protect hearing are, generally, modified by a 'reasonably practicable' defence, but it is noteworthy that in certain respects — such as the duty to provide personal hearing protection, the duty to ensure that all relevant equipment, other than personal hearing protection, is fully and properly used, and the duty to ensure that adequate noise assessments are carried out — the duties are not so modified.

12. Dangerous Substances (Notification and Marking of Sites) Regulations 1990

These regulations apply to any site upon which more than 25 tonnes of dangerous substances (as listed in the Classification, Packaging and Labelling of Dangerous Substances Regulations) are kept at any one time. They oblige the person in control of such sites to notify the local health and safety enforcing authority, and also the fire authority, giving the information specified in the regulations. Warning signs must also be displayed at the sites.

The object of the regulations is to ensure that the safety and fire authorities are in possession of information that will assist them in organising their inspection programmes, and also in alerting the emergency services personnel as to the hazards they are likely to encounter at a particular site where dangerous substances are stored.

EC individual Directives

13. The Workplace Directive

The main thrust of this Directive is in its annexes which require minimum safety standards in respect of the many matters identified in them.

The matters identified in the first, and more stringent, of the annexes (that relating to premises brought into use for the first time after 1 January 1993) are approximately 20 in all:

stability and solidity
electrical installations
emergency routes and exits
fire detection and fire fighting
ventilation of enclosed workplaces
room temperature
natural and artificial room lighting
floors, walls, ceilings and roofs of rooms
windows and skylights
doors and gates

> traffic routes
> escalators and travelators
> loading bays and ramps
> rest rooms
> rest rooms for pregnant women and nursing mothers
> sanitary equipment
> first aid rooms
> organisation of workplaces for the needs of handicapped workers
> special provisions for outside workplaces.

The Directive does not attempt to stipulate quantifiable standards but requires that the standard of provision shall be suitable and appropriate for the particular circumstances.

The HSC has proposed Workplace (Health, Safety and Welfare) Regulations and Approved Code of Practice to implement this Directive. These proposals include repealing or revoking all or part of 35 acts, regulations and welfare orders, particularly affecting the Factories Act 1961 (*see* Chapter 8) but the new regulations would introduce a system similar to that contained in the 1961 Act for all workplaces. Existing workplaces would, until 1 January 1996, continue to be governed by the standards of the previous laws, where these were applicable.

14. The Work Equipment Directive

The HSC has proposed regulations for implementing this Directive. Coverage includes:

(a) *Selection of work equipment.* Every employer is to be required to have regard, when selecting equipment, to working conditions and the hazards in the premises.

(b) *Suitability of work equipment.* Work equipment must be so constructed or adapted as to be suitable for the operations for which it is used or provided.

(c) *Maintenance.* Work equipment must be properly maintained.

(d) *Specific risks.* Where use of equipment is likely to involve specific risk the use of that equipment must be restricted to those persons given the task to use it, repair it, etc.

(e) *Information and instruction.* All persons who use work equipment must have adequate information, and where appropriate, written instructions.

(f) *Training.* Persons who use equipment must be properly trained.

(g) *EC standards*. Equipment must comply with community requirements.

(h) *Dangerous parts of machinery*. Employers must ensure effective measures are taken (wherever practicable by guards) to prevent access to any dangerous part.

(i) *Other protections against machinery hazards*. These include safety protection in relation to: failure of machinery; temperature of equipment; controls for starting, changing or stopping operations; emergency stop controls; marking of controls; isolation from sources of energy; stability.

(j) *Lighting*. Workplaces will have to be adequately lit.

(k) *Maintenance work*. Wherever reasonably practicable the equipment will have to be stopped.

(l) *Marking*. Work equipment will have to be appropriately marked.

(m) *Warnings*. Work equipment must incorporate any appropriate safety warnings.

It is intended to repeal the guarding provisions of the Mines and Quarries, the Factories, and the Offices, Shops and Railway Premises Acts.

15. Personal Protective Equipment Directive

The proposed regulations are intended to:

(a) amend relevant post-1974 regulations which deal with personal protective equipment (PPE) so that they fully implement the Directive in circumstances where they apply;

(b) cover all aspects of the provision, maintenance and use of PPE at work in other circumstances; and

(c) revoke and replace almost all pre-1974, and some post-1974 legislation which deals with PPE.

16. Manual Handling of Loads Directive

The HSE estimates 27% of reported accidents involve manual handling. Implementing the proposed regulations is nevertheless expected to be very costly to industry. The proposals are accompanied by extensive guidance.

The proposed regulations require employers, so far as is reasonably practicable, to avoid the need for manual handling operations which involve risk or injury. Where it cannot be avoided there must be a suitable and sufficient assessment of all manual handling operations to be undertaken by employees and appropriate steps must be taken to reduce the risk of injury. Where it is reasonably practicable to do so, employees must be informed as to the weight of each load and the heaviest side of any load whose centre of gravity is not positioned centrally. It is the duty of employees to make full and proper use of any equipment or system of work provided by the employer and to inform the employer about any physical conditions from which they suffer which might be considered to affect their ability to undertake manual handling operations safely.

17. Work with Display Screen Equipment Directive

Employers must analyse workstations to evaluate their safety, with particular regard to risks to eyesight, physical problems and problems of mental stress. Appropriate measure must be taken to remedy such risks. Workers must be properly trained and informed of any health and safety risks to which they are exposed. Workers must be given sufficient rest breaks. Workers are entitled to have an appropriate eyesight test and must be provided with any special 'corrective appliances' which such tests prove to be necessary.

The HSC proposes to implement this Directive through Health and Safety (Display Screen Equipment) Regulations and guidance. A schedule to the regulations gives minimum requirements for workstations (reproducing the Annex to the Directive). The proposals are for the protection of the 'user' of VDU equipment, being a person '. . . who habitually uses . . .'. Identifying the circumstances to which the definition applies may be problematic. It is also questionable whether the employer should (as the EC requires) pay for eyesight tests or corrective appliances.

Progress test 9

1. Which of the post-1974 regulations implement EC Directives? **(5, 6, 7, 8, 11)**

2. What are the principal requirements of the Control of Substances Hazardous to Health Regulations? **(9)**

3. To what workplaces do the Electricity at Work Regulations apply? **(10)**

4. Which of the post-1974 regulations set out above provide for public safety? **(6, 7)**

5. Which of the regulations require a 'safety case' to be made out? **(7)**

6. What matters are covered by the 'individual' EC Directives? **(13–17)**

10

Implementation and enforcement of the 1974 Act

1.   Introduction

Responsibility for implementation and enforcement of the 1974 Act lies with the Health and Safety Commission (HSC) and the Health and Safety Executive (HSE); certain responsibilities and powers are also given to the Secretary of State (normally the Secretary of State for Employment). This chapter will identify the constitution, responsibilities and powers of the HSC and the HSE with particular reference to powers to make regulations and codes of practice, powers and responsibilities of HSE appointed inspectors, and the system of enforcement under the Act.

Establishment and functions of the HSC and the HSE

2.   General

Section 10 declares that there shall be two bodies corporate: the Health and Safety Commission and the Health and Safety Executive and sets out their constitutions.

3.   The Health and Safety Commission

The HSC is a 'quango', established to specialise in occupational health and safety and thus to rectify the problems which the Robens Report had attributed to the previous situation where responsibilities for occupational health and safety had been spread over a number of Ministerial portfolios. The HSC is largely independent, acting on behalf of the Crown, but reporting to Parliament through relevant Secretaries of State.

4. Composition of the HSC

The HSC consists of a full-time chairman and between six and nine other members, all appointed by the Secretary of State. Before appointing members the Secretary of State is required to hold consultations: in respect of three members with employers' organisations; in respect of three members with employees' organisations (i.e. trade unions); and before appointing the other members with organisations representing local authorities and other organisations, including relevant professional bodies.

5. The Health and Safety Executive

The HSE must consist of three persons, appointed by the HSC with the approval of the Secretary of State. One is to be appointed to be the director of the HSE; the others are to be appointed after consultation with the director of the HSE.

Detailed provisions concerning the appointment, tenure of office, remuneration, etc., of members of the HSC and HSE are set out in Schedule 2 of the Act.

6. Role of the HSC

It is the general duty of the HSC 'to do such things and make such arrangements as it considers appropriate for the general purposes of' Part I of the Act (s.11). Section 11(2) (somewhat paraphrased here) requires the HSC to:

(a) assist and encourage persons concerned with furthering the purposes of the Act;
(b) make arrangements for carrying out research, publishing the results thereof, and the provision of training and information in connection therewith;
(c) make arrangements for the provision of information and advice to government departments, and employers and employees and organisations representing them;
(d) submit proposals for the making of regulations.

The HSC is required to report to the Secretary of State on its proposals, ensure that its activities accord with proposals the Secretary of State has approved, and give effect to any directions given to it by the Secretary of State.

7.   Role of the HSE

It is a duty of the HSE to provide staff for the performance of HSC functions. In practice this means that a proportion of the work of the HSE's inspectorate is concerned with conducting the research and identifying the information required to enable the HSC to remain properly informed. Notwithstanding this, the HSC is also empowered to appoint and pay persons to provide specialist advice, and to pay for research (s.13).

The HSE is further required to provide information to any Minister of State in connection with any matter with which he is concerned, and to provide him with advice, where relevant expertise is available in the HSE, even if the matter is not relevant to any of the general purposes of the Act. It would appear, therefore, that the HSE could be requested to give an expert opinion on such matters as whether plant and equipment used on merchant ships engaged in fishing was comparable, in safety terms, with that used onshore, or whether mechanical toys could be deemed to be safe.

The HSE may be required by the HSC to investigate and report on any accident or occurrence which the HSC considers necessary or expedient to investigate for any of the purposes of the Act, including the making of regulations, whether or not the HSE is directly responsible for enforcement of the Act in the situation in question.

8.   Responsibilities for enforcement

It is the duty of the HSE to make adequate arrangements for the enforcement of the relevant statutory provisions, except to the extent that some other authority has been made responsible, or by agreement with the HSC assumed responsibility for their enforcement (s.18(1)). The Secretary of State may make regulations giving local authorities specified enforcement duties (s.18(2)(a)). Local authorities have retained their duties of enforcing health and safety legislation in those premises which were formerly within the scope of the Offices, Shops and Railway Premises Act 1963, and were given responsibility for enforcing the 1974 Act in those premises by the Health and Safety (Enforcing Authority) Regulations 1977. By the Health and Safety (Enforcing Authority) (Amendment) Regulations 1985 they were given responsibility for a large number of other 'low risk' premises and work situations (e.g. leisure premises).

Section 19 empowers enforcing authorities to appoint (and terminate the appointment of) inspectors.

Regulations and codes of practice

9.   Powers of the Secretary of State

Section 15 of the 1974 Act empowers the Secretary of State to make regulations for the purposes of Part I of the Act, i.e. to secure the health and safety of persons at work, to protect other persons from risks created by the activities of people at work (s.1(1)), and to update the earlier safety legislation (s.1(2)).

10.   Purposes for which regulations may be made

Schedule 3 specifies purposes for which regulations may be made, but s.15(2) makes it clear Schedule 3 in no way restricts the general regulation-making power.

The schedule covers such matters as the regulation or prohibition of manufacture, use or supply of any plant or substance; the testing labelling, or marking of articles; the transport of articles or substances; and the licensing of activities. Regulations may also be made about the premises in which people work, the taking of fire precautions, and the provision of protective clothing.

Regulations must not conflict with EC requirements, e.g. prohibit the import into the UK of articles or substances contrary to the EC's objective of securing free movement of goods between Member States.

11.   Scope of regulations

Section 15 identifies certain matters which may be dealt with by, and limitations which may be imposed on, the application of regulations. In particular regulations may vary statutory provisions. Thus the existing statutory provisions may be repealed or modified (and indeed have been!), and situations may be removed from the ambit of the general duties of the 1974 Act itself, by regulations. Similarly exemptions from the requirements of any of the relevant statutory provisions may be granted (this latter power has been used fairly extensively in respect of mining legislation in relation to specified mines). The Offshore Safety Act 1992, s.1(2) makes specific provision for regulations concerning the offshore oil industry.

12. Breach of regulations

Regulations may also state the persons or classes of persons who are to be guilty of offences in the event that regulatory duties are breached, make provision for defences available in proceeedings, exclude proceedings on indictment, and restrict the punishment which may be imposed.

13. Proposals for regulations

Section 50 empowers the Secretary of State to make regulations further to proposals submitted by the HSC, or independently of such proposals. However, the Secretary of State may not act on proposals other than those submitted by the HSC without having consulted the HSC. Regulations do not become operative unless they have been laid before Parliament.

14. Codes of practice

Section 16 empowers the HSC to approve and issue such codes of practice (whether prepared by it or not) as are, in its opinion, suitable for the purpose of providing practical guidance as to the requirements of any of the general duties of health and safety regulations, or of any of the existing statutory provisions. It can also, where it considers this appropriate, approve codes of practice which have been issued by other bodies.

15. Approval of a code of practice

While approved codes of practice take their authority from the actions of the HSC rather than the Secretary of State, the HSC is nevertheless required to obtain the consent of the Secretary of State before approving a code of practice. Moreover, before seeking the consent of the Secretary of State, the HSC must consult any government department that appears to the HSC to be appropriate (usually the Department of Employment). Any other government department which the Secretary of State identifies as appropriate must also be consulted.

When the HSC approves a code of practice it must issue a written notice identifying the code, stating the date on which its approval is to become effective, and specifying the statutory or regulatory provisions for which it provides practical guidance. The HSC may withdraw its approval from a code of practice.

16. Regulations and codes of practice

Many regulations brought into force under the 1974 Act have been accompanied by codes of practice. It has become the practice for the HSC to publish draft regulations and codes in the form of a consultative document, to seek the widest possible comment, as part of the process of drawing up, and bringing into force these instruments.

17. Breach of a code of practice

Failure to observe a code is not in itself an offence (s.17). However, where in any criminal proceedings someone is alleged to have committed an offence by reason of a contravention of any requirement or prohibition imposed by or under a statutory provision to which an approved code of practice has properly been related, then that code may be relevant to the proceedings. Where a code appears to the court to be relevant that code is admissible in evidence in the proceedings. If it is proved that there was a failure to observe any provision of the code which is relevant to any matter which it is necessary for the prosecution to prove in order to establish a contravention of the law, that matter shall be taken as proved unless it is proved that the law was complied with otherwise than by observance of the code. Thus if the prosecution shows that the accused has not observed the code, then a presumption is raised that the law to which the code relates has been broken, but this presumption may be rebutted by the accused showing that he has observed the law in some other, and equivalent, way.

Powers of inspectors

18. Appointment and exercise of powers

Inspectors appointed under s.19 of the 1974 Act, and also local authority inspectors responsible for enforcing occupational health and safety, may enforce the 1974 Act and other relevant statutory provisions and regulations. Inspectors appointed under s.19 must be appointed in writing and the instrument of appointment must specify which of the powers conferred on inspectors by the relevant statutory provisions are to be exercisable by the person appointed. An inspector is entitled to exercise only such powers as are specified in the instrument of appointment and then only within the field of responsibility of the authority which appointed him. Thus local authority inspectors can only exercise their powers in premises and situations which are within the jurisdiction of local authorities. Where it is intended that HSE inspectors shall exercise powers which the HSE has acquired under agency agreements (e.g. with the Department of Transport in relation to railway legislation), this must be stipulated either in the instrument of appointment, by amendment of it (under s.19(3)) or in a separate document. An inspector may be required to produce his instrument of appointment or an authenticated copy of it, when exercising his powers (s.19(4)).

19. Powers of inspectors

Section 20 sets out the powers of an inspector. Under s.20(2) these are broadly:

(a) at any reasonable time (or in a situation which in his opinion is, or may be dangerous, at any time) to enter any premises which he has reason to believe it is necessary for him to enter;

(b) to take with him a constable if he has reasonable cause to apprehend any serious obstruction;

(c) on entering any premises in the course of his duty to take with him —
   (i)   any other person duly authorised by his (the inspector's) enforcing authority; and
   (ii) any equipment or materials required for any purpose for which the power of entry is being exercised;

(d) to make such examination and investigation as may in any circumstances be necessary;

(e) to direct that premises shall be left undisturbed for as long as is reasonably necessary for the purpose of any examination or investigation;

(f) to take measurements and photographs;

(g) to take samples of any articles or substances found in any premises, and of the atmosphere in, or in the vicinity of the premises;

(h) to cause an article or substance found in premises to be dismantled or subjected to testing (but not to damage or destroy it if this is avoidable) where he believes these commodities to have caused or to be likely to cause danger to health or safety;

(i) to take possession of any article or substance he believes to be dangerous and to detain it for so long as is necessary for any of the following purposes:

    (i) to examine it and do to it anything he is empowered to do;

    (ii) to ensure that it is not tampered with before his examination is completed;

    (iii) to ensure that it is available for use as evidence in any proceedings in relation to enforcement of the relevant statutory provisions;

(j) to require any person to answer any relevant questions and to sign a declaration as to the truth of the answers given;

(k) to require the production of, inspect, and take copies of or of any entry in —

    (i) any books or documents which the relevant statutory provisions require to be kept;

    (ii) any other relevant books or documents;

(l) to require any person to afford him such facilities and assistance with respect to any matter or things within that person's control or in relation to which that person has responsibilities:

(m) any other power which is necessary.

Arguably these powers are wider than those given to a police constable. In common law jurisdictions constables normally need a special warrant in order to enter premises, and in the USA it has been held that federal health and safety inspectors need a warrant before entering premises, should the occupier insist on the point. The statutory authority of inspectors under s.20 is such that no such proposition could be raised in Great Britain. Similarly the powers of the police in Great Britain to take evidence are probably more constrained by the Police and Criminal Evidence Act 1984 than those of HSE and local authority inspectors operating under s.20.

20. Constraints on the exercise of inspector's powers

Section 20 does, however, actually or potentially, place some constraints on the exercise by inspectors of their powers. Section 20(3) enables the making of regulations as to the procedure to be followed when taking samples, including the way in which samples, are to be dealt with when taken. Section 20(4) provides that when inspectors propose to exercise their powers under s.20(2)(h) to dismantle or test something then they must (subject to questions of national security), if so requested by that person, carry out these processes in the presence of the person who has responsibilities in relation to the premises. They must also consult such persons as appear to them to be appropriate to find out what dangers, if any, there may be in dismantling or testing the thing (s.20(5)). Where inspectors take possession of something under s.20(2)(i) they must leave at the premises, either with a responsible person, or if that is impracticable, fixed in a conspicuous position, a notice giving particulars of the article or substance of which they have taken possession. Wherever it is practicable for them to do so, they must take a sample of any substance they intend to take into possession, and give that sample to a responsible person at the premises in question.

No answer given by a person under s.20(2)(j) is admissible in evidence against that person or the husband or wife of that person in any proceedings (s.20(7)).

Enforcement of the law

21. General advisory role of the inspectorate

An important feature of the British safety inspectorates has been the emphasis placed on giving advice rather than merely invoking the law. The merits of the approach become apparent when the relationship between the British inspectorate and those at the workplace is compared with the adversary relationship which can exist in other jurisdictions, such as the USA.

The advisory role is authorised by s.11(2)(c) which imposes upon the HSC the duty to provide information and advice. This duty is carried out by the publication of explanatory leaflets, and more substantial reports and works of guidance.

The inspector must be circumspect in giving advice because, in the final analysis, legal requirements can only be determined in court, by a judge interpreting the law. Inspectors do, however, provide information as to available expert literature, and may, upon occasion, express an opinion about how situations might be improved.

22. Level of enforcement

Prior to the implementation of the 1974 Act if an inspector did not get cooperation from an employer in maintaining workplace standards, the only way forward for the inspector was the expensive and time-consuming process of prosecution. Moreover, in most instances a dangerous state of affairs could not be stopped pending the outcome of the prosecution. The 1974 Act enables inspectors to deal speedily and effectively with both hazardous situations and persistent non-compliance with the statutory standards, by serving improvement and prohibition notices. The level of effective enforcement has risen greatly since the 1974 Act, although there has been no great increase in the number of prosecutions. Prosecutions have tended to be reserved either for situations where there has been personal injury, or where, even though there has been no accident, there has been very unacceptable behaviour. This is in the spirit of the Robens Report, which recommended that the criminal process should only be used where there had been a wilful or reckless disregard for safety.

23. Improvement notices

Inspectors may serve an improvement notice when they are of the opinion that a person is contravening one or more of the relevant statutory provisions or has contravened one or more of those provisions in circumstances that make it likely that the contravention will continue or be repeated (s.21). The notice states the inspector's opinion, identifies the statutory provision(s) which has been broken, gives reasons for the view that it is broken and requires that the situation be remedied within the period stated in the notice. The notice must be served on the person under the duty to ensure that the statutory standard in question has been met. For example, if the inspector's concern is that the organisation has either no, or an unsatisfactory, safety policy it will specify s.2(3) as being contravened; as the s.2(3) duty is placed on the employer, the notice will be served on the employer.

24. Prohibition notices

Section 22 enables an inspector to serve a prohibition notice when of the opinion that activities which are, or are likely to be, carried on involve a risk of serious personal injury. The activities must be ones to which relevant statutory provisions apply. But it is not necessary for the inspector to identify that a statutory duty is being flouted or broken — the criterion is the apparent danger, not the violation of the law. As no particular legal rule need be invoked by the inspector it is not relevant to require the service of the notice on a person with identified statutory duties. Therefore the notice is served on the person 'in control' of the activities to which the notice relates: who this should be will be a factual matter to be determined by the inspector.

25. Content of prohibition notices

The notice must state that the inspector is of the opinion that there is a danger of serious personal injury; specify the matters which in the inspector's opinion give, or as the case may be, will give rise to the risk; where statutory duties appear to be contravened, specify the provisions in question; give the inspector's reasons for having formed the opinion that these provisions are being broken; and direct that the activities shall not be carried on by, or under the control of the person on whom the notice is served unless the situation has been remedied.

26. Time scale

A prohibition notice either takes effect at the end of the period specified in the notice (a deferred notice) or immediately. In practice the majority of notices are immediate prohibition notices.

27. Additional matters

Sections 23 and 24 provide additional information about notices.

(a) Section 23 clarifies that a notice may include directions about the measures which are to be taken to remedy any contravention or danger and such directions may be framed by reference to an approved code of practice. The notice may specify alternative ways of dealing with the situation, leaving a choice to the person on whom the notice is served.

(b) Notices relating to the structure of a building must not impose requirements more onerous than the building regulations currently in force; notices which might lead to measures affecting the means of escape in case of fire must not be served unless the inspector has consulted the fire authority.

(c) An immediate prohibition notice, once served, may not be withdrawn. So the controller on whom it is served remains at risk should work be resumed before the required standard has been achieved, or, if work has been resumed, the standard is allowed to fall again below that required by the notice.

(d) The time granted for complying with an improvement notice or a deferred prohibition notice may be extended by an inspector.

28. Appeals

A person upon whom a notice is served may appeal to an industrial tribunal against it (s.24); regulations stipulate that the appeal must be lodged within three weeks of the service of the notice (the Industrial Tribunals (Improvement and Prohibition Notices Appeals) Regulations 1974). The tribunal may either affirm the notice, modify it or cancel it. Where an appeal is brought against an improvement notice the bringing of the appeal suspends the notice until the appeal is finally disposed of, or the appeal is withdrawn. In the case of a prohibition notice the appeal only suspends the notice if the tribunal so directs. Assessors may be appointed to assist the tribunal in evaluating the notice.

Appeal against a notice may be taken from the industrial tribunal to the High Court and ultimately to the House of Lords. The number of appeals against notices is not high in relation to the number of notices which are served and the proportion of successful appeals is small.

> In *Belhaven Brewery Company Ltd* v. *A McLean (HM Inspector of Factories)* [1975] the appellants appealed against an improvement notice which required screens to be provided to prevent access to transmission machinery and other parts of the company's automatic kegging plant. The appellants claimed that the work would be more expensive than they could afford. The tribunal held that the requirement was only to do what was reasonably practicable and it had no regard to the suggestion that the work would be too costly for the particular employer.
>
> On the other hand in *West Bromwich Building Society Ltd* v.

Townsend [1983] a notice had required fitting bandit screens. The tribunal found that the risk to employees from robberies was more than minimal and the measures required by the notice were both physically and financially within the society's capacity; so the tribunal had upheld the notice. The High Court found that in reaching its decision the tribunal had erred because it had not weighed the risk at the particular premises against the cost of providing the screens. Had it made this evaluation it would have concluded that, though possible for the employer to install the screens, it was not reasonably practicable for them to do so.

29. Criminal procedures

Service of a notice does not activate the criminal law; however, failure to comply with a notice, whether an improvement or a prohibition notice, is a criminal offence. Contravening a prohibition notice can result in up to two years imprisonment; the penalty for contravention of an improvement notice is a fine.

30. Inspectors' responsibilities

The commitment of inspectors to the use of their powers to serve notices, especially immediate prohibition notices, has been commendable, bearing in mind that such notices may involve organisations on whom they are served in very great expense — often more expense than might be incurred by a prosecution in a magistrates' court. HSE inspectors cannot but be aware that if they do not observe highly professional standards when serving a notice an action for damages might be brought against them personally. Should such an action be brought against an inspector the relevant enforcing authority may, but need not necessarily, indemnify the inspector (s.26). In a climate in which the public is increasingly likely to seek redress against public bodies whenever there is the least suggestion of failure properly to carry out public duties, the possibility of civil litigation cannot be ignored. There is no recorded case of either an inspector, or the HSE, being sued under the 1974 Act.

Work of customs officers

31. Assistance for HSE inspectors

The work of HSE inspectors in enforcement of s.6 of the 1974 Act is assisted by customs officers who are empowered by s.25A to seize and detain any imported article or substance. Though customs officers may only detain such goods for two working days this is sufficient time to enable HSE inspectors to decide whether to serve a notice or take other enforcement measures in relation to the articles and substances in question.

Obtaining and disclosing information

32. Powers of the HSC

Section 27 empowers the HSC (with the consent of the Secretary of State) to serve on any person a notice requiring that person to provide specified information, either to the HSC or the relevant enforcement authority. Information thus obtained must only be used for the purposes of the HSC or HSE.

33. Confidentiality of information

Section 28 applies both to information obtained under s.27 and to any other information provided by persons in compliance with a requirement imposed by any of the relevant statutory provisions. It provides such information must not normally be disclosed without the consent of the person who provided it. Section 28(3) provides exceptions to this safeguard enabling information to be disclosed for the purposes of functions conferred under the relevant statutory provisions, and to officers of certain other public bodies, such as the police. There is a particular restriction on the disclosure of trade secrets.

34. Disclosure of information

Notwithstanding the rigorous emphasis of the provisions of s.28 on the confidentiality of information obtained by the HSC and the HSE, s.28(8) requires disclosure of information to employees or their representatives for the purpose of assisting in keeping them adequately informed about matters affecting their health, safety and welfare. For this purpose the following descriptions of information must be supplied:

(a) factual information which the inspector has obtained which relates to the premises where they are employed, or to anything which is in the premises or was or is being done there; and
(b) information with respect to any action which the inspector has taken or proposes to take in or in connection with those premises in the performance of his/her functions.

Where an inspector supplies such information the same information must be given to the employers of the persons in question.

Provisions as to offences

35. Institution of proceedings
Section 38 of the 1974 Act provides that in England and Wales proceedings for an offence under any of the relevant statutory provisions may not be instituted except by an inspector, or by or with the consent of the Director of Public Prosecutions. This provision remains in force although the Crown Prosecution Service has been created since 1974. Section 39 empowers inspectors to prosecute before a magistrates' court even though they are not qualified lawyers. Proceedings, even to final appeal to the House of Lords, may well be in the name of the inspector who initiated the prosecution. In Scotland offences are prosecuted through the Procurator Fiscal.

36. Types of offence
Section 33 of the Act sets out the circumstances in which offences may be committed. The section is not well framed, but broadly it is an offence to fail to discharge a general duty or to contravene any health and safety regulation, or to contravene an improvement or prohibition order. There are also other offences such as obstructing an inspector, disclosing information, making a false statement, intentionally making a false entry in any register etc. required by law, or forging a document.

37. Penalties available

The majority of these offences are 'either way' offences; that is to say they may be prosecuted either summarily or upon indictment. The normal maximum penalty on summary conviction has been £2,000, but will be £5,000. In respect of offences committed after 6 March 1992 (the commencement of the Offshore Safety Act 1992, s.4), magistrates are empowered to impose penalties of up to £20,000 for breaches of ss.2–6 of the 1974 Act, breaches of improvement of prohibition notices, or of a court's remedial order, and any court may impose up to six months' imprisonment for breaches of a notice or court order. The penalty where trial is on indictment is usually an 'unlimited' fine (i.e. the court's jurisdiction is unlimited). In a few instances the Crown Court may impose a prison sentence of up to two years.

A prison sentence may be imposed:

(a) where the accused has done without a licence something which requires a licence (e.g. stripping asbestos — *see* the Asbestos (Licensing) Regulations 1983);
(b) contravened a term of, or a condition or restriction attached to, a licence;
(c) acquiring or attempting to acquire, possessing or using an explosive article or substance in contravention of any of the relevant statutory provisions;
(d) contravening a requirement or prohibition imposed by a notice;
(e) using or disclosing any information obtained further to ss.27 or 28 of the Act (i.e. obtained by the HSC or the HSC by notice issued with the consent of the Secretary of State, or other information obtained in relation to enforcement activities).

While most prosecutions are tried summarily, the majority of the offences are either way offences. It has been held that when an either way offence under the Act is tried summarily the usual limits on the time within which summary prosecutions must be brought do not apply.

38. Use of penalties by the courts

It might be thought that the powers of the Crown Court to impose very heavy fines, coupled with the majority of the offences being triable either way, would result in very substantial penalties being imposed for health and safety offences. However, there has in recent years been some dissatisfaction, which the HSE has shared, that the level of fine is not sufficiently high to bring home the seriousness of health and safety offences. There appears not to have been an imprisonment under the legislation, though there have been suspended sentences, particularly in the context of asbestos licensing requirements.

39. Alternatives to penalties

On convicting a person, in addition to, or as an alternative to, imposing a penalty for an offence, the court may order that person, within such time as may be fixed, to take such steps as may be specified in the order, to remedy matters (s.42).

40. Common law not available

Inspectors may not prosecute under the common law. Therefore, while homicide charges might be brought where workplace accidents have resulted in death, such proceedings could not be instituted or conducted by the HSE or local authority inspectors. Such prosecutions would be instituted in England and Wales by the police and conducted through the Crown Prosecution Service. The police are likely to learn that someone has been killed either through the involvement of emergency services (e.g. calling an ambulance through the telephone service) or the coroner's inquest.

Progress test 10

1. What are the principal responsibilities of: (a) the HSC; (b) the HSE?   **(6, 7)**
2. Which has the greater powers, HSE inspectors or the police? **(19, 40)**
3. What are the principal differences between improvement and prohibition notices?   **(23, 24)**
4. What information must an inspector provide to workers? **(34)**
5. What rights has an HSE inspector to proscute a case?   **(35)**
6. In what ways is the inspector's advisory role inhibited?   **(21)**

11
Worker involvement

1. Introduction
In the 1960s it was believed that workplaces would be safer if they had safety committees. There were attempts to enact legislation requiring such committees in every factory employing more than 50 persons. Many progressive organisations voluntarily introduced them.

From Robens to regulations

2. The Robens Committee
The debate about worker involvement was a reason why the Robens Committee was set up; the Committee's terms of reference included consideration of what changes were necessary in 'the nature and extent of voluntary action' for health and safety. The Report advocated involvement by management of workers to counter the apathy which the Committee believed to be a principal cause of accidents at the workplace.

3. Worker involvement
Parliament accepted the value of worker involvement. Nevertheless one of the matters most vigorously debated was whether provision should be made for every workplace or only for workplaces at which there was a trade union presence. The 1974 Act contained two separate enabling provisions: one for worker representation through trade unions (s.2(4)); the other for representation through employee-elected persons (s.2(5)). Section 2(6) imposed a broad obligation on employers to consult with

worker safety representatives and s.2(7) made provision for safety
committees.

4. Implementation strategy

It would have been possible to have implemented both s.2(4)
and s.2(5) and permitted organisations to decide which system to
adopt. However, a Labour government of the late 1970s,
committed to developing the role of trade unions, repealed s.2(5)
and then encouraged the implementation of s.2(4). The draft
regulations as proposed in the initial Consultative Document
satisfied neither trade unions nor employers. The final
regulations, the Safety Representatives and Safety Committees
Regulations 1977, did not differ greatly from the original draft
and would appear to be a compromise between the aspirations of
the two sides of the collective bargaining process at that time.

5. Alternative systems

It remains lawful to operate an alternative system to that laid
down in the regulations, at either unionised or non-unionised
workplaces; however, the lack of statutory provision for
non-unionised workers makes it difficult for them to have any
system of representation other than one which their employer may
choose to provide.

Emphasis on safety representatives

6. Appointment of safety representatives

Section 2(4) enables regulations for the appointment of safety
representatives, and it states that safety representatives:

> shall represent the employees in consultations with the employers
> . . and have such other functions as may be prescribed.

It makes no specific mention of any relationship between safety
representatives and safety committees, though membership of a
safety committee might be one of the functions of safety
representatives.

7. Employers' obligation to consult

Section 2(6) reiterates the emphasis of s.2(4), making it the employer's primary obligation to consult with safety representatives. The subsection then goes on to state the purposes for which, but not the means by which, such consultation must take place. The employer is required to consult:

> with a view to the making and maintenance of arrangements which will enable him and his employees to cooperate effectively in promoting and developing measures to ensure the health and safety at work of the employees, and in checking the effectiveness of such measures.

8. Safety committees

Section 2(7) makes minimal provision for safety committees:

> In such cases as may be prescribed it shall be the duty of every employer, if requested to do so by the safety representatives ... to establish, in accordance with regulations made by the Secretary of State, a safety committee having the function of keeping under review the measures taken to ensure the health and safety at work of his employees and such other functions as may be prescribed.

Thus the employer is only required to set up a safety committee if safety representatives ask him to do so, and regulations have prescribed that safety representatives may require a committee. The committee need only exercise the functions prescribed by the regulations.

Rights of trade unions

9. 'Recognised trade union'

Section 2(4) enables regulations to give rights to 'recognised trade unions'. The value of the rights under s.2(4) to trade union members depends on the legal significance of the expression 'recognised trade union'.

It is necessary to turn to other employment protection legislation to give a meaning to the words 'recognised trade union', an expression related to status in negotiation with an employer. The Trade Union and Labour Relations Act 1974, s.28(1), states that a trade union is an organisation of workers (whether permanent or temporary):

> whose principal purposes include the regulation of relations between workers and employers or between workers and employers' associations, or include the regulation of relations between its constituent or affiliated organisations.

10. Certification of trade unions

If a trade union is on the list of unions maintained by the Certification Officer it may, under s.8 of the Employment Protection Act 1975, apply for certification by the Certification Officer as an independent trade union. The certificate will be granted if the union meets the criteria of independence given in s.30 of the 1974 Trade Union and Labour Relations Act. For this purpose it must be a trade union which:

(a) is not under the domination or control of an employer or a group of employers or of one of more employers' associations; and
(b) is not liable to interference by an employer or any such group or association (arising out of the provision of financial or material support or by any other means whatsoever) tending towards such control.

11. Recognition of trade unions

Recognition is recognition by an employer for any of the purposes set out in s.29:

(a) terms and conditions of employment, or the physical conditions in which any workers are required to work;
(b) engagement or non-engagement, or termination or suspension of employment or the duties of employment, of one or more workers;
(c) allocation of work or the duties of employment as between workers or groups of workers;
(d) matters of discipline;
(e) the membership or non-membership of a trade union on the part of a worker;
(f) facilities for officials of trade unions; and
(g) machinery for negotiation or consultation, and other procedures, relating to any of the foregoing matters, including the recognition by employers or employers' associations in any such

negotiation or consultation or in the carrying out of such procedures.

A certified independent trade union could at one time seek formal recognition by an employer for purposes of negotiation; it could invoke procedures set out in the Employment Protection Act 1975 to obtain a ruling that it had a sufficient presence at a workplace for it to be entitled to be recognised at that workplace (though this would not necessarily ensure that the employer would actually recognise it!). The statutory procedures for recognition have been repealed. Whether a trade union can claim to be recognised is now therefore no more than a matter of fact: it will be recognised only if it can persuade an employer to recognise it for one or more of the matters set out above.

12. The present position

The formal abolition of all statutory protection for closed shop arrangements, and the introduction of statutory provisions which are intended to prevent an employer making any contractual stipulations concerning an employee's membership or non-membership of any trade union, have made it difficult for any union to acquire recognition. It seems unlikely therefore that workers who have not already achieved a system of trade union appointed safety representatives will be able to persuade an employer to grant them the floor of rights set out in the regulations made under s.2(4). Indeed employers who have sympathy with the concept of safety representatives may be reluctant to endorse the statutory system because such *de facto* trade union recognition might in due course involve them in recognition of trade unions for other purposes such as consultation in relation to redundancies (Employment Protection Act 1975, ss.99–107). Thus any new system of safety representatives set up now is likely to be established within a framework laid down by the employer, with perhaps some consultation with the workforce.

Status of safety representatives

13. Role of the safety representative

The safety representative, being a worker's representative is not a part of the employer's management team. Safety representatives must not be confused with the competent persons whom the employer is required to designate by Article 7 of the Framework Directive to carry out safety activities. This provision of the Directive has not hitherto been expressly paralleled in the UK system, but clearly the article has in view management nominees. The safety representative's function is also quite distinct from the function of the safety manager, who is engaged to advise the employer on, or deal with, safety issues. The worker safety representative's role is primarily a policing role, monitoring the performance of management. Carried to ultimate conclusions it may be, in the UK system, a conflict role.

14. Experience required for the post

In many instances trade unions have chosen to give the responsibility of acting as safety representative to shop stewards. It is argued that, as such persons are 'officials' of the union they can bring to the role experience and power. An alternative argument is that the special functions of safety representative are best performed by someone with more narrow technical expertise who is not burdened with the responsibilities which a shop steward carries.

Relationship of scheme with 1974 Act

15. General

The Safety Representatives and Safety Committees Regulations take their authority from legislation which bears criminal sanctions. This is anomolous because the system is essentially concerned with industrial relations as much as safety. Theoretically an inspector might serve an enforcement notice on, or even prosecute, an employer who failed to recognise and consult with safety representatives; the prospect of this happening is very remote.

16. Floor of rights

The regulations are not mandatory as are other regulations made under the 1974 Act. They represent a floor of rights which recognised trade unions might require of an employer; the employer is under no obligation to set up a system for safety representatives — he is required only to recognise those who have been properly appointed. Also, it is open to employer and union to negotiate a system somewhat different from the system set out in the regulations. Even if they agree to adopt the statutory system there are areas in which they will need to negotiate the way in which the system is to operate in the particular workplace.

17. Result of failure to apply regulations

The most likely result of a failure on the part of an employer to set up and maintain a safety representatives system to the requirements of the relevant trade union, or unions, is a breakdown in industrial relations, possibly a strike. Alternatively a claim might be made by a particular safety representative, to an industrial tribunal (*see* below).

The regulatory provisions

18. General

The Safety Representatives and Safety Committees Regulations 1977 were published in conjunction with an Approved Code of Practice on Safety Representatives and two sets of guidance notes, one on the operation of the safety representatives system and the other on the functioning of safety committees. A further approved code of practice published in 1978 dealt with time off for the training of safety representatives. The system has the following provisions.

19. Appointment of safety representatives

Regulation 3(1) empowers a trade union to appoint safety representatives from amongst the employees where one or more employees are employed by an employer by whom it is recognised; this regulation does not take precedence over the provisions in the Mines and Quarries Act 1954, s.180, for safety representatives in coal mines. An appointment takes effect when the employer has been notified in writing and will continue until either the trade union concerned notifies the employer in writing that the appointment has been terminated, or the representative leaves the employer's employment at the workplace(s) for which he/she was appointed or he/she resigns. The method of appointment is for the trade union to decide but regulation 3(4) stipulates that so far as is reasonably practicable the person appointed shall either have been employed by the employer throughout the preceding two years, or have had at least two years' experience in similar employment.

20. Where there is more than one union

Where there is more than one union at a workplace it is not usual for one to cede its rights to appoint representatives to the other; but trade unions often deal with matters concerning a worker who is not a union member, since it is in the union's interest to have the hazard controlled. This is in contrast to compensation claims where a union is most unlikely to concern itself with assisting the claim of someone who is not a member.

21. Numbers of representatives

The code of practice suggests that appropriate criteria for determining numbers of representatives should include:

(a) the total numbers employed;
(b) the variety of different occupations;
(c) the size of the workplace and the variety of workplace locations;
(d) the operation of shift systems;
(e) the type of work activity and the degree and character of the inherent dangers.

Employers cannot resist the appointment of a disproportionate number of safety representatives but might reasonably respond by allowing only minimal time for any particular representative to perform safety functions.

22. Scope of functions

Safety representatives have no function in relation to workers who are not employees of their own employer (except that such workers might be putting their employer's employees at risk) and no right to recognition by, or consultation with, an employer other than their own. These limitations put some restrictions on the operation of safety representative systems when employees are sent to work at premises which are not occupied by their own employer, or otherwise where they are required to work together with employees of another employer.

23. Situations where safety representatives need not be employees

Regulation 8 provides that safety representatives representing members of the British Actors' Equity Association or of the Musicians' Union need not be employees of the employer of members of the group they represent.

24. Functions of safety representatives

Regulation 4 states that a safety representative has certain functions in addition to the function given to them under s.2(4) and (6) of the Act, which is to represent the employees in consultation with the employer. These additional functions are to:

(a) investigate potential hazards and dangerous occurrences at the workplace (whether or not they are drawn to his attention by the employees he represents) and to examine the causes of accidents at the workplace;

(b) investigate complaints by any employee he represents relating to that employee's health, safety or welfare at work;

(c) make representations to the employer on matters arising out of sub-paragraphs (a) and (b) above;

(d) make representations to the employer on general matters affecting the health, safety or welfare at work of the employees at the workplace;

(e) carry out inspections in accordance with regulations 5, 6 and 7 [*see* **33** below];

(f) represent the employees he was appointed to represent in consultations at the workplace with inspectors of the HSE and of any other enforcing authority;

(g) receive information from inspectors in accordance with s.28(8) of the 1974 Act; and

(h) attend meetings of safety committees where he attends in his capacity as a safety representative in connection with any of the above functions.

The code of practice suggests that safety representatives should take all reasonably practicable steps to keep themselves informed of legal requirements, the particular hazards of the workplace and the measures deemed necessary to eliminate or minimise the risk deriving from these hazards, and the health and safety policy of their employer. The code further suggests that they should encourage cooperation between their employer and its employees in promoting and developing essential measures to ensure the health and safety of employees and in checking the effectiveness of such measures.

25. Reporting unsafe systems

The code of practice suggests that safety representatives should bring to the employer's notice (preferably in writing if the matter is a serious one) any unsafe or unhealthy conditions or working practices or unsatisfactory arrangements for welfare at work which come to their attention.

Regulation 11 of the Proposals for Health and Safety (General Provisions) Regulations intends to require every employee to inform his employer 'or any other employee of that employer with specific responsibility for the health and safety of his fellow employees...' (presumably the safety officer rather than the safety representative):

(a) of any work situation which may reasonably be considered to represent a serious and immediate danger to health and safety; and

(b) of any matter which may reasonably be considered to represent a shortcoming in the employer's protection arrangements for health and safety, insofar as that situation or matter either affects the health and safety of the employee concerned or arises out of or in connection with his own activities at work, and has not previously been reported to that employer or to any other employee of that employer in accordance with this paragraph.

26. Safety representatives' legal responsibilities

Regulation 4 provides that no function given to a safety representative by regulations shall impose any duty on him. However, this provision is without prejudice to duties imposed by ss.7 and 8 of the Act. The duties under s.7, to take care for themselves and others, to cooperate with persons such as their employer, and (under s.8) not to interfere with any thing provided for purposes of safety, need to be borne in mind in discussions as to whether safety representatives should be empowered to stop operations which in their view are dangerous. This should not detract from the right of safety representatives or any other worker personally to withdraw from work which is putting them in danger which is not within the terms of his contract, or, even if within the contract, unlawful; even then such withdrawal should be after carrying out shut-down procedures which can safely be undertaken (*see Gannon* v. *Firth Ltd* [1976]).

The guidance notes give reassurance that a safety representative who accepts, agrees with or fails to object to a course of action taken by an employer to deal with a health or safety hazard does not take on legal responsibility for that course of action.

The guidance notes also point out the need for representatives to be able to communicate with management without delay.

27. Protection of safety representatives

A safety representative is in some respects given more authority, but less legal protection, in UK law than a shop steward. On the one hand there is no regulatory provision for shop stewards comparable to the detailed identification of functions of safety representatives. On the other hand the shop stewards enjoy a general protection against discrimination against them by the employer on account of trade union membership or activitives (*see* Employment Protection (Consolidation) Act 1978, ss.23 and 58) which a safety representative, or anyone else seeking to enforce safe systems, does not necessarily enjoy. Thus in *Chant* v. *Aquaboats Ltd* [1978] organising a petition about safety standards was held not to be a trade union activity, and therefore the worker was not protected from discrimination, even though the TU vetted the petition. (*See also Gardner* v. *Peeks Retail Ltd* [1975], and *Drew* v. *St Edmundsbury BC* [1980].) The Framework Directive, Article 11, would seem to require UK law on discrimination to be clarified on this at least as far as safety representatives are concerned.

28. Protection of employees

Individual employees refusing to carry out work which places them in danger are usually protected against dismissal provided they have the two years' full-time continuous employment (or five years' part-time employment) which is necessary to bring them within the jurisdiction of industrial tribunals for the purposes of unfair dismissal proceedings (*see*, for example, *BAC* v. *Austin* [1978]).

29. Rights to time off and training

Regulation 4(2) provides that an employer shall permit a safety representative to take such time off with pay during the employee's working hours as shall be necessary for the purposes of:

(a) performing his functions as a safety representative; and
(b) undergoing such training in aspects of those functions as may be reasonable in all the circumstances.

A schedule to regulation 4(2) provides that an employer must pay a safety representative remuneration at his normal rate while he is carrying out his safety representative's duties, and if there is no normal rate, then an amount calculated by reference to the average hourly earnings for that work.

30. Failure by the employer to permit time off

Regulation 11 enables a safety representative to present a complaint to an industrial tribunal that:

(a) an employer has failed to permit him to take time off to carry out his functions under regulations 4(2); or
(b) has failed to pay him for the time in which he was carrying out those functions.

A complaint must be presented to an industrial tribunal within three months of the date when the failure occurred or within such further period as the tribunal considers reasonable in a case where it is satisfied that it was not reasonably practicable for the complaint to be presented within the period of three months. Where an industrial tribunal finds a complaint that time off has not been allowed is well founded, it shall make a declaration to that effect and may make an award of compensation to be paid by the employer to the employee. The compensatory award is to be of such amount as the tribunal considers just and equitable in all the circumstances having regard to the employer's default in failing to permit time off to be taken by the employee and to any loss sustained by the employee which is attributable to the matters complained of. Where a complaint concerning failure to pay is established then the tribunal must make an order requiring the employer to make the due payment.

31. Other disputes

The procedure of complaint to a tribunal might prove a way of settling a dispute in which the allegation is that the employer either refuses to recognise the appointment of the complainant as a safety representative or to agree the amount of time needed for the performance of the representative's safety functions.

32. Code of practice proposals

The Code of Practice on Time Off for the Training of Safety Representatives proposes that as soon as possible after their appointment safety representatives should be permitted time off with pay to attend basic training facilities approved by the TUC or by the independent union or unions who appointed the representative. Moreover, further training, similarly approved, should be undertaken where the safety representative has special responsibilities or where such training is necessary to meet changes in circumstances or relevant legislation.

The Code proposes that when a trade union wishes a safety representative to receive training it should inform management of the course it has approved and supply a copy of the syllabus, indicating its content, if the employer asks for it.

The number of safety representatives attending training courses at any one time should be that which is reasonable in the circumstances, bearing in mind such factors as the availability of courses and the operational requirements of the employer. Unions and management should endeavour to reach agreement on the appropriate numbers and arrangements and refer any problems which may arise to the relevant agreed procedures.

White v. *Pressed Steel Fisher* [1980] concerned a dispute about attendance at a training course. The appellant's union wanted him to attend a course at a local technical college, but the employer wanted him to attend the company's own in-company course which did not include a trade union input because, so the employers alleged, the union had refused to contribute to it. The employers refused permission to attend the technical college, because they considered their own course was appropriate. The industrial tribunal rejected the employee's claim that he had been unreasonably refused time off to attend the course and found that the company's course was adequate for the purposes of the regulations. The EAT noted that, while the code of practice refers to training through a union-approved course, the requirement of union approval was not in the regulations themselves. However, the EAT found that a union refusal to participate in an employer's course was not automatically an answer to a claim for time off to attend a TU course. On the other hand the union refusal to work with the employer did not automatically mean the employer's course was defective. The EAT considered there was not sufficient evidence to know whether the employer's course was adequate and the case was sent back to the tribunal for further consideration of the evidence.

In *Gallagher* v. *The Drum Engineering Co. Ltd* (1991) an industrial tribunal found employers had breached the regulations when they failed to allow safety representatives to take paid time off to attend a TUC course on the implementation of the Control of Substances Hazardous to Health Regulations. It was held unreasonable for the employer to allow only one of the three representatives to attend the particular course: the regulations were new and important, the course was only offered three times a year and there was no evidence that the employer would have been greatly inconvenienced if all the men had attended at the same time.

Training provided by the TUC and unions in the late 1970s and early 1980s ensured that the first generations of safety representatives were well informed — often better informed than first line management, whom employers did not generally train sufficiently to enable them to respond efectively to informed safety representatives.

33. Inspections at the workplace

Regulation 5 entitles safety representatives to inspect the workplace (or part of it) if they have given the employer reasonable notice in writing of their intention to do so and have not inspected it in the previous three months. More frequent inspections may be carried out by agreement. Inspections may also be carried out within the three-month period where there has been a substantial change in the conditions of work, or new information has been published by the HSC or HSE. The employer is required to provide such facilities and assistance as the safety representatives may reasonably require (including facilities for independent investigation by them and private discussion with the employees). The employer may be present at the workplace during the inspection.

Regulation 6 provides for inspections following notifiable accidents, occurrences and diseases. In these circumstances an inspection may be carried out only if it is safe for it to be carried out and the interests of employees in the group or groups which safety representatives are appointed to represent might be involved.

34. Guidance on inspections

The guidance suggest that normal inspections should be carried out on an agreed routine basis and also that there may be advantages in employer and representatives carrying out such inspections together, provided such arrangements do not prevent the representatives from carrying out independent investigations or having private discussions with employees. In the view of the HSC, where a post-accident investigation is carried out, the main purpose should be to determine the causes so that the possibility of action to prevent a recurrence can be considered. For this reason it is important that the approach to the problem should be a joint one by the employer and the safety representatives working together.

35. Inspection of documents etc.

Regulation 7 gives safety representatives the right (provided they have given the employer reasonable notice) to inspect and take copies of any document relevant to the workplace or to the employees the safety representatives represent, being documents which the employer is required to keep by virtue of any relevant statutory provision, except a document consisting of, or relating to, any health record of an identifiable individual.

The employer is required to make available to safety representatives information which is both within the employer's knowledge and necessary to enable them to fulfil their functions except:

(a)   any information the disclosure of which would be against the interests of national security, or

(b)   any information which the employer could not disclose without contravening a prohibition imposed by or under an enactment, or

(c)   any information relating specifically to an individual, unless that individual has consented to its being disclosed, or

(d)   any information the disclosure of which would, for reasons other than its effect on health, safety or welfare at work, cause substantial injury to the employer's undertaking or, where the information was supplied by some other person, to the undertaking of that other person, or

(e)   any information obtained by the employer for the purpose of bringing, prosecuting or defending any legal proceedings.

The employer is not required by this regulation to produce or allow inspection of any document which is not related to health, safety or welfare.

36.   Guidance on disclosure of information

The guidance suggests that safety representatives will need to be given information over and above that given to individual employees by employers in discharge of their duty under s.2(2)(c).

37.   Safety committees

Regulation 9 provides that the prescribed cases referred to in s.2(7) of the Act, where safety committees must be established by an employer, are cases in which at least two safety representatives request the employer in writing to establish such a committee.

The regulation further provides that where an employer is requested to establish a safety committee he shall establish it in accordance with the following provisions:

(a)   they shall consult with the safety representatives who made the request and with the representatives of recognised trade unions whose members work in any workplace in respect of which he proposes that the committee should function:

(b)   the employer shall post a notice stating the composition of the committee and the workplace or workplaces to be covered by it in a place where it may be easily read by the employees;

(c) the committee shall be established not later than three months after the request for it.

38. Guidance on safety committees

In guidance published in association with this regulation, the HSC suggests the detailed arrangements necessary to fulfil the regulations should evolve from discussion and negotiation between employers and safety representatives, since they are best able to interpret the needs of the particular workplace. The HSC further opines that safety committees are most likely to prove effective where their work is related to a single establishment. They also consider that the work of the committee should have a separate identity from that of other works' committees.

EC requirements

39. General

The EC Framework Directive on health and safety at work attaches some significance to worker involvement and envisages a worker safety representative system. Article 3 of the Framework Directive defines a workers' representative as a person elected, chosen or designated in accordance with *national laws and or practices* to represent workers where problems arise relating to the safety and health protection of workers at work.

40. Requirements of the Directive

Article 11 of the EC Directive requires employers to consult with workers and/or their representatives and allow them to take part in discussions on questions relating to safety. It intends that all workers and/or their representatives will have the right to make proposals and engage in balanced participation with employers on safety matters. Employers are specifically required to consult with their workers about:

(a)   any measure which may substantially affect safety and health;
(b)   the designation of workers with special safety responsibilities, such as first-aid or fire-fighting;
(c)   safety risks and the way they are being controlled;
(d)   the enlistment of competent persons from outside the enterprise;
(e)   the planning and organisation of training.

Moreover, workers and or their representatives must be allowed by the employer the opportunity to submit their observations during inspection visits by the enforcing authority.

41. UK response

In the proposed General Provisions Regulations, regulation 15 and the schedule propose to extend the employer's duty to consult with safety representatives as set out in s.2(6) of the 1974 Act. The proposals require the employer to consult with safety representatives in good time with regard to:

(a)   the introduction of any measure at the workplace which may substantially affect the health and safety of the employees the safety representatives concerned represent;
(b)   his arrangements for appointing or, as the case may be, nominating [competent] persons in accordance with [the General Provisions Regulations];
(c)   any health and safety information required to be provided by him to the employees the safety representatives concerned represents;
(d)   the planning and organisation of any health and safety training required to be provided by him to the employees the safety representatives concerned represent; and
(e)   the health and safety consequences for the employees the safety representatives concerned represent of the introduction (including the planning thereof) of new technologies into the workplace.

The schedule reiterates the duty of employers to provide safety representatives with facilities and assistance for carrying out their functions.

No proposals have yet been made to provide for extending the scope of the 1977 regulations to make them apply other than to safety representatives appointed by recognised trade unions.

Outstanding issues

42. Representation of non-unionised employees

It must be doubted whether the *national system* in the UK at present meets the expectations of the EC Directive, since the latter appears to presuppose that there will be a more comprehensive system of representation than the trade union orientation of the UK system provides.

The problem with the UK system is not that the regulations provide for a system of trade union representation; it is that the system imposes no alternative duty on an employer to consult with the non-unionised sector of the workforce. It is true that the general duty in s.2(2)(c) could be deemed to impose on the employer an obligation to provide information to every individual employee, even if there is no trade union at the workplace in question. The s.2(2)(c) duty does not, however, necessarily extend to consultation with individual employees, i.e. entering into dialogue with them.

It seems inescapable that UK law will have to be changed to give a safety representatives system to non-unionised workers, if the Directive is to be honoured. It would not be necessary to reinstate s.2(5) to do this; the general regulation-making power of the 1974 Act is wide enough to support such regulations. Alternatively regulations might be made under s.20 of the European Communities Act 1972.

43. Offshore system

It has been an ongoing cause of dissatisfaction to the trade union movement that the onshore regulations have not been extended to offshore installations, where in any case the workforce tends not to be unionised. A distinct set of regulations has now been made under the Mineral Workings Act — namely the Offshore Installations (Safety Representatives and Safety Committees) Regulations 1989. These require the implementation of a system to allow representatives to be elected without reference to whether the workforce is unionised. Safety representation offshore is further complicated because of the number of different employers with employees present on an installation.

The Offshore Safety (Protection Against Victimisation) Act 1992, which came into force on 16 March 1992, makes provision to protect employees working on offshore installations from victimisation when acting as safety representatives or members of safety committees.

Progress test 11

1. What is a 'recognised trade union'?   **(9, 11)**

2. What are the primary functions of a safety representative? **(24)**

3. Does a safety representative enjoy protection against discrimination? **(27)**

4. What systems for safety representatives other than that created under s.2(4) exist in the UK?   **(5, 19, 23)**

5. When is a safety committee required?   **(37)**

6. Why does the UK system not match the requirements of the EC Framework Directive?   **(42)**

Part three

Compensation for industrial accidents

Part three

Compensation for industrial accidents

Introduction: nature and purpose of civil liability

1. Introduction

Claims for common-law damages are based either on the tort of negligence or on breach of statutory duty. These forms of liability will be discussed in the two succeeding chapters: this chapter will deal with principles which are relevant to these forms of liability. It will cover:

(a) the role and purpose of civil liability;
(b) strict and fault liability;
(c) personal and vicarious liability;
(d) distinction between employers' liability and public liability.

The role and purpose of civil liability

2. General

There has been a longstanding debate about the purpose of litigation for damages for personal injury.

3. Damages are to compensate

Litigation is intended to provide the accident victim with damages to compensate for the injury that has been suffered, though it may be disputed whether a monetary value can be placed on physical injury, as opposed to loss of income which results from physical injury. English law has hitherto rejected awarding sums greater than the loss suffered by the plaintiff in order to punish the defendant for callous, irresponsible or reckless behaviour (but *see A.B. v. S.W. Water Services Ltd* (1992)), although exemplary damages, as such awards are called, are available in other kinds of civil litigation (*see Rookes* v. *Barnard* [1964]).

In the nineteenth century workers argued that payment of damages to injured workers should cause hardship to the wrongdoer to punish for the suffering which had been endured by the accident victim. Subsequently it was realised that there was a conflict between the need to compensate the victim and the desire to punish the wrongdoer; if wrongdoers did not have the funds to pay the damages then accident victims got neither financial compensation nor emotional satisfaction.

4.   Third-party insurance

Until the purpose of civil liability had been clarified, the legality of third-party insurance was doubted: it was argued that a contract of insurance would be illegal if it relieved the insured of the obligation personally to compensate. Later, it was realised that there was merit in using insurance to ensure availability of funds for compensation. In the twentieth century legislation has made third-party insurance compulsory in respect of road traffic generally, and to some extent in relation to work-related injuries.

5.   The Pearson Commission

The debate about the purposes of compensation is not entirely dead. One of the arguments against paying all compensation through the social security system is that litigation is therapeutic for victims; it enables them to enjoy a sense of 'getting even with' the wrongdoer. This, and the overwhelming cost of providing adequate compensation through social security, were the reasons that the Pearson Commission advocated retaining the present common-law system in tandem with the social security system. So while the system of suing for common-law damages for personal injury has been described as 'the forensic lottery' (T.G. Ison (1967)), the right to sue remains.

The Pearson Commission demonstrated that, as far as can be estimated, given the uncertainty over how many cases are settled out of court, about 15% of industrial injury victims obtain common-law damages. But nevertheless, for personal injuries generally, about 50% of money payments (primarily in respect of income maintenance) come from the social security system and less than 20% come from common-law litigation.

6. Victim support groups

The victim's desire to impose a financial penalty on the wrongdoer is illustrated by the victim support groups which are nowadays frequently formed in the aftermath of major catastrophies. These groups publicise the problems of the victims with quite surprising outcomes. One such outcome has been the revival of the suggestion that exemplary damages should be awarded, even if such damages were not paid to the victims, but used for other suitable purposes which the court might name (such as research). Such an idea could, presumably, only be implemented by legislation.

A controversial outcome of the publicity which catastrophies receive is that victims of them often get favourable out-of-court settlements. Alleged wrongdoers presumably conclude that it is better, and perhaps cheaper, to settle rapidly, without admission of liability, rather than face ongoing publicity in the litigation process. By contrast, the solitary victim of an accident may face lengthy and expensive proceedings.

7. For what injuries is compensation paid?

Damages are awarded in respect of personal injury. Personal injury is interpreted widely to include fatal accidents; it includes other accidental injury and injury suffered by reason of deterioration in health, i.e. disease.

The former Workmen's Compensation Acts which provided compensation for any *accident* arising out of and in the course of employment, but only provided compensation for *certain prescribed diseases* contracted in like circumstances, gave rise to a great deal of case law about the meaning of the word accident. Suffice it to say that an accident was defined as some unlooked-for mishap or untoward event which was not expected or desired by the victim: an accident normally happens only once and has fairly immediate consequences. Diseases generally occur over a period of time from continual exposure to adverse conditions.

Historically much disease has been caused to the workforce by exposure to dust: this has typically caused respiratory diseases and skin complaints such as dermatitis. Changing work patterns, and advances in medical science, have shifted the focus to deafness caused by noise, muscular and skeletal strain caused by repetitive work and poisoning caused by toxic substances such as lead. The realisation that work can cause cancer and related diseases, such as asbestosis, also causes concern.

8. Difference between accident and disease

There is little purpose here in distinguishing accidents from diseases, since either may entitle the victim to claim common-law damages. In practice it remains more difficult for the victim of long-term exposure to bad working conditions to recover damages than it is for one who has suffered an accident whose occurrence was at a particular time and probably witnessed. However, back injuries are difficult to prove, even where allegedly caused by an accident rather than repetitive strain — because there is often a lack of evidence of the occurrence!

9. Assessment and payment of damages

Compensatory damages are intended to put the defendant in the position in which he would have been had he not sustained the injury. There are generally two aspects to a claim: unliquidated damages and special damages.

10. Unliquidated damages

The claim for unliquidated damages is generally supported by medical evidence. On the basis of the evidence, and also by reference to the 'tariff' established by other judges in like cases, the judge puts a monetary figure on the pain, suffering and loss of amenity suffered by the plaintiff.

11. Special damages

These damages are for the financial burden which the injury has imposed on the plaintiff. Principal items of special damages are the cost of medical attention and care attendance, the cost of adapting to the injury (e.g. installing a lift in a house) and the loss of earned income. The plaintiff is allowed to look into the future and claim in respect of financial benefit which might have been expected to accrue to him if the accident had not occurred; this is an exception to the general reluctance of courts to award damages for economic loss negligently caused.

12. Relationship with social security

The Law Reform (Personal Injuries) Act 1948, s.2(1), required that deductions be made of half of the benefits received for a five-year period (if the disability lasts this long) as sickness benefit, invalidity benefit, non-contributory invalidity pension, injury benefit or disablement benefit. This is now relevant only to small claims. In other cases the Social Security Act 1989, s.22 requires the compensator completely to reimburse the Secretary of State out of sums otherwise payable to the victim whether by way of damages or out of court settlement.

Under s.5 of the Administration of Justice Act 1982 any saving to the injured person which is attributable to his maintenance wholly or partly at public expense in a hospital is set off against any income lost to him as a result of the injuries sustained.

13. Loss of expectation of life

Formerly substantial damages were awarded for 'the lost years' where the victim's life expectancy was shortened as a result of the injury. The Administration of Justice Act, s.1(1), has considerably curtailed such claims by providing:

(a) no damages shall be recoverable in respect of any loss of expectation of life caused to the injured person by the injuries; but

(b) if the injured person's expectation of life has been reduced by the injuries, the court, in assessing damages in respect of pain and suffering caused by the injuries, shall take account of any suffering caused or likely to be caused to him by awareness that his expectation of life has been so reduced.

Section 1(2) provides that s.1(1)(a) does not affect the right to claim for loss of income, confirming the House of Lords decision in *Pickett* v. *British Rail Engineering Ltd* [1980]. The plaintiff was the victim of asbestosis contracted at work. He died before his appeal on *quantum* of damages could be heard; the House held an award should have been made for loss of income appropriate to the length of his life expectancy prior to the accident. Their Lordships were no doubt mindful that any other finding would have been unfavourable to the widow who might otherwise have been left with less provision than if she had made a claim in her own right under the Fatal Accidents Act.

14. Periodical payments

Identifying the appropriate amount for an award is a difficult task, necessitating a calculation of the plaintiff's needs, over an uncertain period of time, when the prognosis of the plaintiff's future physical condition may be unclear, and inflation may affect the value of the award. The Supreme Court Act 1981, s.32A, assists the court to award provisional damages in cases where there is a chance that the injured person will develop some serious disease or suffer some serious deterioration in his physical or mental condition as a consequence of the injury under consideration. Where the award is provisional the plaintiff may return to court to make a further claim if the contingency occurs.

The courts welcome any arrangement between the parties, in the form of structured settlements, for investment of money to enable periodical payments to be made to meet the needs of the plaintiff; while courts are reluctant themselves to rely on actuarial evidence in calculating awards, they are happy that the parties should rely on this kind of evidence to agree a suitable arrangement for endorsement by the court.

15. Fatal accidents

The Fatal Accidents Act 1976 acknowledges the needs of widows and other dependents deprived by a fatal accident of income support from the deceased. It must be established:

(a) if the victim had been injured rather than killed he would have had a claim in his own right (i.e. the claimant must establish liability of the defendant to the deceased in negligence or for breach of statutory duty);
(b) the claimant must come within the class of persons to whom the statute gives rights (i.e. be either a spouse or child, or other person within the recognised list of relationships);
(c) the claimant must actually have been dependent on the deceased for income maintenance (e.g. an adult married child would not normally be able to claim); and
(d) awards are calculated in relation to the income support which the deceased might have been expected to provide.

A claim under this legislation is normally brought by the personal representative of the deceased; this person need not, of course, be a person actually entitled under the Act.

Section 1A of the Fatal Accidents Act enables a claim of a small sum for bereavement; such sums are only payable to the benefit of the husband or wife of the deceased, or to the parents of a minor who had never married.

16. Limitation of actions

Normally a plaintiff may not start an action for personal injury more than three years after the cause of action arose, i.e. the date when the accident occurred. In cases arising from exposure to circumstances which cause ill-health, the cause of action ought logically to arise at the time of the exposure, but if this rule were applied the limitation period might have expired long before the victim was aware that he might sue (*see Cartledge* v. *Jopling & Sons Ltd* [1963]). Parliament has revised the limitation rules to assist persons in this situation. The task proved difficult and the problem had to be addressed on more than one occasion to produce legislation that was satisfactory. The position is now governed by the Limitation Act 1980, ss.11(4)(b), 14 and 33.

17. Knowledge of right to sue

Section 11(4)(b) prevents time running until the plaintiff has knowledge that he has a right to sue.

Section 14 defines knowledge for this purpose as knowledge of the following facts:

(a) that the injury in question was significant;

(b) that the injury was attributable in whole or in part to the act or omission which is alleged to constitute negligence, nuisance or breach of duty; and

(c) the identity of the defendant; and

(d) if it is alleged that the act or omission was that of a person other than the defendant, the identity of that person and the additional facts supporting the bringing of an action against the defendant.

When the plaintiff has the relevant knowledge he must start the action within three years unless he can persuade the court to exercise its power under s.33 further to extend the period; the court will only exercise this discretion if it is equitable to do so and the defendant would not be prejudiced by the extension of time.

Strict and fault liability

18. General

The debate about the purposes of civil liability has led to questioning whether civil liability should be strict or fault liability. If the purpose is entirely compensatory then arguably damages should always be recoverable by an injured person regardless of whether the injury was the result of his own folly, the fault of another person, or occurred without fault.

19. Liability of the state

The Pearson Commission pointed out that the state's liability to pay social security benefits is 'no fault liability': the claimant who can establish that he suffers from the incapacity is entitled to the benefit. The primary source of income maintenance for incapacity arising from work-related injuries is the social security 'no fault' system, providing benefits, in the short term at least, from the general sickness benefit scheme. Since the implementation of the Social Security and Housing Benefits Act 1982, payments due to employees from the state scheme for incapacitating sickness in respect of the first 28 weeks of incapacity are paid to the employee by the employer. The Statutory Sick Pay Act 1991 restricted the employers' entitlement to recoup payments made to employees under this scheme, in most instances (there are exceptions for small employers) to 80% of the benefits paid. Thus an element of strict liability for income maintenance of employees has been placed on employers, independently of any contractual scheme for income maintenance which the employer may operate and irrespective of whether or not the incapacity has been caused by work or is in any way related to it.

20. Common-law system of damages

The common-law system of compensatory damages is a fault-based system. The plaintiff must establish that the defendant's conduct was at fault in order to win his case. Where the claim is based in negligence the plaintiff must establish that the defendant's conduct was negligent. The possibility of imposing strict liability in common-law industrial injury claims was proposed to, and rejected by, the House of Lords in *Read* v. *J Lyons & Co Ltd* [1946] where the plaintiff had suffered personal injury in an explosion in the munitions factory where she worked. The matter was put by Lord Macmillan:

> The action is one of damages for personal injuries ... I am of opinion that, as the law now stands an allegation of negligence is in general essential to the relevancy of an action of reparation for personal injuries.

In rejecting the proposition that there might be special rules of strict liability imposed on anyone who engaged in hazardous activities his Lordship continued:

> Strict liability, if you will, is imposed upon him in the sense that he must exercise a high degree of care, but that is all. The sound view, in my opinion, is that the law in all cases exacts a degree of care commensurate with the risk created.

21. Damages as a result of disease

It is often difficult for the victim of disease to recover damages because of the problems associated with establishing that the disease was caused by work. The ruling of the House of Lords in *Bonnington Castings Ltd* v. *Wardlaw* [1956] is of assistance to plaintiffs in establishing that unlawful working conditions have caused their illness. The respondent, who had worked for eight years in the appellants' foundry, contracted pneumoconiosis through inhaling air containing silica dust. Some of the dust came from swing grinders because the dust-extraction plant for these grinders had not been kept free from obstruction as required by statutory regulations. Their Lordships held the respondent should recover damages for breach of statutory duty as the dust from the swing grinders had contributed materially to his condition.

This approach was developed in *McGhee* v. *National Coal Board* [1972] where the House considered the case of a worker who had suffered a skin disease apparently attributable to cycling home from a workplace where (in breach of the employer's statutory duty) there were no washing facilities. It was established that the lack of washing facilities increased the risk of catching the disease, but not that the plaintiff would not have suffered from it if his employers had provided washing facilities. Their Lordships nevertheless allowed the plaintiff's claim.

It thus appears that if the circumstances of an employer's breach of duty could cause the plaintiff's ill-health the courts are prepared to find a causal link sufficient to sustain a claim in damages.

22. Appreciation of the danger

Another problem which frequently besets the plaintiff in ill-health cases is of showing that the employer ought to have appreciated the risk at the date when the worker was exposed to it. Illnesses which manifest themselves today may have been caused by exposure to dangers many years ago; in the past the dangers may not have been appreciated. The victim can only impose liability on a defendant for conduct which was unlawful at the time the injury occurred; in relation to some causes of ill-health which have been much litigated the courts have established the date at which employers ought first to have been aware of the risk to which they were exposing their workers. In the case of noise-induced deafness the courts have refused to attach liability for exposure to noise before the mid 1970s.

23. Risk outside the workplace

Finally the difficulty of establishing the cause of ill-health is compounded if the particular disability from which the plaintiff suffers is one, like asthma or deafness, which might have been caused by exposure to risk outside the workplace.

24. Breaches of statutory duties

In situations where claims are based on breach of statutory duty, strict liability may be imposed on defendants. The plaintiff is unlikely to have to establish that the defendant's conduct has been negligent: the only alleged 'fault' of the defendant is failure to ensure that the duty imposed by the statute has been observed. The plaintiff must bring the evidence necessary to show the statutory duty has been broken: what the plaintiff has to prove will vary according to the requirements of the provision relied upon, but negligent conduct is rarely a criterion of liability.

Vicarious liability, imposed upon employers in respect of the wrongdoing of their employees is another example of strict liability.

Personal a ous liability

25. General

Most employ orporations; while the law recognises such legal entities ns' it is somewhat fanciful to imagine them as actually pe g any actions, since they have no physical being. Howev law places duties on corporations personally.

26. Types of organisationa ility

In civil law two kinds o nisational liability have been recognised: the personal liab of the organisation and its liability for the acts of others (vi us liability). Strictly speaking vicarious liability has no place in inal law, but if a strict duty is imposed by the criminal law, and t person on whom it is placed is not allowed either to delegate responsibility for performance of that duty or to bring evidence that another person is the actual wrongdoer, the effect will be much the same as under the civil law relating to vicarious liability. However, in this chapter personal and vicarious liability will be considered solely in the context of the civil law.

27. Demise of the doctrine of common employment

The doctrine of common employment formerly prevented an injured employee from claiming damages from his employer if the actual wrongdoer were a fellow servant in the service of the victim's own employer at the time when the injury was suffered. In *Wilsons & Clyde Coal Company Ltd* v. *English* [1937] the House of Lords imposed liability on an employer in circumstances where the, by this time discredited, doctrine of common employment should logically have protected him from liability. Their Lordships achieved this by discovering a 'non-delegable' duty on the employer to provide a safe system of work. The matter was put by Lord Wright:

> ... I do not mean that employers warrant the adequacy of plant, or the competence of fellow-employees, or the propriety of the system of work. The obligation is fulfilled by the exercise of due care and skill. But it is not fulfilled by entrusting its fulfilment to employees, even though selected with due care and skill. The obligation is

threefold, 'the provision of a competent staff of men, adequate material, and a proper system and effective supervision' . . .

I think the whole course of authority consistently recognises a duty which rests on the employer, and which is personal to the employer, to take reasonable care for the safety of his workmen, whether the employer be an individual, a firm, or a company, and whether or not the employer takes any share in the conduct of the operations.

28. Duty to provide a safe system of work

Subsequent case law added other facets to this personal duty, such as the requirements of training and supervision, but the essence of the duty is to provide a safe system of work. The abolition of the doctrine of common employment might have seen the demise of the concept of the personal duty: that it did not is because an employer can only be made vicariously liable for the actual wrongdoings of an employee when acting in the course of his employment. The employer's personal duty therefore remains important:

(a) where the wrongdoer is not an employee, though the courts are reluctant to find an employer liable for the wrongdoing of one who is not their employee (e.g. *Davie* v. *New Merton Board Mills Ltd* [1959]);

(b) where the wrongdoer was not acting in the course of employment, e.g. a practical joker who tripped a fellow worker was not in the course of employment when thus skylarking, but the employer was liable for keeping in his employment someone with the known propensity for practical joking (*Hudson* v. *Ridge Manufacturing Company Ltd* [1957]);

(c) a hazard may be created because no person is detailed to a task, or persons given the task cannot perform it because they lack adequate equipment, training or supervision (*see Jones* v. *Manchester Corporation* [1952].

29. Various forms of liability

The employer does not incur *personal* liability unless his conduct has been negligent in failing to provide a safe system. On the other hand, an employer may be *vicariously* liable for the wrongdoing of his employee even though that employer has exercised every degree of care possible. For example, in *Lister* v. *Romford Ice & Cold Storage Co. Ltd* [1957] employers were found liable for the negligence of their lorry driver in running down his mate although the employers were themselves faultless.

30. Vicarious liability

The prerequisites of vicarious liability are:

(a) the wrongdoer must have been an employee (*see* 31);
(b) the employee must have committed a tort (which will generally, but not necessarily, be the tort of negligence) (*see* 32); and
(c) when committing the tort that employee must have been acting in the course of his employment (*see* 33).

It is, since the abolition of the doctrine of common employment, no longer relevant whether the victim was also an employee, or another worker, or a member of the public.

31. Status of employee

It was noted when outlining the development of safety law that the task of identifying a test by which the status of employee might be determined has exercised the courts for more than a hundred years. The origin of the modern multiple test is *Ready Mixed Concrete South East Ltd* v. *Minister of Pensions* [1968] where a firm had dismissed all its lorry driver employees and purported to re-engage them as self-employed drivers.

McKenna J held that there were three conditions necessary to establish that a contract of employment existed:

(a) the worker agreed to provide his own work and skill in the performance of a service for the employer;
(b) there was an element of control exercisable by the employer;
(c) that the other terms of the contract must not be inconsistent with the existence of a contract of employment.

In the event, the facts that the drivers were buying their own lorries, thus giving them a considerable capital investment in the enterprise, and that they were allowed to delegate the work to other persons, led his Lordship to find the drivers were not employees.

Subsequent case law has focused on identifying contractual terms which may be inconsistent with there being a contract of employment. These have included the intention of the parties

(*Massey* v. *Crown Life Insurance Company* [1978]), and an obligation on the employer to provide, and the worker to accept, work (*Nethermere (St Neots) Ltd* v. *Gardiner & Taverna* [1984]), but no single factor is conclusive and the decision of the trial court or industrial tribunal is a question of fact which cannot normally be challenged on appeal (*O'Kelly* v. *Trusthouse Forte plc* [1984]).

The question of the status of the worker is only in dispute in a very small proportion of cases.

32. The wrongful act of the employee

Vicarious liability does not arise unless the employee has committed a tort, normally, but not necessarily, the tort of negligence. An employee's conduct will be considered in the context of the training he has had, and the resources available to him. There may be cases where the employer is deemed to be personally rather than vicariously liable because he has placed more responsibility on the employee than the circumstances warrant. For example, in *Jones* v. *Manchester Corporation* [1952] a hospital was found at fault for allowing a junior doctor to administer an anaesthetic without supervision from a more experienced practitioner (though in this case the liability was still vicarious — for the wrongdoing of the senior man!).

33. In the course of employment

In the older cases the courts were frequently concerned narrowly to define the task which the employee was engaged to do and to find that if the employee had deviated from that task he was no longer in the course of employment. Nowadays the courts tend to take a broader view and find that the employee is in the course of employment if what he is doing is for the employer's benefit. Thus formerly an employee would not be in the course of employment if he did something other than what he was employed to do, e.g. a conductor driving the bus (*Beard* v. *London General Omnibus Company* [1900]). Similarly employees sent on an errand ceased to be in the course of their employment when they deviated from the route on 'frolic of their own' (*Storey* v. *Ashton* (1869)).

In contrast to these older cases a warehouseman was in the course of his employment when he, though not employed as a driver, moved a lorry which was in the way (*Kay* v. *ITW Ltd* [1967]), maintenance men remained in the course of their employment when they took a meal break and also went off (on a motorbike) to fetch extra tools (*Harvey* v. *O'Dell Ltd* [1958]), and a tanker driver remained in the course of his employment when he smoked a cigarette (a forbidden action) while delivering petrol (*Century Insurance Co.Ltd.* v. *Northern Ireland Road Haulage Transport Board* [1942]).

34. Basis of doctrine of vicarious liability
The doctrine of vicarious liability really rests on the policy that the employer should pay for injuries caused when something is being done for his benefit; *Rose* v. *Plenty* [1976] recognised this. A boy was injured by the negligent driving of a milkman he was assisting to deliver milk: the milkman knew that it was forbidden for him to seek the assistance of young persons, but the employers were, in the view of the majority of the Court of Appeal (Lawton LJ dissenting), liable because the milkman, though doing something which was prohibited, was nevertheless working for the employers' benefit. Lord Denning MR said:

> In considering whether a prohibited act was within the course of the employment, it depends very much on the purpose for which it is done. If it is done for the employers' business, it is usually done in the course of his employment, even though it is a prohibited act...

A fairly extreme example of employees being deemed to be in the course of employment is *Smith* v. *Stages* (below).

35. Action against actual wrongdoer
The fact that the employer may be vicariously liable does not prevent an action being brought against the actual wrongdoing employee (though the victim cannot recover damages twice for the same injury). Sometimes the victim may join both employer and employee as co-defendants, though this will normally only be an attractive strategy if the employee is a professional person, like a doctor, or a driver, who has his own insurance cover. If both employer and employee are brought before the court, responsibility may be allocated between them according to the extent to which each is at fault. If an employer is found liable in these circumstances the liability placed upon him is personal.

Distinction between employers' and public liability

36. General

Compensation law has distinguished between employers' and public liability. Early case law distinguished the employers' liability to one who had a contract of employment with them from their liability to those who rendered services under other arrangements, whether or not provided under a direct contract between the employers and the workers concerned. The contract of employment (or contract of service) had an implied term that the employers would take reasonable care for the safety of their employee.

37. Action in contract

It is still possible for an injured employee to frame a personal injury claim against the employer in contract (*Matthews* v. *Kuwait Bechtel Corporation* [1959]). This option has a superficial attraction where the accident victim was engaged in the UK but was, at the time of the accident, working overseas. But the courts may, in such cases, recognise that the employer has little power to ensure workers are safe (*see Cook* v. *Square D Ltd* (1991)).

38. Maintenance of injured workers

The Workmen's Compensation Acts imposed liability on employers to make payments towards income maintenance of injured workers. This liability only arose in relation to certain of their workers who were their employees.

39. Difference between contract and other relationships

Twentieth-century case law, particularly before about 1970, further demonstrated the differences between employment relationships based on a contract of employment and other relationships. Cases like *Wilsons & Clyde Coal Company Ltd* v. *English* [1937] identified special obligations for the employer in respect of the safety of employees. Similarly civil actions for breach of statutory duty normally benefited only employees of the defendant since these duties were usually imposed on employers to protect their employees. The historic limitations on liability continue to be reflected in the statutes which require liability insurance.

40. Compulsory liability insurance

The Employers' Liability (Compulsory Insurance) Act, 1969 s.1(1), requires that:

> Every employer carrying on any business in Great Britain shall insure and maintain insurance, under one or more approved policies with an authorised insurer or insurers against liability for bodily injury or disease sustained by his employees, and arising out of and in the course of their employment in Great Britain in that business ...

The circumstances in which liability to pay damages may arise remains governed by case law. The statute only determines when insurance monies should be available to meet liability which the courts impose. The provision:

(a) requires insurance only in respect of injuries to employees of the employer — it makes no provision in respect of other persons;
(b) the policy only has to cover 'accidents arising out of and in the course of their employment'. It may not cover for example, accidents on the way to work, on the employer's premises during lunch breaks, or after clocking out.

41. Effectiveness of the legislation

The effectiveness of this legislation in providing funds must depend on the extent to which the legislative provisions are observed. The HSE and other occupational health and safety inspectors are authorised to ask for evidence that an effective policy is in force, but there is no fund comparable to that operated by the Motor Insurers' Bureau in respect of road traffic insurance, to meet claims against a person who does not have the cover which the law requires.

42. Additional legislation

This Act must be considered in conjunction with the Employer's Liability (Defective Equipment) Act 1969. This enables employees to claim against their own employer in respect of injury caused by equipment which is defective due to the negligence of someone other than the employers (typically the manufacturer). Section 1(1) provides that where:

(a) an employee suffers personal injury in the course of his
     employment in consequence of a defect in equipment provided
     by his employer for the purposes of the employer's business;
     and
(b) the defect is attributable wholly or partly to the fault of a third
     party (whether identified or not), the injury shall be deemed to
     be also attributable to negligence on the part of the employer...

This statute makes the employer strictly liable for the fault of
another (i.e. it is a statutory extension of vicarious liability). The
employer may seek an indemnity from the actual wrongdoer.

43. Extent of insurance cover

Wise employers will take out more third-party liability insurance than these statutes require. They are likely to insure at
least against liability to persons other than employees injured on
their premises or by the activities of their employees. If they are
manufacturers they will also need to consider product liability
insurance.

Road traffic legislation also requires that drivers of vehicles
have insurance to cover the vehicle for the purposes for which it
is being driven. Employers need to ensure that they are not held
liable for injuries caused by their employees when driving their
own vehicles in the course of their employment without insurance
cover appropriate for the circumstances.

> In *Smith* v. *Stages* [1989] the House of Lords held an
> employer liable to compensate an employee for personal
> injury suffered when being driven by a fellow employee
> from a workplace in Wales to their work base in the
> Midlands, in an uninsured vehicle. The employees were
> held to be in the course of their employment although they
> were supposed to travel by train, and at the time of the
> accident they were in a paid rest break at the end of a very
> long period of work without sleep. As the employer was
> paying them during the hours in question they were
> deemed to be in the course of employment. The decision
> undoubtedly ensured compensation was available to the
> accident victim. It may, however, be considered that this
> was only achieved by transfering what was really liability
> under road traffic insurance to employers' liability. This

may not have been unjust: possibly the employer should
have insisted that the vehicle was properly insured, or,
better still, taken effective steps to prevent his employees
from starting on a long cross-country drive directly after
the completion of a 90 hour work shift.

Progress test 12

1.   What is the primary purpose of civil litigation following
personal injury?   **(3)**

2.   What matters are generally covered in awards of 'special
damages'?   **(11)**

3.   To what extent is compensation made for 'loss of
expectation of life'?   **(13)**

4.   How does the Limitation Act apply in disease cases?   **(16, 17)**

5.   How do the courts assist plaintiffs to overcome the problem
of establishing causation in disease cases?   **(21)**

6.   In what circumstances is an employer 'vicariously liable'?
(30)

13
Liability in negligence

1. Introduction

Most personal injury claims are founded in negligence. This is partly because there are few situations to which the tort of negligence is not applicable, and partly because judges are unsympathetic to attempts to establish other forms of liability for personal injury. (*See Bolton* v. *Stone* [1951] and *Read* v. *Lyons* [1948].)

The exceptions to the general rule occur when the plaintiff either alleges that the defendant intended to injure him or else builds his case on the defendant's breach of statutory duty. Breach of statutory duty will be considered in the following chapter; other exceptions to the general rule can be dealt with very quickly here.

2. No strict liability at common law

In the Court of Appeal in *Letang* v. *Cooper* [1965] (where the plaintiff had been run over while sunbathing in a car park!) Lord Denning MR stated:

> If one man intentionally applies force directly to another, the plaintiff has a cause of action in assault and battery . . . If he does not inflict injury intentionally, but only unintentionally . . . only cause of action is in negligence, and then only on proof of want of reasonable care.

There is little likelihood of an employer being found personally liable for assault and battery. Similarly an employer is not likely to be vicariously liable for assault and battery committed by one of his employees. In *Warren* v. *Henleys Ltd* [1948] where a garage forecourt attendant struck a customer whom he believed to be leaving without paying for the petrol he had received, it was held that the employee was not in the course of his employment when he struck the customer.

3. From employers' liability to negligence

In *Donoghue* v. *Stevenson* [1932] the House of Lords established that there was a general concept of tortious liability for negligence. This case did not overrule earlier case law on liability for negligent conduct. For the immediate future the new tort was perceived as relevant to various categories of relationships of which master/ servant and occupier/visitor relationships were examples and to which *Donoghue* v. *Stevenson* itself added the manufacturer/ consumer relationship. In the 60 years which have elapsed since *Donoghue* v. *Stevenson*; the category approach has ceased to be valuable. Old cases on employers' liability have not necessarily been overruled, but it must be asked whether the distinctions these often suggest between employers' liability and other forms of negligence liability still exist.

4. The ingredients of negligence

In order to succeed in an action for negligence the plaintiff must prove:

(a) the defendant owed the plaintiff a duty of care;

(b) the defendant broke that duty by negligent conduct;

(c) the defendant's negligent conduct caused damage to the plaintiff.

The duty of care

5. Basis of the duty of care

Whether the defendant is under a duty to take reasonable care not to injure the plaintiff is a matter of law for the judge.

The essence of Lord Atkin's dictum in *Donoghue* v. *Stevenson* was that a person had to take reasonable care not to injure his neighbour. This raises two questions. First, who is the 'neighbour' to whom this duty of care is owed? Secondly, what has to be done to discharge the duty? Strictly the first question relates to the duty issue while the second question relates to the conduct issue, but it has not proved easy to keep the two distinct.

The difficulty was not assisted because his Lordship's speech bound the two issues together with a foresight test thus:

> Who then is my neighbour? The answer seems to be — persons who are so closely and directly affected by my act that I ought reasonably

to have them in contemplation as being so affected when I am directing my mind to the acts or omissions which are called in question.

6. Development of the duty of care

In the years which immediately followed *Donoghue* v. *Stevenson* the content of the duty was generally considered to depend on the category of relationship under consideration. Judges felt bound to declare not merely that plaintiff and defendant were neighbours, but also which category of neighbour situation the parties were in, in order to determine what the defendant was required to address when exercising care.

Thus the duty which the employer owed to his employee was regarded as legally of a different order to the duty which the occupier owed to a visitor, and the nature of the occupiers' duty at that time depended on whether the visitor was an invitee or a licensee. Indeed case law between 1932 and 1960 tended to emphasise the differences between the categories of duty situations, rather than rationalise them into a general law of negligence.

In *Wilsons & Clyde Coal Co Ltd* v. *English* [1937] Lord Wright's characterisation of the employers' duty served to distinguish it from other neighbour relationships. His Lordship stated:

> The obligation is threefold, 'the provision of a competent staff of men, adequate material, and a proper system and effective supervision'.

Victims of industrial accidents could, after this decision, attach their employer with a legal responsibility for competent staff, adequate plant and equipment, and in due course instruction and supervision. On the other hand the visiting workman was disadvantaged after *London Graving Dock Co. Ltd* v. *Horton* [1951] held that a visiting workman who continued to work knowing of a risk (in that case inadequate staging on scaffolding) must be deemed to have accepted the risk, and be barred from claiming damages for injury resulting from this hazard.

The unsatisfactory state of occupiers' liability led to the Occupiers' Liability Act 1957; the distinction between invitees and licensees was abolished and statutory provision was made for situations such as had occurred in *Horton*'s case.

7. The Occupiers' Liability Act 1957

The Act rationalised the duty which the occupier of premises owed to his visitors (s.1(1)). Section 2(1) of the Act stated that the occupier owed the same duty, the ' "common duty of care" to all his visitors . . .' Section 2(2) provided:

> The common duty of care is a duty to take such care as in all the circumstances of the case is reasonable to see that the visitor will be reasonably safe in using the premises for the purposes for which he is invited or permitted by the occupier to be there.

This simplification of the occupiers' duty reduced the duty issue to a simple matter of whether the plaintiff was a lawful visitor to, and the defendant was the occupier of, the premises where the plaintiff suffered his injury. Once the plaintiff and defendant are shown to be in the category of visitor and occupier, the matter of what the occupier has to do to discharge his duty is a question of fact peculiar to the circumstances of the particular case and of no significance to the development of case law generally. Moreover, s.1(1) makes it clear that the occupiers' duty extends to the activities being conducted on the premises (confirming *Slater* v. *Clay Cross Co Ltd* [1956]).

8. Abolition of categories?

Rationalisation of occupiers' liability encouraged a breaking down of the categories of liability and a rationalisation of the content of the duty which employers owed to their employees.

In the 1950s, after *Horton*'s case, visiting workmen who suffered injury had often pleaded that they had become employees of the occupier while executing the task they had come to perform. This argument was raised after the Act in *Savory* v. *Holland Hannen and Cubitts (Southern) Ltd* [1964]. The plaintiff was the employee of a subcontractor called to a building site to blast rock to enable the laying of foundations. The defendants were supposed to provide men to help the plaintiff, but allegedly failed to do so. The plaintiff slipped and suffered injury; he claimed that for the task in hand he had become the employee of the defendant contractor and that they accordingly owed him the duty which an employer owed to his employees. The Court of Appeal, though Diplock LJ, had no difficulty in disposing of this argument:

... since the passing of the Occupiers' Liability Act 1957 ... that is an incorrect approach to the question of negligence in a case like this. The question for the court is not whether the plaintiff was in the category of servant to the defendants pro hac vice. The only question is whether, in all the circumstances, the defendants used reasonable care for the safety of the plaintiff.

9. Simplification of employers' duty

The content of the employer's duty of care was considered by the House of Lords in *Qualcast (Wolverhampton) Ltd* v. *Haynes* [1959] where the plaintiff, an experienced metal moulder employed by the defendants, burnt his foot with molten metal. He was wearing ordinary boots. The county court judge found for the plaintiff, subject to 75% contributory negligence, because he considered he was bound by authority to hold that the defendants' duty included an obligation to instruct the plaintiff to wear protective clothing; the Court of Appeal upheld this decision. The House of Lords found for the defendants for, in their view, the defendants were not required to give instruction to an experienced workman. On the content of the employers' duty of care Lord Somervell commented:

> Whether a duty of reasonable care is owed by A to B is a question of law. In a special relationship such as that of employer to employee the law may go further and define the heads and scope of the duty. There are cases in your Lordships' House which have covered this ground, I would have thought by now exhaustively ... There would seem to be little if anything that can be added to the law ... Now that negligence cases are mostly tried without juries, the distinction between the functions of judge and jury is blurred. A judge naturally gives reasons for the conclusion formerly arrived at by a jury without reasons. It may sometimes be difficult to draw the line, but if the reasons given by a judge for arriving at the conclusion previously reached by a jury are to be treated as 'law' and citable, the precedent system will die from a surfeit of authorities.

His Lordship therefore shifted the emphasis from the legal content of the duty to the analysis of the facts of the particular situation; but he considered that the existing case law on the content of the employers' duty had become too deeply embedded to be ignored. Contemporary judicial statements nevertheless tended to emphasise that the cases merely illustrated what was essentially an unqualified duty to take reasonable care. Indeed Lord Somervell himself said in *Cavanagh* v. *Ulster Weaving Co Ltd* [1960]:

> courts of first instance . . . will proceed more satisfactorily if what I have called the normal formula — that is reasonable care in all the circumstances — is applied whatever the circumstances.

10. Back to general principles

In *Home Office* v. *Dorset Yacht Co Ltd* [1970] the House of Lords had to consider whether the Home Office owed any duty to take care to prevent borstal boys from damaging the plaintiffs' property. Lord Reid took the opportunity to comment on the duty issue in negligence generally:

> . . . there has been a steady trend towards regarding the law of negligence as depending on principle so that, when a new point emerges, one should ask not whether it is covered by authority but whether recognised principles apply to it . . . I think that the time has come when we can and should say that it ought to apply unless there is some justification or valid explanation for its exclusion. For example causing economic loss is a different matter . . .

11. Simply reasonable care?

It is difficult to ignore the cases which gave a special legal content to the employers' duty, and so distinguished it from other duty situations. It is, however, suggested that little is gained by relying on them today. Following the *Dorset Yacht* case the duty is rarely put in issue in personal injury cases; the court is primarily concerned with whether the defendant's negligent conduct caused the injury the plaintiff has allegedly suffered. The relationship between the parties, be it occupier and visitor, employer and employee, or indeed some other relationship, will be relevant when deciding whether the defendant's conduct has shown reasonable care for the plaintiff.

Breach of duty of care

12. General

A duty of care is broken by negligent conduct; whether conduct is negligent is a matter of fact established by evidence. Decisions

on fact do not create precedents but judicial statements provide
criteria by which situations may be evaluated. Such criteria become
precedents. In the following paragraphs some of the criteria will
be considered.

13. The reasonable man

The classic description of negligent conduct was laid down by
Alderson B in *Blyth* v. *Birmingham Waterworks Co.* (1856):

> . . . as the omission to do something which a reasonable man would
> do or doing something which a reasonable man would not do.

14. Reasonable care in all the circumstances

This criterion, used in the Occupiers' Liability Act, is more
frequently used today than the 'reasonable man' test, but both
suffer from the same limitation, namely the decision as to what is
reasonable rests with the judge.

15. Objectivity

The conduct in question is evaluated objectively without
reference to the special characteristics of the defendant (*Vaughan*
v. *Menlove* (1837)); for example, a learner driver is expected to
perform to the standard of an experienced driver (*Nettleship* v.
Weston [1971]). When an organisation carries out an activity as part
of a commercial undertaking, that organisation holds itself out as
an expert and is expected to achieve the standards of an expert.
In *The Lady Gwendolen* [1965] brewers transported stout from
Dublin to Liverpool in their own ship. After an accident caused by
poor navigation, they sought to avoid liability by pleading they
were not navigators. Nevertheless Winn LJ had no hesitation in
finding them liable:

> The law must apply a standard which is not relaxed to cater for their
> factual ignorance of all activities outside brewing: having become
> owners of ships, they must behave as reasonable shipowners.

16. Foresight

At the core of Lord Atkin's neighbour statement is the concept
of reasonable foresight: foresight is both the basis of the duty and
the criterion of the acts or omissions of the defendant. Again the
test is objective, so the actual evaluation is that of the judge, with

hindsight, upon careful analysis, rather than that of the defendant who often makes decisions in traumatic situations which give little opportunity for careful evaluation. It is not easy to reconcile the case law.

The defendant only has to be able to foresee that his conduct creates a risk of injury to others; it is not necessary that he should be able to foresee the actual sequence of events. In *Ogwo* v. *Taylor* (below) it was sufficient that a householder could foresee that his actions might result in a fire which would endanger firemen; it was not necessary that he should foresee the exact sequence of events.

In *Hughes* v. *Lord Advocate* [1963] post office engineers left an open manhole unattended and two children crawled under tarpaulin and then apparently knocked a lamp, which they found on the site, into the manhole. This caused an explosion which resulted in one of the children suffering severe burns. The House of Lords held that the respondents were liable for the injuries he had suffered. The lamp was a known source of danger; it was not material that the injury was caused through an unforeseeable sequence of events.

On the other hand in *Doughty* v. *Turner Manufacturing Co. Ltd* [1964] a workman at the defendants' factory knocked an asbestos cover into molten liquid and a few seconds later there was an explosion and the plaintiff was injured. It was later discovered that such an explosion could take place because of a chemical reaction engendered by intense heat. The plaintiff contended that as there was a foreseeable risk of being burned by splashing there was a foreseeable risk of being burned by the molten liquid. The defendants were not liable; the actual damage suffered was not foreseeable; it was, the Court of Appeal held, of quite a different type from anything which might have been foreseen.

17. The state of the art

What is foreseeable depends largely on technical knowledge available at the time when the plaintiff was injured. Advances in technical and scientific knowledge make foreseeable today occurrences which would not have been foreseeable a few years ago. Post-accident investigations disclose the cause of that accident and enable others to learn from the experience. In *Roe* v. *Minstry of Health* [1954] the two plaintiffs entered hospital for minor surgery and left permanently paralysed. Investigation established that the ampoules of anaesthetic used had hair line cracks enabling disinfectant to percolate through to contaminate the anaesthetic. The Court of Appeal found that it had not been foreseeable that such an accident might occur. Lord Denning noted:

> It is easy to be wise after the event and to condemn as negligence that which was only a misadventure . . . Doctors, like the rest of us, have to learn by experience; and experience often teaches us in a hard way. Something goes wrong and shows up a weakness, and then it is put right . . . We must not look at the 1947 accident with 1954 spectacles.

His Lordship continued, however:

> Never again, it is to be hoped, will such a thing happen. ... If the hospitals were to continue the practice after this warning, they could not complain if they were found guilty of negligence.

18. Forseeable through experience

It may be the defendant's own experience which made the particular injury in question foreseeable. In *Stokes* v. *Guest, Keen & Nettlefold (Bolts and Nuts) Ltd* [1968] the plaintiff's late husband had been sprayed, in the course of his work, with cutting oils. He died of scrotal cancer. The deceased was the second employee of the defendants to die of this disease. Furthermore, the company employed a skin specialist who was a nationally accepted expert in skin cancer. Swanwick J considered the case law and continued:

> From these authorities I deduce the principles, that the overall test is still the conduct of the reasonable and prudent employer, taking positive thought for the safety of his workers in the light of what he knows or ought to know; . . . but where there is developing knowledge, he must keep reasonably abreast of it and not be too slow to apply it; and where he has in fact greater than average knowledge of the risks, he may be thereby obliged to take more than the average or standard precautions.

His Lordship found the employers liable.

19. Constructive knowlege

The enterprise is deemed to know what is generally known. It

is not relevant that the particular defendant might not be aware
of risks. Thus in *Vacwell Engineering Co. Ltd* v. *British Drug House
Chemicals Ltd* [1971] an explosion occurred when the defendant
allowed a certain chemical to come into contact with water. The
defendants were found liable for the damage caused: while they
were not themselves aware of it, the risk was acknowledged in
older textbooks.

20. Industrial practice

The defendants will be liable if they do not maintain the
standards observed by others in like business; however, evidence
that defendants are operating in the customary manner may not
exonerate them. The courts may declare that the general practice
is a negligent one. In *Cavanagh* v. *Ulster Weaving Co. Ltd* [1960] a
labourer who was carrying cement across a roof slipped and fell.
An expert testified that the system adopted was 'perfectly in accord
with good practice'. It was nevertheless held that the employers
had been negligent: evidence as to the trade practice was not
conclusive.

21. Duty to plaintiff personally

The conduct required from the defendant to discharge the
duty may vary from one plaintiff to another, so that if the
defendants are aware of some personal factor making a particular
person specially vulnerable they may have to take special steps to
protect that person. In *Paris* v. *Stepney Borough Council* [1951] a
one-eyed man worked in the defendant's garage. A piece of metal
flew into his good eye and caused him to become totally blind.
While it was not usual for persons like him to be provided with
goggles, the House of Lords had no hesitation in finding that the
defendant ought to have provided eye protection to the plaintiff.

The converse also applies; if the plaintiff is a skilled person
who knows the hazards of his work, it may not be necessary for the
defendant to train or supervise him. It has already been noted that
in *Qualcast (Wolverhampton) Ltd* v. *Haynes* [1959] the House of Lords
declined to find that employers had been negligent merely because
they had failed to instruct a skilled man to wear protective clothing.

Everything hinges on the facts of the case. In *Bux* v. *Slough
Metals Ltd* [1974] the plaintiff had worked for many years without
eye protection before a manager introduced the goggles which the

then relevant eye-protection regulations required the employer to provide. Within a short time the plaintiff reverted to working without the goggles and lost his sight. The Court of Appeal found the employers were negligent in failing to instruct and persuade the plaintiff to wear the goggles. However, the plaintiff's damages were considerably reduced because of his own contributory negligence in not wearing the goggles which he was under a statutory duty to wear.

22. Cost benefit
When events show the defendant has not provided a safe system of work, whether this failure is negligence will to some extent depend on the cost of removing the hazard as opposed to the likelihood of injury being suffered and the likelihood of that injury being serious. In *Paris* an important factor was that goggles are relatively cheap, and not only is there a considerable possibility of eye injury for someone working (as was Mr Paris) under a vehicle, but eyesight is precious, particularly so for someone with only one eye. Similarly in *Roe* Lord Denning was impressed that the preventative measure (i.e. colouring the sterilising fluid) was a cheap and simple one. On the other hand an employer may not be negligent in failing to take every precaution for the safety of an employee who has to respond to an emergency itself involving serious personal injury (*Watt* v. *Hertfordshire County Council* [1954]).

23. Errors of judgment
Defendants are not liable for the consequences of errors of judgment. The distinction between errors of judgment and negligent conduct was made in *Whitehouse* v. *Jordan* [1981] while giving little guidance as to how the two types of conduct are to be distinguished. The case was of brain damage suffered at birth because a doctor incorrectly decided to attempt a forceps delivery. The House of Lords held that all that was certain was that there had been an error of judgment: it could not be said that there had been negligence, because a person might make an error of judgment while acting with care. This decision might be significant where the alleged wrongdoing is that of an employee for whose negligence the employer might be liable, but it might well be

irrelevant where an employer is alleged to have a faulty system of work.

24. Safe system

Where the defendant is an employer, the essential question will be, was the defendant operating a safe system? For the system to be safe resources (including human resources) sufficient and appropriate for the task must be put in place at the outset and retained in operation for so long as the situation requires. *McDermid* v. *Nash Dredging and Reclamation Co. Ltd* [1987] is a salutory reminder of this. The plaintiff was a deckhand employed by the defendant; he had to untie hawsers attaching a tug to a dredger and, when he had finished the task, knock twice on the wheelhouse door to tell the captain it was safe to start the tug. The plaintiff was seriously injured when the captain started the tug without waiting for the signal. The House considered that the defendant employer should be liable for failure to operate a safe system of work. Lord Brandon explained:

> The provision of a safe system of work has two aspects: (a) the devising of such a system and (b) the operation of it.

25. Liability to visiting workers

The qualifications of the occupiers' duty, in the Occupiers' Liability Act 1957, s.2(3), (4) and (5), remain of significance in personal injury litigation. They are discussed in paragraphs 26–32 below.

26. As regards special risks ordinarily incident in the calling
Section 2(3)(b) provides that:

> An occupier may expect that a person, in the exercise of his calling, will appreciate and guard against any special risks ordinarily incident to it, so far as the occupier leaves him free to do so.

Applying this rule an occupier might not, for example, be liable to a window cleaner who relied on the insecure frame of a sash window, and consequently fell to the ground. In a case on these facts, decided before the Act, the occupiers of the premises were not liable. As Lord Reid remarked:

> . . . a peculiar danger in window cleaning arises from the fact that

sometimes the sash moves down unexpectedly so as to deprive the man of his hold, and the evidence shows that it is not very uncommon for this to happen and to cause a serious accident.

The case did demonstrate, however, the relationship between the occupiers' liability and the employers' liability for the House of Lords had no doubt that the employers were at fault for not providing a safe system of work — which in this instance meant ensuring the worker was provided with a safety harness (*General Cleaning Contractors Ltd* v. *Christmas* [1952]).

27. The position as regards the self-employed

If the worker is self-employed then he is obliged to take responsibility for his own safety as the Court of Appeal's decision in *Roles* v. *Nathan* [1963]) demonstrates. Two self-employed chimney sweeps were called to a central heating boiler which was smoking. When the problem continued after the initial cleaning, an expert was called in and he expressly warned the sweeps not to work in the vicinity when certain vent holes were open, particularly if the boiler were alight. The sweeps ignored this advice and were found dead one morning after the boiler had been used. In the widows' action, the Court of Appeal found the occupiers were not liable, even though there had apparently been some negligence on their part in allowing the boiler to be lit. Lord Denning expressed the opinion that *Christmas* remained good law:

> The risk of a defective window is a special risk, but it is ordinarily incident to the calling of a window cleaner, and so he must take care for himself, and not expect the householder to do so. Likewise, in the case of a chimney sweep who comes to sweep the chimneys or to seal up a sweep-hole. The householder can reasonably expect the sweep to take care of himself so far as any dangers from the flues are concerned.

28. Duty of care to workmen

However, a subsequent line of cases culminating in a House of Lords decision in *Ogwo* v. *Taylor* [1988] have now established that the occupier owes a duty of care to workmen to avoid exposing them to unnecessary risks, at least if the visitors are firemen. Indeed the House of Lords ruling in *Ogwo* suggests that the general common law may prevail over the Act if the common law is more exacting.

In *Ogwo* v. *Taylor* [1988] a householder set fire to the loft of
his house. A fireman who entered the loft to hose the fire
was badly burned by the steam. His claim for damages was
initially founded both on the statutory duty under s.2 of the
Act and on the common law of negligence. The Court of
Appeal saw no necessity to consider s.2 because:

> . . . it is common ground that the duty of the defendant to the
> plaintiff at common law as the person who started the fire
> negligently is no lower, and may well be higher, than his duty
> to the plaintiff as the occupier of the premises (per Neill LJ).

The House of Lords accepted this approach and focused on
the common law. In the principal speech, Lord Bridge
considered *Salmon* v. *Seafarer Restaurant Ltd* [1983], a case
concerning the occupier's liability to a fireman when a gas
explosion followed a chip pan fire. His Lordship read, and
adopted the headnote, from that case:

> The fire had been caused by the defendants' negligence and
> since it was foreseeable that the plaintiff would be required to
> attend the fire and would be at risk of the type of injuries he
> received from the explosion which was caused by the
> negligence, the defendants were liable for those injuries and
> damages were recoverable by the plaintiff.

Relying on this analysis the House of Lords found that the
householder was liable at common law.

These later cases seem to throw doubt on whether *Nathan* was
rightly decided given that there was some negligence on the part
of the occupier. They also raise questions as to the relevance of the
Occupiers' Liability Act 1957, s.2(3)(b), if it is subsumed in the
general common law, which may exact a higher standard of care.

29. Qualifications to the liability of the occupier

Section 2(4) places two qualifications on the liability of the
occupier. It reiterates that in determining whether the occupier
has discharged the duty of care to a visitor regard must be had to
all the circumstances and states 'so that (for example)' two
circumstances to be considered are whether the visitor has been
warned of a danger, and whether the danger is due to work
undertaken by an independent contractor.

30. Warnings

The occupier may discharge his duty by warning a visitor of a danger, but only if the warning is enough to enable the visitor to be reasonably safe (s.2(4)(a)). The Court of Appeal particularly noted in *Nathan* that the chimney sweeps had been warned of the dangers of working in the fumes which built up if the sweep-hole was open. Section 2(4)(a) appears to be intended to exonerate the occupier only where the circumstances are such that once warned the visitor can avoid the danger. The provision must now be read in conjunction with the Unfair Contract Terms Act 1977, s.2(1), which provides that an occupier of business premises (as indeed anyone else to whom business liability attaches):

> . . . cannot by reference to any contract term or to a notice given to persons generally or to a particular person exclude or restrict his liability for death or personal injury resulting from negligence.

While the Occupiers' Liability Act 1984 extends liability to trespassers the provision which that Act makes for the occupier to discharge his liability by giving a warning of a risk does not appear to be restricted by the caveat of s.2(1) of the 1977 Act.

31. Liability for independent contractors

Section 2(4)(b) states:

> Where damage is caused to a visitor by a danger due to the faulty execution of any work of construction, maintenance or repair by an independent contractor employed by the occupier, the occupier is not to be treated without more as answerable for the danger if in all the circumstances he had acted reasonably in entrusting the work to an independent contractor and had taken such steps (if any) as he reasonably ought in order to satisfy himself that the contractor was competent and that the work had been properly done.

This provision appears merely to reiterate that occupiers are not vicariously liable for the wrongdoings of independent contractors. Where a hazard has been created on the occupiers' premises by an independent contractor, the occupier will only be liable if they have been personally negligent in matters such as the selection of, or the monitoring of the work of, the contractor.

32. Risks willingly accepted

Section 2(5) states:

The common duty of care does not impose on an occupier any obligation to a visitor in respect of risks willingly accepted as his by the visitor (the question whether a risk was so accepted to be decided on the same principles as in other cases in which one person owes a duty of care to another).

The issue of whether this subsection reversed the controversial House of Lords decision in *London Graving Dock Co. Ltd* v. *Horton* [1951] was resolved by the Court of Appeal in *Bunker* v. *Charles Brand & Son Ltd* [1969]. In *Bunker* the defendants were the main contractors excavating a tunnel for the London Underground system; the plaintiff was an employee of a contractor called in to modify a machine in the tunnel. The plaintiff suffered injury clambering to the point at which he had to work. The appeal court found that, while the plaintiff knew of the risk he was taking, he could not be deemed to have accepted it because his obligation to his employer to carry out the work meant he was not free to refuse to take the risk.

Damage

33. General

In order to succeed in an action for negligence the plaintiff must establish both that he has suffered damage and this damage was caused by the defendant. Questions may also be raised as to whether the loss was foreseeable.

34. Medical evidence

In personal injury claims the plaintiff's case largely depends on medical evidence showing that the plaintiff has suffered physical incapacity as a result of an accident or because of work conditions which have induced ill-health. This evidence will assist the judge in quantifying the damages.

35. The causation issue

The plaintiff must also satisfy the court that it was the defendant who caused the damage for which he is claiming damages. This, the causation issue, can be one of the most complex issues in the case.

A case which dramatically illustrates the causation issue is

Barnett v. *Chelsea and Kensington Hospital Management Committee*
[1968]. The plaintiff's husband visited the casualty department at
the defendant hospital, complaining of vomiting. He was merely
told to consult his own doctor; later in the day he died of arsenic
poisoning. The widow failed in her claim against the hospital for,
although they had been negligent in not treating her husband,
their negligence had not caused his death. They had not administered the fatal dose of poison and, even if they had given him
treatment, they could not have saved his life.

36. Plaintiff's own conduct as an influence

In *McKew* v. *Holland & Hannen & Cubitts (Scotland) Ltd*
[1969] the court found it necessary to distinguish the
accident which the plaintiff had suffered at the workplace
from a second incident in which the plaintiff suffered
further injury and found that there was no chain of
causation between the first and the second injuries. The
plaintiff had injured his leg at work; some days later, as he
was descending a steep staircase with no handrail, his leg
gave way and he fell suffering further damage. The House
of Lords held that the defendants had not caused the second
accident: the chain of causation had been broken by the
plaintiff's unreasonable conduct in attempting the stairs
with his known incapacity.

McKew demonstrates a problem which frequently arises, namely
determining in situations where the plaintiff's own conduct has
undoubtedly had some influence on events whether the injury was
entirely the plaintiff's own fault or whether the plaintiff and the
defendant should share responsibility. For example, in *Qualcast*
their Lordships considered that the plaintiff worker was sufficiently experienced to operate safely within the system the
employers had established, so the plaintiff's injury was caused
entirely by his own conduct. On the other hand, in *Bux* the Court
of Appeal considered that there was some negligence on the part
of the defendants in operating their system of work.

37. Exoneration from liability

The courts do not normally find negligent conduct on the part
of defendant employers and then exonerate them from liability

for injury suffered by their employee. An exception is *McWilliams* v. *Sir William Arrol & Co. Ltd* [1962]. The plaintiff was the widow of a steel erector killed when, not wearing a safety harness, he fell from where he had been working. Although the respondents were found to be in breach of statutory duty in not providing the safety equipment, they were not held liable for the death because evidence showed the deceased was not in the habit of wearing a safety harness even when it was available! The defendants' fault was not deemed to have caused the death.

38. Possibility of causation
It has been noted that where the plaintiff proves he has suffered ill-health and establishes that due to the defendants' negligence he has worked in conditions which could have caused illness of the kind of which he complains, the courts are disposed to find that the working conditions caused the illness.

39. Length of chain of causation
Some kinds of damage are not recoverable because the chain of causation between the injury and the damage suffered is too long even though there has not been, as in *McKew*, an intervening action by the plaintiff (or a third party) to break that chain.

40. Foresight and remoteness
It is often difficult to separate the duty and the damage issues: the problem can be re-formulated by asking: What is it that it is the defendant's duty to take care to prevent? The answer is that the defendant must take care not to cause injury which is foreseeable: injury will not be foreseeable if there is only a remote possibility that it will be suffered.

In *McGovern* v. *British Steel Corp.* [1986] the plaintiff was employed on a walkway on scaffolding: the walkway was bordered by toe-boards one of which got knocked out of place. The plaintiff tripped over it, but was unharmed: he then decided to put it back in place although there was no question but that it was too heavy for him to lift safely. He injured his back. The trial judge found that the acccident was unforeseeable and there was no liability in negligence.

On the other hand in *Bradford* v. *Robinson Rentals Ltd* [1967]

when an employee was required to make a difficult
cross-country journey in a vehicle without heating, at a time
when the weather forecast predicted severe cold and snow,
it was foreseeable that the employee would suffer frostbite
and the employers were liable when he did.

It is difficult to reconcile cases where it has been foreseeable
that some injury may be caused but the actual damage suffered
was not foreseeable. It is suggested that the following rationalisation (*see* **41–3**) may be made.

41. Extent of injury suffered

There is a so-called eggshell skull rule under which the
defendant must take the victim as he finds him, i.e. if because of
some unusual personal weakness the plaintiff suffered more
severe injury than a normal person would do, the defendant must
bear the cost of the injury actually suffered.

In *Smith* v. *Leech Brain & Co. Ltd* [1962] a man was, due to
the negligence of his employers, splashed on the lip with
molten metal; he died of cancer. In finding the employers
liable to pay for the fatal injury, Parker LCJ said at:

> The test is not whether these employers could reasonable have
> foreseen that a burn would cause cancer and that he would die.
> The question is whether these employers could reasonably
> foresee the type of injury he suffered, namely the burn. What,
> in the particular case, is the amount of damage which he suffers
> as a result of that burn depends upon the characteristics and
> constitution of the victim.

Employers were similarly liable for an unforeseeably
serious injury suffered in *Robinson* v. *Post Office and Another*
[1974]. The plaintiff, a Post Office technician, slipped when
descending an oily ladder and gashed his shin. His doctor
gave him an injection which produced a very serious
reaction. The doctor had not followed the correct medical
procedure but the Post Office was nevertheless held
responsible for the injury whose seriousness was due to the
susceptibility of the plaintiff: the doctor's failure was neither
the cause of the injury nor a breach in the chain of
causation.

42. Unforeseeable sequence of events

It has been noted that in *Hughes* v. *Lord Advocate* [1963] their Lordships did not entertain the argument that the defendant should not be liable because the sequence of events was not foreseeable in a context when it was foreseeable that an accident could occur.

43. Unforeseeable kind of injury

In *The Wagon Mound (No.1)* [1961] the Privy Council found that a defendant should not be liable when the kind of damage suffered was not foreseeable: the case concerned damage to a wharf and a ship anchored there as a result of fire caused by oil discharged into water. In the view of the Council damage by oil was foreseeable but damage by fire was damage of a different sort and was not foreseeable. Application of this ruling creates difficulties: the argument is that oil damage is different from fire damage; however, in both instances the damage would be to property. Further it might be argued that if damage is foreseeable it is not relevant that the way in which that damage is brought about is not foreseeable. (But *see Doughty* v. *Turner Manufacturing Co. Ltd* [1964] above.)

44. Successive injuries

In *McKew* the defendant was not liable for a second accident which the plaintiff suffered through his own lack of care. Sometimes questions arise as to whether a second event terminates the defendant's liability for the first, so that the defendant is liable only for the period of time between the two events. The courts have laid down different rules according to whether the second event is another accident for which there is human responsibility, or whether it is an illness which is a natural occurrence. In *Baker* v. *Willoughby* [1970] the plaintiff suffered an injury to his leg and before his claim for damages reached trial he suffered gunshot wounds. This second accident caused such serious injury that the leg was amputated. The House of Lords rejected the contention that liability for the first injury should terminate at the time of the second accident. They held that the defendant should bear responsibility for the remainder of the plaintiff's normal life; the person responsible for the second accident would bear responsibility for depriving the plaintiff of such facility as the first accident had left.

On the other hand in *Jobling* v. *Associated Dairies Ltd* [1982] the appellant sustained a back injury when he fell at work. This accident was attributable to the defendant's fault. Three years later the plaintiff was found to be suffering from a quite unrelated disease affecting his neck. The disease rendered him incapable of work. The House of Lords held that damages awarded against the defendants should not include any sum for loss of wages for the period after the disease rendered the plaintiff unfit to work.

Progress test 13

1. What are the three factors which the plaintiff must prove in order to win a claim in negligence? **(4)**

2. What is the legal content of the duty of care? **(9)**

3. What is meant by the statement, 'the defendant's conduct is evaluated objectively'? **(15)**

4. Is a defendant liable for 'errors of judgment'? **(23)**

5. Explain how the courts take a 'cost benefit approach' to deciding whether the defendant's conduct has been negligent. **(22)**

6. The defendant's conduct must have 'caused' the injury the plaintiff has suffered. Explain. **(35)**

14

Civil liability for breach of statutory duty

1. Introduction

This chapter will explain the rules governing claims for damages for personal injury caused by breach of statutory duty. Where a statutory provision will support an action for breach of statutory duty, the plaintiff frequently claims both common-law negligence and breach of statutory duty.

2. Classes of statutory duties

There are two broad categories of statutory duty which will have to be considered:

(a) Duties created by Parliament primarily for enforcement in the criminal courts. The statutes which create them are properly a part of public rather than private law. For the purposes of the present chapter the duties are those in the 'relevant statutory provisions'.
(b) Duties created by Parliament solely to provide remedies for the victims of personal injury. These statutes are not part of public law since their purpose is to regulate private rights. They are statutory modifications of common law liability.

3. Distinguishing features of statutory duties

Each duty is distinct and different from any other duty, but actions founded on statutory duties do have these features in common:

(a) The duty relied on was created by Parliament not the courts. Defining the duty is therefore an exercise in statutory interpretation and every word has to be carefully considered.
(b) The duty, though originally created by Parliament, may have been interpreted by judges. Such interpretations create

precedents binding in any further consideration of the issue, and of persuasive authority on the interpretation of like statutes.

(c) Liability is not necessarily liability for negligent conduct. Parliament has rarely chosen negligence as the criterion of liability: often liability is strict. Lord Wright put the matter thus in *Caswell* v. *Powell Duffryn Associated Collieries Ltd* [1940] AC 152:

> It is a common law action based on the purpose of the statute to protect the workman, and belonging to the category often described as that of cases of strict or absolute liability. At the same time it resembles actions in negligence in that the claim is based on a breach of a duty to take care for the safety of the workman.

Civil liability for breach of relevant statutory provisions

4. General

The right to bring a civil action for damages for a workplace injury caused by breach of one of the relevant statutory provisions is governed by s.47 of the 1974 Act. This section identifies three general classes of situation:

(a) it makes clear that there shall be no reliance in civil litigation on any of the general duties created by ss.2–8 of the 1974 Act (s.47(1)(a));

(b) it confirms the then existing rights to found civil actions on certain of the earlier health and safety provisions, such as the Factories Act 1961, and regulations, such as the construction regulations, made under this legislation (s.47(1)(b));

(c) it creates a presumption that civil actions may be founded on duties in regulations made under the 1974 Act (s.47(2)).

5. Intentions of Parliament

It is not known why Parliament decided that the general duties may not be relied on in civil litigation. A possible reason is that the very generality of the duties might encourage civil litigation. A second possibility is that they so closely match the tort of negligence that there would be little to be gained by relying on them. A third possibility is that the legislature was mindful that the Robens Committee had expressed reservations about the practice of using regulatory provisions as the basis of compensation actions because:

> The general psychological effect is that attention is diverted from the primary objective of accident prevention to the altogether different question of compensation for injury suffered.

6. Expansion of the range of duties

Nevertheless in the 1970s it would have been unacceptable to have removed the existing rights which were very important for ensuring compensation for the victims of industrial accidents and in s.47(2) Parliament made a commitment to the perpetuation of the system, by creating a presumption that regulations made under the 1974 Act would carry both criminal and civil liability. Thus, while, with the passage of time, the earlier statutory provisions are being progressively repealed, new regulations have created new rights and in the near future the proposals to implement the Framework and individual Directives will add considerably to the range of duties which may be litigated. Indeed the potential for litigation and problems of interpretation may be great; e.g. under the General Provisions Regulations employers have a strict duty to identify and respond to risks, and similarly the Safety, Health and Welfare Regulations require attention to many hazards without clearly identifying performance standards.

7. Right to bring civil action

Today it is usual for Parliament to state expressly whether civil actions are to lie but the rights to litigate for breach of the duties contained in the pre-1974 health and safety legislation were created by judges interpreting the intention of Parliament. This earlier case law not only determined which statutory duties might be invoked in civil litigation, it also established what the plaintiff had to prove to win a claim based on such a duty. Much of the case law given below pre-dates the 1974 Act, for it was then that the framework for litigation was established.

The right to bring civil actions for breach of statutory duty lay in relation to a number of the provisions of the Factories Acts and the mining legislation and regulations made under these Acts, but not every provision of industrial safety legislation has been interpreted as giving civil rights. For example, in *Biddle* v. *Truvox*

Engineering Co Ltd [1952] it was held that a person who sold or let defective factory machinery contrary to s.17(2) of the Factories Act 1961 was not civilly liable to a workman injured by reason of the defect.

8. Significance of pre-1974 provisions

Given the phasing out of the earlier legislative duties, their importance as a basis of civil liability is slowly declining but for the time being some of the pre-1974 provisions remain of significance. Of particular importance are s.14 (guarding of dangerous machinery), s.28 (safety of floors, passages and stairs), s.29 (safe means of access and safe place of employment), and certain regulations like the various construction regulations. Some provisions, like s.63 of the Factories Act 1961 (removal of dust and fumes) have already been repealed and replaced by more up-to-date regulatory provisions. However, s.63 has been particularly significant in claims in respect of dust-related diseases, such as pneumoconiosis, and these diseases often do not manifest themselves until many years have passed. It is possible therefore that civil claims may continue to be based on it for some years to come.

It would be tempting to believe that the value of this form of litigation is less nowadays than in earlier years because the growth of the tort of negligence has made injured workers less reliant on the statutory provisions. Indeed, although a number of regulatory codes have been brought into force since 1974 there is a dearth of case law on their interpretation in civil litigation. This does not necessarily mean they have not been successfully invoked since it is not possible to say how many cases may have been settled out of court. Additionally many of the new regulations are concerned with control of particular substances (e.g. the Control of Lead at Work Regulations) or substances more generally (e.g. Control of Substances Hazardous to Health) where the risk is often of deterioration of health over a long period of time. Since plaintiffs can only rely on regulatory standards in relation to injury suffered after the particular regulations came into force it may yet be some time before regulations are invoked in civil actions.

9. Precedental value of earlier judicial statements

Even though the statutory duties themselves have ceased to be relevant, in some cases judicial statements made in the course of interpreting them may continue to have some precedential value. The meanings which have been given to words like 'factory', 'manual labour' and 'available' may well, following the normal rules of statutory interpretation, be of persuasive authority when these words, or expressions, are used in other similar legislation. It has been noted, when considering the ambit of the 1974 Act, that the expression 'reasonably practicable', which is used so frequently in the 1974 Act, was used in pre-1974 legislation and *dicta* on its meaning in the earlier statutes is generally accepted as indicative of its meaning in the 1974 Act itself.

Similarly, 'provided' has been subject to interpretation in earlier regulations such as those for eye protection, and created case law which may be significant in a new context, since the proposals for regulations to implement the EC Directive on personal protective equipment are entirely concerned with the extent of the employers' duty to 'provide' such equipment.

It is a factual matter whether the employer is holding equipment in a place sufficiently accessible to the worker to have discharged his duties in relation to its provision. In *Finch* v. *Telegraph Construction and Maintenance Co. Ltd* [1949] where goggles were, unknown to the workers, kept in the foreman's office, it was held that the duty to provide them had not been performed. In contrast in *Bux* v. *Slough Metal Co Ltd*, where the employer had made known to the workers that goggles were available in the store the duty was deemed to have been performed.

What the plaintiff must prove

10. General
Given the existence of a civil right of action, either under the pre-1974 legislation or under regulations made since 1974, the task of the plaintiff is not an easy one. Indeed it has been judicially remarked, by Lord Hailsham in *F.E. Callow (Engineers) Ltd* v. *Jackson* [1971], that:

Some of the protection to the workman which at first sight might be thought available turns out on closer scrutiny to be illusory.

The plaintiff must prove:

(a) he belongs to the class of persons whom the statute is designed to protect (**11–16**);
(b) that the defendant was the person on whom the duty was imposed (**17–19**);
(c) that the defendant was in breach of the duty (**20–3**);
(d) that the breach caused the damage (**24–5**).

11. Status of the plaintiff

The plaintiff must have been working in the circumstances to which the statutory provision applies, and be of the class of persons to whom the duty is owed, when the injury was suffered.

12. 'Factory'

Section 175 of the Factories Act 1961 gives a general interpretation of the expression 'factory'. If the premises where the injury was suffered were not within the Act, or the plaintiff was not a manual labourer, the Act cannot be invoked.

In *Weston* v. *London County Council* [1941] the plaintiff was a pupil at a technical institute who was injured when operating an unguarded woodcutting machine there. The judge held that the institute was not a factory, and, moreover, the plaintiff was not employed there. Wrottesley J said:

> . . . I do not think that anyone could suggest that this institute falls within that general definition . . . , they are not occupied in a process which is incidental to any of the purposes mentioned, and it appears to me that they are there for the purposes of instruction.

On the other hand, in *J and F Stone Lighting and Radio* v. *Haygarth* [1968] (a criminal case), the House of Lords had to decide whether a room on shop premises used for the repair of radio and television sets was a place where persons were employed in manual labour and therefore within the Factories Acts. Their Lordships gave careful consideration to the expression 'manual labour', which has been used in a variety of statutory contexts. Lord Morris of Borth-y-Gest said:

There is, I think, a clear and unbroken line of authority to the effect that in such a situation regard must be had to what is the main substantial work which a person is employed to do.

On the facts of the case, their Lordships concluded that the worker in the premises in question was engaged in manual labour and therefore the premises were a factory.

13. Plaintiff must be an employee

Normally the plaintiff must be an employee of the defendant. In *Hartley* v. *Mayoh & Co.* [1954] the defendant's factory caught fire and the plaintiff's husband was electrocuted while fighting the fire during the course of his duty as a fireman. The widow's action relied on regulations made under s.76 of the Factories Act: it was held that these regulations were for the protection of persons employed by the defendant and were not therefore intended to protect persons such as her husband.

14. Exceptions

However, not all provisions of the Act protect only the employees of the defendant. For example, it is required in s.29 of the 1961 Act that:

> There shall, so far as is reasonably practicable, be provided and maintained safe means of access to every place at which *any person* has at any time to work.

In *Whitby* v. *Burt, Boulton & Hayward Ltd and Another* [1947] the plaintiff was employed by a firm which was called in by the defendant factory occupier to repair war damage to the factory. While removing corrugated iron sheets from under a glass skylight the plaintiff fell because of a defect in timber where he was working. The court held that the plaintiff was entitled to rely on what was then s.26 of the 1937 Act. Denning J said, bearing in mind that the provision related to every place where *any* person had to work:

> I hold, therefore, that for the safeguarding of people in factories s.26 applies and puts the responsibility on the occupier even though the building operations are being carried out by a contractor.

The House of Lords reached the same conclusion in *Wigley* v. *British Vinegars Ltd* [1962] where the plaintiff was a visiting window cleaner. The Health Safety and Welfare Provisions will repeal s.29, and it will not be replaced, since s.2(2)(d) of the 1974 Act is deemed to cover the situation. General duties in the 1974 Act carry no civil liability.

15. Other parts of the premises

Similarly s.14(1) of the Factories Act 1961 imposes the duty to guard dangerous machinery in relation to 'every person employed or working on the premises'. This provision has been held to impose a duty on an occupier in respect of an employee who was in a part of the premises where he was forbidden to go — in fact chasing a pigeon up a shaft — *Uddin* v. *Associated Portland Cement Manufacturers Ltd* [1965]. The like provision of the Offices Shops and Railway Premises Act 1963 was similarly interpreted in *Westwood* v. *Post Office* [1973].

16. Statutory interpretation

These last cases serve as a salutory reminder that in exercises of statutory interpretation it is necessary not only to look at the scope of the Act generally but also to look at the particular duty relied on in order to determine the plaintiff's rights.

17. Status of the defendant

The plaintiff must sue the person upon whom the duty is placed. The problem is to identify that person. The individual duties under the Factories Act state the objectives to be achieved, but do not stipulate the person upon whom the responsibility for achieving them rests. In most instances this is the occupier of the premises, but there may still be disputes as to who is the occupier.

In the criminal case of *Turner* v. *Courtaulds Ltd* [1937] the company was charged, as occupier of a factory, with an offence under the electricity regulations then in force; it was alleged that they had the duty to make dead the switchboard before certain work was carried out. The failure to perform this duty caused a fatal accident. The work was being carried out by contractors and the switchboard had not been 'handed over' to the defendants.

The magistrates dismissed the charge finding the defendant was not the occupier at the time of the accident. The appeal court reversed this decision holding the company was the occupier.

However, in *Rippon* v. *Port of London Authority and J Russell & Co. Ltd* [1940] it was held that the person who was occupier under the Act was not necessarily the occupier for the purpose of regulations made under the Act. The first defendants were the owners of a dry dock and the second defendants were ship repairers repairing a vessel lying in the dock. The plaintiff, an employee of the second defendants, was walking down steps in the dock, when one of the steps gave way causing him to fall and sustain serious injury. It was held that the two defendants should share liability for the plaintiff's injury: the first defendants, as owners of the dry dock, remained in occupation of the premises and were liable for breaches of the relevant provisions of the Factories Act; the second defendants were occupiers for the purposes of repairing the ship and were liable for breach of relevant shipbuilding regulations.

18. The burden of the statutory duty

Similar difficulties can arise where it is controversial whether the statutory duty is imposed on the enterprise or on one of its employees, often the plaintiff himself. Thus in *Harrison* v. *National Coal Board* [1951] it was held that while duties relating to mines are imposed on the mine owner when expressed impersonally, duties relating to shotfiring are duties of the shotfirer. In a controversial House of Lords decision, *Imperial Chemical Industries Ltd* v. *Shatwell* [1965], it was held that the employers were neither personally nor vicariously liable for injuries which two shotfirers inflicted on themselves when operating in breach of regulatory duties: the duties were imposed on the men not their employer.

19. Duty rests on both plaintiff and defendant

On occasion where the duty is placed on an employer, the employer may be in breach if the regulatory provision is not observed, although the practicalities of the situation are that only the plaintiff himself could perform the duty.

In *Ginty* v. *Belmont Building Supplies Ltd* [1959] the employer was a roofing contractor subject to building regulations which required him to provide and *use* boards for work on asbestos roofs. The employer provided the necessary boards but the plaintiff worker failed to use them and fell through the roof on which he was working. It was found that the plaintiff's failure to use the boards had resulted in the defendant being (vicariously) in breach of his duty. In the event this availed the plaintiff nothing, for the plaintiff was in breach of his own duty to use the boards. Pearson J stated:

> . . . if one finds that the immediate and direct cause of the accident was some wrongful act of the man, that is not decisive. One has to inquire whether the fault of the employer under the regulations consists of, and is co-extensive with, the wrongful act of the employee. If there is some fault on the part of the employer which goes beyond or is independent of the wrongful act of the employer, and was a cause of the accident, the employer has some liability.

His Lordship instanced that the employer might have failed to provide proper training or supervision; however, on the facts there was no fault of the employer which went beyond or was independent of the plaintiff's own omission.

The case may be distinguished from *Boyle* v. *Kodak Ltd* [1969] where employer and employee similarly shared regulatory duties to ensure that 'every ladder shall so far as practicable be securely fixed so that it can move neither from its top nor from its bottom points of rest'. The plaintiff employee fell, and was injured, when using a ladder which had not been lashed: it was held that the employers' duty extended to instructing and training the employee to ensure that he observed the statutory requirements. As the employers had failed to carry out this aspect of the duty, they had to accept some responsibility for the accident.

20. Defendant's standard of conduct

The standard of conduct required from the defendant in civil liability is the standard imposed by the legislature for enforcement in the criminal courts. However, the interpretation of the legislature's intentions has often been made in civil courts, and impacted back to the enforcement of the duties in the criminal courts.

21. The words of Parliament

The starting point is the words chosen by Parliament. Sometimes Parliament appears to have created strict liability, i.e. it has simply stipulated the result that has to be achieved without qualifying words. For example, s.14(1) of the Factories Act 1961 stipulates 'Every dangerous part of any machinery . . . shall be securely fenced . . .'. Other provisions qualify the duty with concepts such as reasonable practicability; so s.29 requires 'There shall, so far as is reasonably practicable, be provided . . .' safe means of access to every place of work. None of the Factories Act provisions impose absolute duties; there are some defences, and even apparently strict duties may have provisos which give scope for narrowing the definition of the duty. Thus s.14(1) relaxes its requirement by a proviso in respect of machinery which 'is in such a position or of such construction as to be as safe to every person employed or working on the premises as it would be if securely fenced'.

22. Inconsistency of judicial approach

It is difficult to extract from a study of cases any consistent approach to the task of interpreting the regulatory provisions. The judges have sometimes veered towards a theory of statutory negligence, refusing to find liability unless the defendant has been at fault; on other occasions they have imposed very strict liability on an apparently faultless defendant.

At the one extreme, in *Brown* v. *National Coal Board* [1962], the House of Lords had to interpret s.48 of the Mines and Quarries Act 1954 which requires the mine manager to take 'such steps . . . as may be necessary for keeping the road . . . secure'. Lord Radcliffe took the view that the manager's duty was no more than to take care, and there would therefore be no liability in the absence of fault:

> It seems plain to me that if a manager's duty is to ask himself from time to time 'What steps are required now to keep the roadway secure?'he can only pose or answer that question in the light of the

best obtainable information as to the circumstances, geophysical or otherwise, that he is to deal with and knowledge of skilled and up-to-date engineering science and practice. If he answers the question in those terms and acts acordingly, he cannot, in my view be said to be in breach of his duty, even though there is a state of insecurity or a roof fall.

In contrast, in *John Summers & Sons Ltd* v. *Frost* [1955] the House of Lords held, in interpreting what is now s.14(1) of the Factories Act 1961, that a grindstone wheel moving at 1,450 revolutions per minute was dangerous, although the evidence showed that it would be impossible to provide a guard which would make the machine usable. The reasoning of Viscount Simonds is sufficiently interesting to warrant quoting at length:

> In particular, I think it is clear that the obligation imposed by the section to fence securely . . . is an absolute obligation. And by that, I mean that it is not to be qualified by such words as 'so far as practicable' or 'so long as it can be fenced consistently with its being used for the purposes for which it is intended' or similar words. I come to this conclusion for the following reasons . . . First, it appears to me to be an illegitimate method of interpretation of a statute, whose dominant purpose is to protect the workman, to introduce by implication words of which the effect must be to reduce that protection. Secondly, where it has been thought desirable to introduce such qualifying words, the legislature has found no difficulty in doing so . . . Thirdly, it was decided as long ago as 1919 . . . that the obligation . . . was absolute and that, if the result of a machine being securely fenced was that it would not remain commercially practicable or mechanically possible, that did not affect the obligation: the statute would, in effect, prohibit its use . . . Fourthly, the proviso to s.14(1) affords a strong indication that the substantive part of it imposes an absolute obligation: for, unless its effect is absolutely to prevent the operator from coming into contact with a dangerous part of the machine, there would be little meaning in the provision of an alternative which has just that effect. Fifthly, the absolute obligation imposed by s.14(1) is subject to the regulation-making power of the Minister . . .

One way in which the courts have interpreted the strict liability of fencing provisions such as s.14(1) has been to read in a proviso that the defendant will only be liable if it is 'reasonably foreseeable' that the machine is dangerous if unfenced. In *Hindle* v. *Birtwhistle* [1897] it was held that because it was reasonably foreseeable that a shuttle might fly out of a loom, either as a result of careless handling or impurity in the material, the machine ought to be fenced. However, case law on reasonable foresight in relation to fencing provisions has by no means always been invoked to the advantage of the worker.

> In *Burns* v. *Joseph Terry & Sons Ltd* [1950] a machine was guarded by a rail about four feet above the floor, but parts above this rail were only partially guarded. Above the machinery was a shelf. The plaintiff climbed a ladder to empty the shelf and got his hand caught in the machinery. In a claim for breach of s.13(1) (fencing of transmission machinery) the Court of Appeal found that the defendant was not liable because the machinery was fenced against reasonably foreseeable dangers.

23. Duty to do what is 'practicable'

The view that an element of fault ought properly to be present in defendants before they are made liable for breach of duties is reflected in the interpretation of duties in which the defendants are required to do what is 'practicable'. The courts have considered that what is practicable must be judged by the state of technical and, where relevant, medical knowledge at the time when the defendant is alleged to be in breach of duty. Thus in *Richards* v. *Highway Ironfounders (West Bromwich) Ltd* [1955] the Court of Appeal found that the defendants were not in breach of their duty under the first limb of s.47(1) of the Factories Act 1937, although they had failed to take all practicable, or any, measures to protect the plaintiff against the inhalation of dust and had failed to provide appliances, although the nature of the process made it practicable so to do. The Court of Appeal so held because at the time in question it was not known that the dust created by the process in which the plaintiff was working was injurious. They were liable under the second limb of s.47(1), which required them to take protective precautions whenever dust was in substantial quantities!

A similar interpretation was placed on the first limb of s.47(1) of the 1937 Act by the Court of Appeal in *Adsett* v. *K and L Steelfounders & Engineers Ltd* [1953], in that instance in relation to the state of technical knowledge. The defendants having failed to provide a satisfactory dust extraction system until some time after the plaintiff had first been at risk, Singleton LJ commented:

> I realise that . . . the question is whether they had taken all practicable measures, but it must be remembered that, until the defendants discovered the system of installing an extractor under the grid, there was no such system in existence. Can it, then be said that the system which they discovered was practicable long before such discovery? . . . it would appear to be hard on the defendants if, in those circumstances, they were made liable for not discovering sooner something which, for the benefit of the community, they discovered in 1941 . . .

24. Cause of the injury

The plaintiff will not succeed in his claim unless he has suffered an injury caused by the risk the provision was intended to control. The problem of causation has been especially evident in relation to the fencing provisions of the Factories Act. In *British Railways Board* v. *Liptrot* [1969] it was held that since the fencing requirement only related to dangerous parts of a machine it could not be relied on by a plaintiff who had suffered injury because the machine as a whole was unsafe. In *Eaves* v. *Morris Motors Ltd* [1961] it was held that fencing required for a part of machinery did not help a plaintiff where injury had been caused by a workpiece moving under power and held in the machine by a chuck, nor did it include injury caused by materials in the machinery. In *Sparrow* v. *Fairey Aviation Co. Ltd* [1964] it was held that the worker is not protected if what comes into contact with the dangerous part of a machine is a handtool used by the worker, as distinct from the worker's body or clothing. And in *Nicholls* v. *Austin (Leyton) Ltd* [1946] it was held that the provisions did not protect the worker from materials, such as pieces of work, thrown out from the machine.

25. Controversial interpretations

Most controversial of all, in *Carroll* v. *Andrew Barclay & Sons Ltd* [1948] the House of Lords held that the fencing provisions were intended to protect the worker from getting into the machine, not to protect the worker from injury by pieces of flying material ejected from the machine: so in this case s.13 did not provide a remedy where an accident was caused by the breaking of a belt. Further, in *Close* v. *Steel Company of Wales Ltd* [1962] the plaintiff could not recover damages for breach of s.14(1) in respect of injury suffered when the bit of an electric drilling machine shattered and entered his left eye. While bits frequently shattered, there was no evidence of such an accident having happened before because the pieces were generally light and did not fly out with force. The House accepted the proposition that 'the fence is intended to keep the worker out, not to keep the machine or its product in' and did not think that this interpretation should be modified in cases where it was foreseeable that workers might be injured by materials, parts of the machine or workpieces, ejected from the machine.

Defences to breach of duty

26. General
The defendant may be able to plead a defence, either one of the general defences to civil liability, or a defence made available by the statutory provision itself in the context of criminal liability, provided this has been allowed by the legislation in question (s.47(3) of the 1974 Act).

27. In civil actions
Special defences available in criminal proceedings may therefore not be readily available in civil actions. For example, the Classification, Packaging and Labelling of Dangerous Substances Regulations 1984 give a person injured by breach of these regulations a right to sue (regulation 15(1)(b)), but while in criminal proceedings the defendant would have the defence that he took 'all reasonable precautions and exercised all due diligence' to avoid the commission of the offence, s.47(3) of the 1974 Act would seem to mean that that defence would not be available in civil litigation, since the regulations do not state that it will be so available.

28. Defence of 'due diligence'
A number of the new regulations allow the defendant in criminal proceedings to avoid liability where it is established 'due diligence' has been exercised, but the use of this defence is by no

means universal. Many of the post-1974 regulations have been pitched at the level of what is reasonably practicable, which is a defence available to the employer, against criminal liability (s.40) and might historically have been invoked, in civil liability (*Nimmo* v. *Alexander Cowan & Sons Ltd* [1968]). It may be, however, that s.47(3) has denied the employer of this defence to civil liability under regulations made subsequent to the 1974 Act. The regulations proposed to implement the Framework and individual Directives would appear to be of strict liability.

Statutory modification of the common law

29. General

Parliament has, upon occasion, made statutory provision for situations where judge-made case law has failed to cater adequately for accident compensation. The two areas relevant to this work where the legislature has intervened are occupiers' liability and consumer protection. The statutory modification of occupiers' liability has been discussed.

30. The Consumer Protection Act 1987

The Consumer Protection Act 1987 must now be considered. Part I of that Act, passed to enable UK law to comply with an EC Directive on product liability, imposes strict liability for unsafe goods. It was intended to make an alternative and better provision than the tort of negligence for those who suffered injury as a result of defective goods: by releasing them from the burden of proving that the goods were defective because of the defendant's negligent conduct.

31. Who is protected?

The legislation enables any person to sue in tort in respect of death or personal injury or any loss of or damage to any private property (s.5). A worker injured in the workplace, though not normally considered to be in the category of 'consumer', might nevertheless be able to bring an action under the Act.

32. Who is liable?

The Act places liability upon producers (s.2). A producer is a person who has manufactured a product or, in the case of a substance which has not been manufactured, but has been won or abstracted, the person who won or abstracted it, or the person who carried out an industrial process in respect of it (for example, in relation to agricultural produce) (s.1(2)). The Act does not apply to the producer of game or agricultural products which have not been subject to an industrial process at the time they were supplied (s.2(4)). The producer of a product in which components or raw materials are comprised is not necessarily liable for faults in the components (s.1(3)): the Act intends liability to lie with the producer of the unsafe part. Liability may be imposed on any person who holds himself out as being the producer of the product, for example by putting his name on the product, or on any person who has imported the product into the EC. The Act recognises that the plaintiff may have difficulty in identifying the producer of the defective product so the plaintiff may in appropriate circumstances look to the supplier or others in the chain of distribution. The supplier may be left bearing liability if unable to identify other persons, such as the producer, who ought more properly to bear the responsibility.

33. What is a product?

For the purposes of the Act product means any goods or electricity, and includes anything that forms part of, or is a component of, another product. The general interpretation section (s.45) states that goods includes substances, growing crops and things comprised in land by virtue of being attached to it and any ship, aircraft or vehicle.

34. When are goods defective?

Section 3 provides that a product will be deemed to be defective if: 'the safety of the product is not such as persons generally are entitled to expect'.

In determining what persons might be entitled to expect, circumstances which are to be taken into account include the manner in which, and purposes for which, the product has been marketed (s.3(2)(a)); what might reasonably be expected to be done with or in relation to the product (s.3(2)(b)); and the time when the product was supplied by its producer (s.3(2)(c)). It might well be, therefore, that a producer would not be liable for injury caused if products intended for domestic use were subjected to the same use as 'heavy duty' models normally supplied to industrial users. This would suggest that if an employer acquired domestic equipment for use at the workplace, any subsequent injury suffered by a person employed at that workplace would be attributed to the employer's negligence rather than to the statutory liability of the producer of the goods. If the equipment had been brought to the workplace by the worker himself, as might be the case in respect of certain relatively small handtools, the employer might still be negligent in permitting the worker to do this.

35. Defences

Section 4 of the Act provides the following defences to the producer of defective goods:

(a) that the defect is attributable to compliance with any requirement imposed by or under any enactment or with any
Community obligation; . . .

This defence is quite narrow. It does not mean that if goods comply with relevant regulatory standards they cannot be the subject of liability under this Act. The paragraph only provides a defence where the regulatory standard is the cause of the defect. For example, if the product were manufactured in compliance with relevant electrical standards, the producer would not be liable if damage were suffered because these standards proved inappropriate. If, however, the injury was suffered because the plastic casing housing the product was inadequate the producer would not be able to rely on his compliance with the electricity regulations to exempt him from liability.

The following defences all relate to circumstances in which the goods came into use and are fairly self-explanatory:

(b) that the person proceeded against did not at any time supply the
product to another; or

(c) that the following conditions are satisfied, that is to say —

(i) that the only supply of the product to another by the
person proceeded against was otherwise than in the course
of a business of that person's; and

(ii) that [the defendant was not the producer or if he were he
did not act with a view to a profit]; or

(d) that the defect did not exist in the product at the [time when the defendant supplied it].

The so-called 'state of the art' defence is more controversial:

(e) that the state of scientific and technical knowledge at the relevant time was not such that a producer of products of the same description as the product in question might be expected to have discovered the defect if it had existed in his products while they were under his control.

This defence enables the producer to establish that the defect was not generally appreciated within the industry at the time at which the particular unsafe product was put on the market. The defence is very relevant to chemical substances and, as far as the consumer market is concerned, is of especial value to the pharmaceutical industry. If the defendant successfully raises this defence the plaintiff is thrust back on the law of negligence to establish that the defendant was at fault in not being aware of the risk. It is not unknown for judges to declare an industry negligent, but the task of the plaintiff to achieve such a ruling must inevitably be a hard one.

The producer of a component of a product may raise the defence that the defect was not in the component but was attributable to the design of the end product or to compliance by the defendant producer with instructions given by the producer of the subsequent product (s.4(1)(f)).

36. Application of the Act

Part I of the Act applies to products put into circulation after 1 March 1988 and liability may be attached to the producer for up to ten years after the product has been put into circulation, though clearly the longer the product has been in circulation the more probable that the producer will be able to establish that the defect was not there when the product was put into circulation.

The liability described above is completely independent of criminal liability: Part II of the 1987 Act deals separately with criminal liability.

37. Relationship with other statutory provisions

The Employers' Liability (Defective Equipment) Act 1969 enables the injured employee to sue his employer, rather than the manufacturer of any defective equipment which had caused him injury in the course of his employment. The employee might consider the 1969 Act provides more valuable rights than the 1987 Act. Apart, however, from the fact that the two pieces of legislation are not necessarily coterminous in relation to workplace accidents (e.g. the terms 'product' and 'defective equipment' might not bear the same meaning), the plaintiff under the 1969 Act cannot succeed unless he can show that the manufacturer of the defective product had been negligent, whereas under the 1987 Act liability is strict.

It would appear that there is a considerable similarity between articles and substances to which s.6 of the 1974 Act relates and the products to which the 1987 Act relates, but there is no civil action for any person who suffers personal injury as a result of a breach of s.6 of the 1974 Act. On the other hand, the 'state of the art' defence might be less significant at the workplace than in the general market, bearing in mind the duties which s.6 of the 1974 Act imposes on manufacturers and suppliers (and others) of articles and substances for use at the workplace, to carry out research and testing before they are put into use, and the duties which the Control of Substances Hazardous to Health Regulations impose on employers in relation to substances used at the workplace.

Progress test 14

1. What provision does the Health and Safety at Work Act make for civil liability for breach of statutory duty? **(4)**

2. What must a plaintiff prove to succeed in an action for breach of statutory duty? **(10)**

3. To what extent is 'foresight' relevant to breach of statutory duty? **(22)**

4. What defences are there to actions for breach of statutory duty? **(26)**

5. How does the Consumer Protection Act fundamentally alter common law liability?   **(30)**

6. Has the plaintiff necessarily lost a product liability claim if the defendant successfully pleads the state of the art defence? **(35)**

15

General defences to civil liability

1. Introduction

There are two general defences to civil liability:

(a) *volenti non fit injuria*; and
(b) contributory negligence.

These defences have in common that the defendant alleges that the plaintiff's conduct has been such as to affect the defendant's liability.

Volenti non fit injuria

2. The plaintiff was *volens* of the risk

The defence of *volenti non fit injuria*, which translates loosely as assumption of risk, rarely succeeds in employment situations. In *Smith* v. *Baker* [1891] the House of Lords distinguished knowledge (*sciens*) from acceptance (*volens*) and found that, although a plaintiff might know of a risk, he might not have accepted it. If he had no power to remove the risk, his only way of avoiding it would have been to terminate his employment. A similar decision was reached in *Bunker* v. *Charles Brand & Son Ltd* [1969], a case brought by a visiting worker against the occupier of premises. Following these two cases there have been very few cases where the courts have found that a plaintiff worker accepted the risk which led to his injury. Where the defence succeeds it completely releases the defendant from liability.

3. Plaintiff at fault

Where the plaintiff worker has been at fault difficult questions can arise as to whether or not the fault has been so great as to make the plaintiff rather than the employer responsible for his injury. Thus in *Qualcast (Wolverhampton) Ltd* v. *Haynes* [1959] an experienced employee who failed to use protective equipment was unable to attach any liability to his employers for the injury which he suffered as a result of his conduct. It was not a case of the employee accepting the employers' negligence: the fault was entirely that of the employee.

The situation is less clear where two workers have created a risk when working together and as a result of their conduct one or both of them is injured. In this case, while the employer is perhaps faultless, he might be made vicariously liable for the negligence of the one worker which caused injury to the other. This factual situation has been before the House of Lords on at least two occasions.

In *Stapley* v. *Gypsum Mines Ltd* [1953] the employers had instructed the deceased (Stapley) and another employee (Dale) to bring down the roof of part of the gypsum mine to make the working place safe. The workers could not achieve this but the deceased continued to work in the area and was killed when the roof fell. It was argued for the employers that the accident was the result of the negligence of the worker and they should not bear any liability. The House of Lords, on a careful consideration of the facts, found that Dale's negligence, in failing to take proper steps to bring the roof down, had to some extent caused the accident and for Dale's negligence the employers were vicariously liable.

Their Lordships came to a different conclusion in *Imperial Chemical Industries Ltd* v. *Shatwell* [1965]. George and James Shatwell were two shotfirers who, in disregard of both their employers' instructions and statutory duties imposed on them personally, created a risk which resulted in personal injury to them both. In George's action against the employers it was held that they were not vicariously liable; *Stapley*'s case was considered to be an authority only on the matter of causation, the defence of *volenti* not being considered. Their Lordships found that on the facts the brothers had been *volens* of the risk they were creating. The plaintiff had fully appreciated the risk the brothers were taking; moreover, the statutory duty which had been broken was one which was placed on the plaintiff employee personally. So the employers were not liable.

4. Rescue situations

The defence rarely succeeds where the plaintiff has gone outside the scope of his employment in order to assist in an emergency situation, or to carry out a rescue. In rescue cases, however, the defendant will be the person whose negligence caused the danger, and this may not be the employer of the plaintiff. So in *Haynes* v. *Harwood* [1935] the defendant's horse was negligently left where it might cause injury to children. A child threw a stone and the horse bolted. The plaintiff policeman managed to stop the horse but was seriously injured. It was held that the defence that the policeman was *volens* of the risk could not be raised by the defendant.

Contributory negligence

5. General

Contributory negligence is a defence which the defendant may raise: it is not for the court to raise the issue even though the evidence may suggest the plaintiff was partly to blame (*Fookes* v. *Slaytor* [1979]). At common law proof of the plaintiff's negligence was a complete defence and the plaintiff was left remediless. The Law Reform (Contributory Negligence) Act 1945 now governs the situation and it provides for the apportionment of liability between plaintiff and defendant in cases of contributory negligence by the plaintiff. Section 1(1) provides that the damages recoverable:

> . . . shall be reduced to such extent as the court thinks just and equitable having regard to the claimant's share in the responsibility for the damage . . .

Section 1(2) requires the court to find and record the total damages which would have been recoverable if the claimant had not been at fault. In practice the plaintiff's damages are reduced by a percentage comparable to the degree of fault which the court finds in the plaintiff.

6. 'Negligence' and 'fault'

The title of the Act refers to 'negligence', but s.1(1) uses the word 'fault' and states that damages shall be apportioned:

> Where any person suffers damage as the result partly of his own fault and partly of the fault of any other person or persons . . .

Section 4 states:

> 'Fault' means negligence, breach of statutory duty or other act or omission which gives rise to a liability in tort or would, apart from this Act, give rise to the defence of contributory negligence.

7. Interpretation of 'fault'

It has also been held that fault applies both to conduct causing the accident and to conduct affecting the severity of the injury. This interpretation has arisen from a number of road accident cases concerning the wearing of seat-belts (e.g. *Froom* v. *Butcher* [1975]) and crash helmets (*O'Connell* v. *Jackson* [1972]); in these cases wearing the protective equipment would not have avoided the collision but it would have made the consequences of the collision less severe. While this approach does not appear to have been expressly adopted in industrial accident cases it has in a sense been acknowledged: in *Bux* v. *Slough Metals Ltd* [1974], for example, where the plaintiff suffered eye injury when not wearing goggles, it was not suggested that goggles would have prevented the plaintiff being splashed with molten liquid — they would, however, have protected the plaintiff from serious injury. Although the argument was not presented in this way, the plaintiff's contributory negligence in not wearing available goggles did result in his damages being reduced.

8. Availability of the defence

Section 4 makes it clear that the defence is available in both common-law negligence and breach of statutory duty claims. The fault of the plaintiff is more likely to be negligence, though there are, as has been noted, occasions (e.g. *Ginty* v. *Belmont Building Supplies Ltd* [1959]) where plaintiff and defendant are both in breach of statutory duty. In such cases the plaintiff's damage may be reduced. In some less frequent cases the defendant may sometimes escape all liability if his duty is no more than coterminous with the duty which the plaintiff has broken (as in *Ginty*).

9.   Plaintiff's standard of care

Where the defendant argues that the plaintiff's conduct has been negligent a question then arises as to the standard of care the plaintiff ought to exercise. Should his conduct be judged by the same standard as is applied to the conduct of the defendant? In road accident cases, where both plaintiff and defendant are drivers, it is clear that the conduct should be to the same standard in each case. It is not certain that this is so where the plaintiff is an employee and the defendant is his employer: it was not the view expressed by the House of Lords in *Caswell* v. *Powell Duffryn Associated Collieries Ltd* [1940]. In this case the plaintiff was the mother of a miner who was killed in the defendants' mine by reason of the defendants' breach of their statutory duty to fence machinery. Lord Atkin put forward this argument:

> The argument is that safety obligations are placed upon employers for the purpose of protecting not only workmen who are careful but also those who are careless: and that the object of the legislature is defeated if the right to sue for injuries caused by the breach of the safety regulations is denied to the careless workman for whose benefit amongst others the legislation was specially enacted.

While Lord Porter did not go so far as this, he did suggest that the standard of care expected of the worker might not be the high standard expected of persons in other circumstances. He said:

> The skill gained by a worker may enable him to take risks and do acts which in an unskilled man would be negligence, and on the other hand the fatiguing repetition of the same work may make a man incapable of the same care, and therefore not guilty of negligence, in doing or failing to do an act which a man less fatigued would do or leave undone...

10.   Regard to all the circumstances

Neither of their Lordships was making a statement of general application to all industrial accident cases: their statements were made in the context of, and would seem to have no relevance beyond, breach of statutory duty cases. Moreover, it must be borne in mind that they were made at a time when contributory negligence completely defeated a claim for damages. Now that this is no longer so it is arguably better for the court to apply a common standard of care but take into account the argument of Lord Porter when apportioning damages. That the Act should have this effect was argued by Denning LJ in *Davies* v. *Swan Motor Co (Swansea) Ltd* [1949]:

> The legal effect of the Act of 1945 is simple enough. If the plaintiff's negligence was one of the causes of his damage, he is no longer defeated altogether. He gets reduced damages. The practical effect of the Act is, however, wider than its legal effect. Previously, to mitigate the harshness of the doctrine of contributory negligence, the courts in practice sought to select, from a number of competing causes, which was *the* cause — the effective or predominant cause — of the damage and to reject the rest. Now the courts have regard to all the causes and apportion the damages accordingly.

There is evidence that this is what in fact happens. For example, in *Laszczyk* v. *National Coal Board* [1954], while the plaintiff was held to be contributorily negligent, being in breach of a statutory duty binding on himself, the court noted that he was at the time acting under instructions from his superior, and his damages were reduced by a mere 5%.

Progress test 15

1. What are the principal defences to common law liability? **(1)**

2. Why did the defence of assumption of risk succeed in *ICI* v. *Shatwell*? **(3)**

3. What statute governs the defence of contributory negligence? **(5)**

4. How does the statute define 'fault'? **(6)**

Part four

Systems and procedures at the workplace

Part four

Systems and procedures at
the workplace

16
Safe systems at the workplace

1. Introduction

The previous chapters have been concerned with the rules of law created by Parliament and judges in relation to the prevention and compensation of personal injury. The remainder of this book will consider procedures and systems which the law, or good management practice, require for the achievement of safe workplaces.

2. The importance of systems

The law places emphasis on systems. The common law of negligence expects organisations to operate to safe systems. The 1974 Act, in its general duties, demands a systematic approach to safety; recent regulations such as the Control of Substances Hazardous to Health Regulations 1988 require employers systematically to assess situations and then respond in systematic ways. Similarly the EC's Framework and individual Directives stress the need for safe systems. While, increasingly, the need for a systematic approach is written into regulatory provisions, the law is unlikely totally to dictate management systems and, even where there are statutory systems for control of hazards, they are unlikely to be put into, and kept in, effect without systematic management of plant and personnel.

The safety policy

3. General duty

It was noted when considering employers' general duties to their employees that s.2(3) of the 1974 Act requires employers to prepare and, as often as appropriate, revise a safety policy and to bring this policy to the notice of all of their employees. The general requirements of s.2(3) will in future be supplemented by the regulations to implement the Framework Directive; these will require employers to put into writing both their assessment of, and response to, the risks to which employees are exposed while at work. Comprehensive written safety systems will therefore in future be required for all but the smallest organisations.

4.   Content of the safety policy
Section 2(3) makes three specific requirements of an employer in respect of the safety policy:

(a) a general statement of policy (**5–7**);
(b) the organisation for safety (**8–12**);
(c) the arrangements for carrying out the policy (**13–14**).

The essence of a safety policy is that it has to be tailor-made for an organisation by that organisation. Nevertheless the following comments may be made.

5.   Statement of policy
What is required is a general statement of intent. The language and apparent philosophy of s.2(3) may seem a little dated in the 1990s, in the era of corporate plans because it does not ask that the employer have a safety plan for progression over time: it merely requires that the employer make a statement of commitment to safety. In practice many organisations have produced a single side of paper, doing little more than stating that the employer intends to comply with the Act, and often going on to say that they expect all employees and other persons to comply with the duties which the Act imposes on them. This brief statement usually bears the signature of a senior member of management as further indication that the senior managers of the organisation are committed to the policy.

6.   Safety policy and the corporate plan
The corporate plan will undoubtedly have set out the company's aims and objectives, probably for a five-year period, indicating the goals the organisation intends to achieve in terms of development of markets, expansion of turnover, reduction of

production costs and so on. Arguably a safe organisation ought at least to cross reference its safety policy to its corporate plan. The suggestion that safety be built into the corporate plan is the more pertinent bearing in mind that since s.79 of the Companies Act 1967 there has been a possibility that regulations might impose a requirement that the public company's annual report to shareholders include a statement on the company's safety performance in the year under review. While regulations do not appear to have been made, the power to do so is repeated in s.235, and Schedule 7, Part IV of the Companies Act 1985.

7. Impact of safety policy

Experience suggests that the policy statement makes little impact on employees. Whether this is important may be questioned provided employees have been trained to operate the safe systems which it envisages.

8. Safety organisation

The second requirement of s.2(3) is that the employer set out his organisation for safety. Thus the safety policy ought to have appended to it a list of the personnel with safety responsibilities from senior management down, and the chain of communication between these persons. This information may well be best expressed in, or at least supplemented by, a chart.

9. Requirement for 'competent' persons

It may well be that the organisation will have appointed a safety officer/adviser/manager with responsibilities confined to safety. While this person should be identified in the safety policy, it will be misguided to believe that such an appointee, who may be a relatively junior manager, can have total responsibility for safety.

The appointment of 'competent' persons in compliance with the General Provisions Regulations will necessitate the identification of persons, either within the organisation, or without, with special safety responsibilities: it will be logical to name these in the policy.

10. Management responsibility for safety

It is misguided to avoid giving special roles to individuals because 'safety is everyone's business'. It is true that everyone should be aware of, and have regard for safety, but the organisational chart ought to indicate who has management responsibility to make and execute decisions in respect of safety.

A comprehensive organisational system for safety should include line managers, and is likely to include, in addition to the safety manager, both personnel and production managers. It should also indicate a senior manager — probably at board level and perhaps the person who signed the policy statement — to take ultimate responsibility for safety within the organisation. Since the policy will be given to all employees it may be helpful to name the persons with safety responsibilities as well as naming the management roles.

11. Safety representatives

While safety representatives may be mentioned in this chart it should be remembered that they are not persons with management responsibilities for safety. The names of safety representatives might be given to enable employees to know the persons to whom safety issues may be reported. However, including the names of employee safety representatives is going beyond what s.2(3) envisages and employers may consider it preferable to encourage employees to communicate on safety issues directly with management rather than to management through safety representatives.

12. Effect of producing a safety policy

The process of producing a safety policy may cause organisations to look critically at their organisational structure generally and discover weaknesses that are of significance to matters other than safety.

13. Safety arrangements

Management, preferably through specialist safety personnel, should have considered the various tasks which have to be performed in the course of the organisation's ordinary activities, having regard to the situations which do or might occur, identifying where there are hazards and laying down routine procedures for dealing with them. Many organisations have dealt with these matters by annexing to, rather than writing into, their safety policy, codes of practice setting out routines and procedures for dealing with hazardous situations.

14. Matters to be addressed

Safety arrangements are likely to include systems for ensuring that:

(a) only authorised personnel are on the premises, and for ensuring visitors are instructed about, or protected from hazards both for their own safety and for the safety of others;

(b) purchasing procedures are such that products introduced into the workplace are free from hazard, or, if this is not possible risks are identified and controlled;

(c) suitable personnel are selected and personnel are properly trained for the functions they have to perform;

(d) personnel are provided with and trained to use whatever protective equipment is necessary for their work;

(e) plant and equipment is properly used and properly maintained;

(f) adequate arrangements have been made to enable persons and vehicles to pass safely through the property, including members of the public where the public are lawful visitors to the premises;

(g) visiting workers are properly informed as to the hazards and procedures of the site, and detailed arrangements are made to ensure they can work safely and do not endanger others by their work;

(h) maintenance and other similar work is not undertaken without granting a 'permit to work', and once such a permit has been granted its terms are followed by the worker to whom it is granted, and it is observed by other workers;

(i) there are proper emergency procedures to contend with fire and other catastrophies, ensuring, through practice drills, persons recognise the signal to evacuate the premises and know how to proceed when that signal is given;

(j) there is access for emergency services;

(k) there are proper systems for damage control, including, where appropriate, firefighting teams, and, in all cases, first-aid provision;

(l) full consideration is given to the safety of the neighbourhood, including the control of routine emissions from the premises, the control of vehicular traffic, and the protection of the neighbouring community in the event of catastrophe;

(m) arrangements have been made to comply with all the applicable regulatory systems — particularly those required by the Control of Substances Hazardous to Health Regulations;

(n) proper arrangements are made for safety representatives to carry out their functions;

(o) there is a system for evaluating, and if necessary, acting on relevant information received from safety representatives or other persons;

(p) there are systems for keeping the safety policy under review and for the allocation of funds for routine updating and renewal of plant and equipment, for routine training of personnel and for responding to emergencies.

This list is inevitably somewhat vague and general and may not include all the matters to which a particular organisation needs to pay attention. The matters which have to be addressed, and the way in which arrangements are made to deal with these matters, must vary from organisation to organisation and be tailor-made to suit the operation.

15. Preparation process

The safety policy must be in writing and brought to the attention of all employees. It must be updated whenever necessary. While it is not a legal requirement that the policy be drawn up and revised by management in discussion with employees, to involve employees in the exercise is certainly in the spirit of consultation between management and employees which is an important feature both of the 1974 Act and EC Directives. Nevertheless the production and content of the policy is ultimately management's responsibility.

16. Employee involvement

Involving employees in drawing up a policy is one way of alerting employees to the existence and content of the policy. At the very least, however, every employee ought to receive a personal copy of the published policy if the employer is to feel confident that he has discharged the duty to bring the policy to the attention of each employee.

17. Significance of policy

Drawing up a policy should cause an organisation to look critically at its provision for safety. The inspectorate has found the safety policy a useful starting point when conducting a workplace inspection. They will expect the policy and practice to coincide. To satisfy the inspectorate the policy must not merely be a piece of paper whose contents bear no relation to the realities of the workplace.

18. Updating of policy

Given the rapid economic changes which have occurred in recent years, resulting in changed workplace structures both in terms of technology and manpower, there may be many workplaces where a policy which was satisfactory when drawn up is well overdue for updating if it is to be meaningful.

The importance of resource management

19. General

The 1974 Act differs fundamentally from earlier safety legislation in the emphasis which it places on the role of human behaviour in achieving safe systems. The outline account given above of the requirements of a safety policy serve to stress that this is so. The identification of hazards and of systems for their control, and the carrying out of the systems selected, all require careful selection, training and monitoring of personnel. The duty which the Act places on employers to do all that is reasonably practicable to ensure safety at the workplace will not be achieved unless the employer has accepted the close relationship between safe systems and personnel and contracts management.

20. Legal enforcement of duties

While employers may note that the Act places complementary duties on both contractors and individual employees, those duties, like the employers' own duties, bear criminal sanctions and are enforced only by the inspectorate. Employers must utilise management systems to establish and maintain safety arrangements. In so far as employers can invoke the law it will be in contract rather than under the 1974 Act itself.

21. Safety arrangements

The following account will consider first the arrangements which an organisation should make to ensure that its own employees operate safely and secondly the arrangements which should be made by appropriate managers within the organisation to ensure that other organisations with which it deals have a similar concern for safety.

The organisation and its employees

22. General

Safety arrangements should be considered when identifying the specifications for jobs within the organisation; such consideration should largely determine the training needed for persons appointed to, or already on, the staff. In turn, safety performance in relation to these arrangements should both form a part of ongoing staff appraisal, and bear a significant relationship to disciplinary procedures. Throughout the process, from selection to dismissal, the contract of employment will be a material consideration.

23. Selection

When selecting individuals who are qualified and competent to fulfil employment roles safety requirements should be taken into account. Job specifications should be related to safety arrangements.

24. Qualifications required

There are currently relatively few cases in which the law dictates that employment roles with safety responsibilities must be given only to persons with specific qualifications, but this may change. Lead bodies are identifying the subject matter for courses to lead to National Vocational Qualifications. Many of these courses are likely to include some safety training. A lead body is considering the question of training for safety management. It may be some time before the law stipulates the vocational qualifications needed for particular jobs, but the time may soon come when whether a person has such qualifications is taken into account when considering whether they are competent for particular employment roles.

25. Competence

In some cases possession of a recognised qualification may be a necessary prerequisite for appointment; in other cases lack of qualification may create a presumption against suitability for a task. In all cases, however, competence will be something distinct from qualification. Paper qualification indicates only training for the task; competence indicates ability to perform the task. Full competence is likely to come only after experience of doing the work in question. Employers need to look for evidence of the employment record of the candidate, unless they are offering only a junior post.

26. The employment contract

The successful applicant will receive a contract of employment. While the law does not require this to be in writing it does require that an employee who is to work full time (more than 16 hours a week) be given, not less than 13 weeks after starting work, a written statement as evidence of certain of the terms and conditions of the employment. This document need not be the contract of employment, but the systematic employer may prefer to incorporate the material required by the statute (s.1 of the Employment Protection (Consolidation) Act 1978), into a full written contract indicating within it, or by reference to other documents, not only the matters required by the Act, but also terms and conditions which relate to job performance. The matters of relevance to safety include the title of the job, the nature of the task to be performed; the training, if any, that will be provided; the system of appraisal of performance; the length of any probation period, and disciplinary rules and procedures.

27. Importance of the contract of employment

The contract is vitally important because its provisions are the yardstick by which to measure whether or not the employee's work is at a satisfactory standard. Any existing employee who is re-deployed into different work should be provided with a new contractual document to reflect the new terms and conditions of employment.

28. Training

It has for many years been customary to provide induction training for persons newly appointed to a workforce. The cost benefit of prolonged induction programmes may be doubted, since the amount of information that a person new to the job can absorb is probably limited. It is likely to be more effective to keep the induction brief while ensuring that it covers major safety requirements, including the more basic safety rules and emergency procedures.

Following an induction training, the employee should be given a fuller training, over time, relating to the task for which the contract has been given. In the case of jobs with any management responsibilities, this training should cover not only the safety requirements of the job, but also the appropriate rudiments of human resource management, focusing on how to achieve performance by others and what to do if the required performance is not achieved.

29. Ongoing appraisal

When the initial training period is over the employee's performance should be monitored in the context of technical advances. The employee may be expected to be willing to adjust to evolutionary changes in workplace practices, such as the introduction of new plant and equipment or new methods of management, though the employer may need to provide training for this (*Cresswell* v. *Board of Inland Revenue* [1984]).

30. Unsatisfactory performance

An employee's unsatisfactory performance of the contract, in relation to safety, or indeed other matters, may amount to breach of contract, warranting termination of the contract at common law, or enabling the employer to dismiss the employee fairly under the Employment Protection (Consolidation) Act 1978. However, before dismissing an employee the employer should take care to ensure that the evidence of unsatisfactory performance is sufficient to warrant termination of the contract.

31. Termination of contract at common law

An employer may terminate the contract of an employee who has not two years' continuous full-time employment without risk of a complaint being made to an industrial tribunal by the employee who has been unfairly dismissed. In the case of such short-term employees, the employer need only have regard to the terms of the contract of the worker concerned, when considering whether terminating the contract could possibly lead to common-law liability for breach of contract.

If the contract has made adequate provision for a probationary period and appraisal of the employee within that period, and the performance of the worker has in fact been properly monitored in that period, there may be clear grounds for the employer to terminate the contract in the probationary period, without notice and without fear of litigation.

32. Implied contractual terms

It has been held that there is, in addition to express contractual terms, an implied contractual term that the employee will work with the employers to make the employers' operation a viable business concern. This gives employers some scope to adopt rules and systems of work additional to those which are expressly made contractual terms, but on the other hand does not entitle the employee to follow these working rules slavishly to the detriment of the sensible operation of the business. Thus, in *Secretary of State for Employment* v. *ASLEF* [1972], where railway workers, operating a work to rule, insisted on meticulously following the employers' safety rules in such a way as to disrupt the normal train timetable, Roskill LJ said:

> It was not suggested that strictly speaking this (i.e. the rule book) formed part of the contract of employment as such. But every employer is entitled within the terms and the scope of the relevant contract of employment to give instructions to his employees and every employee is correspondingly bound to accept instruction properly and lawfully so given. The rule book seems to me to constitute instructions given by the employer to the employee in accordance with that general legal right.

33. Dismissal in everyone's best interests

In cases where there is not clear evidence of breach of an

express contractual term, the employer may consider that it is in everyone's best interests to terminate the contract with notice, or immediately with wages in lieu of notice. In either case the notice should be the contractual notice period, as set out in the contract, or failing that, the minimum set out in s.49 of the Employment Protection (Consolidation) Act, i.e. one week if the employee has been employed over one month but under two years.

34. Continuous service

It should not be forgotten, however, that if the employee has long service with the employer or an associated employer, then, although the unsatisfactory work is in the context of a new work role, for which a new contract has been given, the new contract is likely to be, for statutory purposes, continuous with other employment within the organisation, so that the employee enjoys the benefit of the unfair dismissal provisions of the Employment Protection (Consolidation) Act.

35. Unfair dismissal

The Employment Protection (Consolidation) Act 1978, s.54, gives an employee with the requisite continuous employment a right not to be unfairly dismissed. If the employee can satisfy an industrial tribunal that he has been dismissed there is a presumption that the dismissal was unfair. The employer can only rebut this by satisfying the tribunal that the reason (or at least the principal reason) for the dismissal was one which the statute permits, and the employer must have acted reasonably in treating that reason as a sufficient reason for dismissal (s.57).

The reasons most likely to be relevant to unsafe conduct are those set out in paragraphs (a) and (b) of s.57(2), namely:

(a)   related to the capability or qualifications of the employee for performing work of the kind which he was employed by the employer to do; or

(b)   related to the conduct of the employee.

36. Employee's incapacity to perform the task

Any inherent incapacity of the employee to do the task required by the contract of employment ought normally to have become apparent and led to dismissal well before the end of the two years' of continuous service which must have elapsed before the employee would have the right to complain to an industrial tribunal. This provision is therefore most relevant where the employee has become incapable, often through deterioration in health, after the appointment, or if the employer has promoted the employee to a level at which that employee is unable to perform satisfactorily.

37. Offer of alternative employment

In cases under paragraph (a) where the problem is of the employee's capacity to do the work, the dismissal is unlikely to be fair unless the employer has properly discussed with the employee the possibilities of alternative employment within the organisation (e.g. *Spencer* v. *Paragon Wallpapers Ltd* [1977]).

38. Employee's misconduct

Paragraph (b) is in effect concerned with misconduct: unsafe conduct will fall within the general ambit of misconduct. Such conduct may disregard express safety rules, e.g. smoking in a 'No smoking' area; or conduct which though not expressly prescribed is clearly unsafe, e.g. a pilot bringing an aeroplane in to make a bad landing (*Alidair Ltd* v. *Taylor* [1978]).

39. Requirement for proper investigation

A dismissal will not normally be fair unless the employer has conducted a proper investigation to find out to the best of his ability the full circumstances of the case, and this investigation should include giving a hearing to the employee whose employment is at stake. Indeed it has fairly recently been reasserted by the House of Lords that even if the employer has a good reason for dismissal, that dismissal may be rendered unfair if the employer dismisses without following appropriate procedures (*Polkey* v. *AE Dayton Services Ltd* [1987]). In the case of a relatively minor safety lapse (e.g. smoking in an area where there is no special danger of fire or explosion) dismissal for a first offence would not be likely to be fair. The employer would be expected to follow the warnings procedure in that employer's disciplinary code. In the case of a major lapse (as was deemed to be the situation

286 Systems and procedures at the workplace

in the *Alidair* case) a single instance of unsafe behaviour might warrant dismissal, provided that the employer had conducted a proper enquiry and was satisfied that the facts were indeed that the employee's conduct had been extremely unsafe.

40. Dismissal and the terms of the employment contract

Whether the employer is entitled to dismiss an employee for either incapacity or misconduct is largely, but not entirely, a matter of evaluating the employee's behaviour in the context of the terms of the contract. The employer's conduct in dismissing would hardly be reasonable if the employee's failure were in the context of the employer having asked the employee to do something that employee's contract had not required, or if the employer had failed to provide training for the task. Moreover, safety rules, like any other disciplinary rules, must be clearly made known to employees and systematically enforced. It would not be fair to dismiss an employee for failing to observe a safety rule which had fallen into abeyance, even though enquiry established that there was clear evidence of the particular employee's unsafe conduct.

41. Employer's unsafe conduct

The employer should bear in mind that there have been successful complaints of unfair dismissal made by an employee who has been required to work in unsafe or unhealthy conditions. The employee will allege that there has been a constructive dismissal within the Employment Protection (Consolidation) Act 1978 s.54(2)(c) which covers the situation where:

> The employee terminates that contract, with, or without notice, in circumstances such that he is entitled to terminate it without notice by reason of the employer's conduct.

In order to succeed the employee must establish that the employer's conduct amounted to a breach of the contract (*Western Excavating (EEC) Ltd* v. *Sharp* [1978]); it has been held that failure to investigate a complaint about unsatisfactory safety equipment did entitle an employee to succeed in a claim for unfair dismissal (*BAC* v. *Austin* [1978]).

Safety and commercial contracts

42. General

There are two major classes of commercial contracts in-relation to which an organisation should certainly ensure that adequate provision has been made for safety. They are (a) contracts for the supply of articles and substances, and (b) contracts for the performance of work.

43. Supply of articles and substances

Section 6 of the 1974 Act imposes on suppliers of articles and substances a duty to ensure that they are, so far as is reasonably practicable, safe at all times when they are being used etc. by persons at work, and there are also duties both in s.2 of the Act and in regulations (e.g. the Control of Substances Hazardous to Health Regulations) on employers to ensure that articles and substances at the workplace are safe for those employed there. Employers, therefore, through their contracts department, their safety manager and relevant line managers, need to ensure that the supplier has complied with his s.6 duties, and that the goods supplied under the contract do conform with the contractual specification both in respect of an initial consignment and, equally importantly, in subsequent consignments. Those responsible for taking delivery of articles and substances both at the warehouse and the individual workstations should be alerted to the need for vigilance on this matter.

It hardly needs to be said that the supplier of the articles and substances must for their part ensure that the goods supplied are both in accordance with their contractual commitments and in compliance with s.6 of the 1974 Act.

44. Contracts for the performance of work

In earlier chapters discussion of the two important criminal cases of *R* v. *Swan Hunter (Shipbuilders) Ltd* and *Mailer* v. *Austin Rover Group plc* stressed the importance of safe systems when two organisations contract for one to provide labour for the performance of services for the other. The cases demonstrate the ways in which ss.3 and 4 require the head contractor, and the other employer of labour, to liaise to ensure that neither workforce is endangered by the ways in which the respective undertakings are conducted, separately or in relation to each other, and also to ensure that visiting workers operate on premises which are safe for the purposes for which they have come on to those premises.

45. Selection of the undertaking

When entering into contracts for the performance of services, as when making contracts of employment, great care should be taken in the selection of the undertaking with whom the contract to undertake the work is made. In particular it should be borne in mind that a low tender for the work may mean (though this is not inevitably the case) that safety has not been costed. Thus it may be advisable to check the safety record of the organisation before making a contract with them.

46. Specification of work systems

In the situations under discussion, the systems under which the work is to be undertaken should be spelled out at the tender stage, or at the very latest in the contractual documents. The occupier of premises contracting for another workforce than his own to come on to, and work on, his premises should stipulate the system in which the work is to be done, both for the protection of his own workers and for the protection of the visitors, and possibly third parties: the work might create neighbourhood risks — as where, for example, construction work is being carried out near a highway.

Both the *Mailer* and *Swan Hunter* cases demonstrate that contractual arrangements that merely set out a plan of work are not on their own sufficient to ensure that safe systems will be operated. In *Mailer*, for example, it had been stipulated that the head contractor's paint thinners should not be used; they were used and this was at least one of the reasons for the catastrophe. In *Swan Hunter* the visiting workforce was not even given the blue book explaining how to weld in confined spaces. It may be doubted, however, whether merely supplying the instruction book as a contractual document would have ensured that the work was carried out in accordance with the system in the book.

47. Provision of safety training

Safe systems in these cases require that the framework is set out in the contract, but it may be necessary to go further and provide the visiting workers with induction training to ensure that they operate safely within the environment in which they have to work: it may not be sufficient for an organisation merely to convey its safety rules and system to another employer. It may be necessary to communicate with the visiting workers directly and in some instances actually provide the training necessary to operate the system documented in the contract papers.

The need to communicate with workers personally about the systems they must operate when visiting a workplace were made clear in the official report of the Piper Alpha disaster. The report disclosed that a very high proportion of the workforce consisted of subcontractors' workers who were not familiar with the Piper Alpha installation and had not been introduced to the emergency procedures for that installation. Many of the victims probably were not familiar with the layout of the installation or the muster points, and may not have been familiar with the arrangements for abandoning the installation.

48. Performance monitoring

Initial training is unlikely to be sufficient; it is likely to be necessary to monitor the performance of the visiting workforce to ensure that the contractual system is complied with. Indeed it may be desirable to write into the contract both a stipulation that subcontractors' workers attend an induction programme on the safety systems needed and a power for the head contractor to monitor the safety performance in the currency of the contract.

49. Failure to observe safety requirements

Failure to observe safety requirements would then clearly be a breach of contract and entitle the head contractor to take steps to remedy the situation. What steps are appropriate will depend on the severity of the situation. In some instances it may be appropriate to require a particular worker to stop work and leave the site; in other situations it may be necessary to stop the whole operation. In the worst situations the conduct of the subcontractors may be so unsatisfactory as to justify requiring them to leave the work unfinished. Similarly the subcontractor should monitor the safety provision made by the head contractor and stop the work if conditions are unsafe. While for both contracting parties there is less room for dispute if the contract has spelt out what each expects from the other, and there is evidence that the express arrangements have not been honoured, there can be no doubt that, provided there is evidence of unsafe conduct, the party suffering from it would be entitled to treat the matter as a breach of the contract and respond accordingly, even if the contract itself were silent on the matter.

50. Requirements under the Framework Directive

Regulations to implement the Framework Directive may require that a person be nominated to be in overall control in circumstances where two workforces work in close proximity.

51. Effects of commercial considerations

Commercial considerations will obviously militate against anything which delays work in progress; this in itself should be a good incentive to arrange a proper system in the first place, bearing in mind that nothing is more likely to cause disruption than an accident!

Safe systems and safety representatives

52. General

The code of practice which accompanies the Safety Representatives and Safety Committees Regulations 1977 advises safety representatives that in performance of their functions they should keep themselves informed of their employers' health and safety policy and the organisation and arrangements for fulfilling that policy.

53. Inspection and consultation

Periodical inspections carried out by safety representatives may identify weaknesses in safety arrangements. Consultation between representatives and their constituents may also identify matters of concern.

An organisation which is safety conscious will wish to use the safety representative system to positive advantage in monitoring its safety performance: it should also be advantageous to management to use the committee as an organ for positive consultation where management is proposing to change operational systems in ways which may impact on safety.

Progress test 16

1. What matters should a safety policy contain? **(4)**

2. What responsibilities has an employee to train employees? **(14, 19, 24, 28)**

3. In what circumstances may an employer fairly dismiss an employee for unsafe conduct? **(35–41)**

4. In what ways may an organisation effectively ensure safe systems between itself and other organisations? **(42)**

5. How can safety representatives help an organisation to achieve safe systems? **(52, 53)**

17
Procedures after an accident

1. Introduction

This chapter is concerned with the steps which an employer is required by law to take, and the systems which should be in place, in order to deal with an accident or dangerous occurrence. It will go beyond the strict legal requirements and discuss steps which good management practice suggest should be taken. It will not be concerned with installations to which the Control of Industrial Major Hazards Regulations 1984 apply; these regulations were discussed in Chapter 9.

2. Emergency procedures

In order to ensure optimum damage control, emergency procedures must be kept in place and individuals must be trained to respond to emergency. The systems needed will vary from one workplace to another, to take into account such factors as the nature of both the workplace and the activity, and the personnel on site.

The matters which will be considered here are:

(a) prevention of further injury;
(b) provision of medical treatment;
(c) reporting of the accident;
(d) investigation of the causes of the accident.

Prevention of further injury

3. Evacuation procedures

An immediate response to emergency must be to remove from

the danger area all persons who might otherwise be placed at unnecessary risk; preferably evacuation should take place as soon as imminent danger is discovered in order to avoid any personal injury occurring. Organisations should have, and are usually required by law to have, emergency warning systems and identified escape routes, and evacuation should have been rehearsed. The mandatory systems are primarily intended to deal with fire but there may be other emergencies, such as terrorist bombing, where using the fire escape drill is the appropriate and effective way of clearing a danger area. Care must be taken to provide safe mustering points, at an appropriate distance from the danger and accessible without exposure to hazard (e.g. without crossing a major highway or other danger zone).

4. Dealing with accident victims

In some accident situations, where the communal risk is minimal, evacuation is not needed and the primary concern is to deal with accident victims; for example, a worker might have received injury to a limb or suffered electric shock. If such an accident has occurred there may be an instinctive reaction to rescue the victim, without stopping to consider whether such intervention might lead to further personal injury. Emergency procedures need therefore to stress the importance of carrying out appropriate shut-down procedures, such as switching off a machine, or cutting off a power supply, before carrying out rescue.

Provision of medical treatment

5. First-aid

The accident victim must receive medical treatment speedily. Circumstances may require that the emergency ambulance service is called, with a view to hospitalisation of the victim, but first-aid should be immediately available. The Health and Safety (First-Aid) Regulations 1981 interpret first-aid as:

(a) in cases where a person will need help from a medical practitioner or nurse, treatment for the purpose of preserving life and minimising the consequences of injury and illness until such help is obtained; and

(b) treatment of minor injuries which would otherwise receive no treatment or which do not need treatment by a medical practitioner or nurse.

6. Provision of first-aid equipment

Regulation 3 requires employers to ensure that there is available such equipment and facilities as are adequate and appropriate in the circumstances for enabling first-aid to be rendered to their employees if they are injured or become ill at work. The requirements of the regulations apply to every workplace, unless a special exemption has been granted (regulation 6), or the situation is within one of the categories identified in regulation 7 (diving operations, merchant shipping and certain mines). The exempted situations are dealt with in other special regulations. It is also the duty of self-employed persons to provide, or ensure that there is provided, such equipment, if any, as is adequate and appropriate to enable them to render first-aid to themselves.

7. Availability of qualified first-aiders

Regulation 3 also requires employers to ensure that there are sufficient suitably qualified persons available to render necesssary first-aid to their employees. Persons nominated 'first-aiders' must normally have been properly trained; that is they must at least have had the training, and obtained the qualifications, the Health and Safety Executive has approved. Exceptionally, there may, however, be circumstances in which it is sufficient to appoint an untrained person to take charge of the situation and the equipment. This will be the case only where either the absence of the first-aider is temporary, or the nature of the undertaking, the size of the workforce, or the location of the establishment (i.e. proximity to other sources of medical assistance, such as a hospital) make this minimal provision acceptable. The code of practice which accompanies the regulations makes it clear that it is unlikely to be sufficient to have only minimal provision for the time that a regular first-aider is on holiday.

8. Information to employees

Employers must inform their employees of the arrangements for the provision of first-aid, including the location of equipment, facilities and personnel.

9. Overview

These regulations replace many older regulatory codes which previously related to specific work places or activities, such as factories or offices. Unlike some earlier regulations, they do not stipulate the exact number of qualified first-aiders needed at any workplace, or the exact equipment to be provided. They leave it ultimately to the employer to decide what is 'adequate and appropriate in the circumstances': the code of practice gives some guidance on these issues.

Reporting of accidents

10. General

The legal requirements in respect of the reporting of accidents and dangerous occurrences are set out in the Reporting of Injuries, Diseases and Dangerous Occurrences Regulations 1985. It will be noted that the regulations cover not only accidents causing personal injury (including fatalities and 'conditions'), but work-related diseases and certain dangerous occurrences (i.e. incidents in which noone was injured).

The provisions of these regulations are detailed and complex; moreover, they are supplemented by a number of detailed schedules. Only a general outline is given here. Employers are likely to find the Health and Safety Executive's leaflet *Reporting an Injury or a Dangerous Occurrence* very useful.

11. Application of the regulations

The regulations apply to all work situations except those listed in Schedule 6 of the regulations. The exempted situations are ones where other statutory provisions apply, including railway, merchant shipping and civil aviation activities, as well as situations governed by the Ionising Radiations Regulations 1985.

12. Who has to report

Regulation 2 imposes the obligation to report upon 'the responsible person'. Where, as will normally be the case, the victim is 'an employee at work', the responsible person is the victim's employer. In the case of the victim being a 'trainee' the duty is on the 'trainer'. In other cases the obligation falls on 'the person for the time being having control of the premises . . . at which the accident . . .' or dangerous occurrence or disease occurred. The occupier's obligation only arises, however, if the occupier is carrying on a trade or business at the premises. In effect the occupier's obligation is in relation to injuries involving the self-employed and members of the public. Employers remain liable to report accidents suffered by their employees, even though these occurred when they were undertaking work at premises where the employer was not the occupier. Finally there are some special situations, such as mines, where the obligation is placed on the manager, and quarries where it falls on the owner.

13. Specified injuries or dangerous occurrences

Regulation 3(1) imposes an obligation to report specified injuries or dangerous occurrences. In effect the specified situations represent the more serious situations. Thus:

  (a) forthwith notify the enforcing authority thereof by the quickest practicable means; and
  (b) within 7 days send a report thereof to the enforcing authority on a form approved for the purposes of this Regulation.

In practice reporting to the Health and Safety Executive (or the relevant local authority) will initially be by telephone and then, within the week, on form F2508.

14. Exemptions from notification

The notification requirements do not apply to injury suffered by patients undergoing treatment in a hospital or surgery, work-related road transport injuries or injuries suffered in road construction or maintenance; or in building operations on a building adjacent to or over a road (Regulation 10).

15. Injuries to be notified at once

Regulation 3(2) specifies the injuries and conditions to which the reporting procedure applies. Those to be notified forthwith are, in general, fracture of a bone; amputation; loss of eyesight; injury (including burns) caused by electric shock; loss of consciousness from lack of oxygen or exposure to a toxic substance; and also any other injury which results in the person injured being admitted immediately into hospital for more than 24 hours.

16. To be notified within seven days

Those to be reported within seven days are any accident which has resulted in over three days' consecutive incapacity for work (Regulation 3(3)).

17. Death of an employee

If an employee dies as a result of a reportable accident within a year of the accident occurring, the employer has to inform the enforcing authority, in writing, as soon as he learns of the death, whether or not the accident was reported (Regulation 4).

18. Specified diseased to be reported

There is a duty to report cases of certain specified diseases. Schedule 2 lists the diseases and the work activities for which they are reportable. The duty to report only rests on an employer, and then only if a doctor has notified the employer in writing that the employee or trainee has been diagnosed as suffering from a relevant disease. A self-employed person has a similar duty to report.

19. Making records

Regulation 7 requires the responsible person to record any event which has had to be reported, and keep this record for at least three years from the date when it was made. The record has to contain the information required by Schedule 3 of the regulations. This is, in the case of a reportable accident or occurrence:

(a) Date and time of accident or dangerous occurrence.
(b) The following particulars of the person affected:
   (*i*) full name;
   (*ii*) occupation;
   (*iii*) nature of injury or condition.
(c) Place where the accident or dangerous occurrence happened.
(d) A brief description of the circumstances.

There are similar requirements for reportable diseases.

20. Dangerous occurrences

Schedule 1 lists the dangerous occurrences which have to be reported, even though there has been no personal injury or notifiable disease resulting from the occurrence. The Schedule is in four parts: the first is general; the remaining parts relate only to mines, quarries and railways. Part I specifies dangerous occurrences in relation to:

(a) lifting machinery;
(b) passenger carrying amusement device;
(c) pressure vessels;
(d) electrical short circuit;
(e) explosion or fire;
(f) escape of flammable substances;
(g) collapse of scaffolding;
(h) collapse of building or structure;
(i) escape of a substance or pathogen;
(j) explosives;
(k) freight containers;
(l) pipelines;
(m) conveyance of dangerous substances by road;
(n) breathing apparatus;
(o) overhead electric lines;
(p) locomotives.

21. Site of occurrence

When an accident or occurrence has to be reported to the enforcing authority the site of the occurrence should not be disturbed until after the relevant inspectors have either visited, and completed their enquiry at the site, or indicated that they do not intend to visit. Nevertheless immediate steps should be taken to isolate the danger, e.g. cut off the power supply, or fence off the area where the accident occurred. Any victim will, of course, have been removed as quickly as possible, but it may be appropriate to mark out, perhaps with chalk, the position and circumstances in which the accident left the victim.

22. Additional reports

In addition to reporting to the enforcing authority good management, and perhaps contractual obligations, suggest the following reports should be made with considerable speed to the following.

(a) *The personnel department.* Applicable only where the victim is an employee.

(b) *Next of kin.* In the case of an employee, the personnel department's records may include the name and address of a person the victim has stated should to be notified in case of accident — this may not, of course, be next of kin! It would be good practice to keep such information on record and to act on it rather than to search for the person whom the law would classify as next of kin. It will be a matter of company policy to decide whether communication with relatives should be through the personnel department or managers more closely associated with the victims.

(c) *Notify head office.* If the accident has occurred at a branch or when working away from the employers' premises this may be expedient. This is a matter which should be addressed when formulating company policy: it may be sufficient to inform the personnel department.

(d) *The organisation's insurance company.* How this report is to be made will no doubt be dictated by the insurance company concerned.

(e) *The employer of the victim.* This will only be applicable where the victim was the employee of another organisation than the occupier of the site where the accident occurred.

(f) *The safety representative.* The Safety Representatives and Safety Committees Regulations give safety representatives a qualified right to inspect where there has been a notifiable accident or dangerous occurrence or a notifiable disease (*see* Chapter 11). There is no obligation on an employer to notify relevant safety representatives of their rights, but it is suggested that it would be good management practice to cooperate with safety representatives in such circumstances.

Carrying out an investigation

23. Management investigation

Quite independently of any investigation which the inspectorate, safety representatives or the insurance company may conduct, management should conduct an inquiry with the objectives of identifying the causes of the occurrence and preventing such an event occurring again. The inquiry will almost certainly include:

(a) interviewing personnel, at both management and junior level, including, but not confined to, taking statements from witnesses;
(b) inspecting the site;
(c) inspecting plant and equipment, and testing substances.

This inquiry may also extend to taking advice from experts not in the employment of the firm.

In *Waugh* v. *British Railways Board* [1980] the House of Lords held that certain accident reports might be called in evidence in any subsequent litigation. In that case a victim's widow sued for damages, alleging that the defendant employers had negligently caused her husband's death. She sought disclosure of a report prepared by the defendants, partly for the purposes of establishing the cause of the accident and partly for the purpose of preparing for litigation. Their Lordships dismissed the defendants' claim that the report was a privileged document, holding that the primary purpose of making the report was not related to litigation.

24. Disclosure of management investigation's results

It seems certain, therefore, that the majority of reports made as a result of in-house investigation following an accident would not be privileged. Nevertheless in the interests of identifying the cause of the mishap and introducing better workplace systems, such reports should be made. It is suggested that a well-managed organisation should not be unduly perturbed by the implications of this case.

Such investigations should result at least in reports to both the safety committee and to management.

Conclusion

25. Overview

Setting up and maintaining safe systems should keep to a minimum the occasions in which accidents and ill-health result from poor working conditions. Unfortunately hazards are all too often only recognised with hindsight, after the event. It is only small consolation that wisdom comes with hindsight and leads to improvements for the future.

Wisdom comes from experience at national as well as organisational level, as a result of rapidly expanding technical knowledge. This, and the desire of the European Community for harmonisation of occupational health and safety laws, makes it likely that before long further EC occupational health and safety Directives will be adopted and in due course reflected in the law of the UK. However, it seems equally likely that for the foreseeable future any amendments to the detail of the law will take place within the framework set out in these pages.

It is to be hoped that with the development of safety awareness, readers of this book will not have to put into effect the procedures set out in its final chapter. But it would nevertheless be wrong not to have the procedures in place to meet the eventuality of a systems breakdown leading to personal injury.

Progress test 17

1. What measures should an organisation take to ensure 'damage control' after an accident has occurred, and in what order should it take them? **(2)**

2. What are the principal provisions of the Reporting of Accidents and Dangerous Occurrences Regulations? **(10)**

3. On whom does the obligation to report normally fall? **(12)**

4. What information must be entered in the accident book? **(19)**

302 Systems and procedures at the workplace

5. What are the provisions of the First-Aid Regulations?   (5–8)

6. Why should an organisation take particular care to ensure that its accident reports are thorough and accurate?   (23–24)

Appendix
Examination technique

Type of assessment

Students' acquisition of knowledge about and understanding of a subject is nowadays often assessed by means other than an end-of-course three-hour written examination.

Coursework assessment often requires the student to demonstrate more than facility with the subject itself: for example, presentation skills and ability to work as a member of a group may also be evaluated. These alternative forms of skills assessment are particularly used in business studies and management courses. Since occupational health and safety is frequently studied in management training courses, it is quite likely that those who have used this book will be subject to this kind of assessment. However, coursework assessment is carried out by the criteria set by the teacher and may, to some extent, reflect the preferences of that teacher. Therefore, it will not be discussed here.

End-of-course written assessment

End-of-course assessment may take the form of the traditional unseen timed paper; or the student may be allowed access to some source material, such as Acts of Parliament. Arguably, the test in which sources may be referred to is harder than the one where the candidate can only rely on memory. Where texts are available, the candidate will score no marks for reciting accurately the material contained in the text, so marks will go exclusively to use of the material in the context of the examination questions. It is very important that the candidate is familiar not just with the text generally but with the particular edition of the text which is to be used in the examination room. It is disconcerting to have, under the stress of the examination, to find one's way round a text whose layout is not familiar.

In many cases examiners allow candidates to take their own texts into the examination. It is likely, however, that the texts will be checked at the door of the examination room to ensure that they have not been marked. It will be as well to find out the rules on this matter early in the course.

The place of safety law in the examination

A three-hour examination exclusively devoted to safety law will be fairly unusual. Candidates are likely to sit an examination of which safety law is only a part: for example, safety may be placed in the general context of labour law, or as part of a law and practice paper.

It is therefore important to discover, at an early stage of the course, the likely balance of the paper: how many safety law questions are likely to occur and whether they are compulsory. Even if safety is only a small part of the syllabus, it is unwise to decide not to learn it (or to favour it at the expense of other areas!). Examination questions may bridge more than one area of study — for example, a problem question in a labour law paper might concern a pregnant black woman who was on sick leave after catching her fingers in a machine. Not knowing the safety law might reduce the candidate's ability to answer an otherwise attractive question. Alternatively, the questions on the area which has been prepared might turn out to be much more difficult than the question in the areas the candidate has decided to ignore.

Type of examination question

Traditionally, questions in law examinations are of one of two types: they are either essay questions or problem questions.

Essay questions
It is most important to identify exactly what the examiner is asking

for and ensure that in the candidate's answer the relevant material is directed to providing that information. To some extent, this is cosmetic but up to half marks can easily be lost by failing to use relevant information for the purpose asked. Clearly the candidate must have a good knowledge of the subject matter but relatively few marks will be gained for simply reproducing the textbook account of the particular subject. Usually, at the very least, the examiner will ask for a 'critical examination' of the material. The candidate who provides a clear outline of the material and a good evaluation of it will gain many more marks than the one who merely regurgitates the material, even if the answer contains a great deal of accurate detail.

Problem questions

The typical problem question is a factual account of an imaginary situation which is likely to lead to legal proceedings. The candidate is asked to advise one or more of the persons involved.

The objects of the problem are:

(a) to identify the candidate's knowledge of the relevant rules of law;
(b) to establish whether the candidate can analyse the facts and relate them to the rules of law;
(c) to establish whether the candidate can give a concise and reasoned account of how a court would apply the law to the facts.

In undertaking this task the candidate should:

(a) study the facts carefully, decide which of the given facts are relevant and note carefully who will be bringing a case against whom (including the instructions in the problem as to whom the candidate is to advise!);
(b) decide whether the proceedings will be in the criminal or the civil courts and make sure that the correct terminology is used (e.g. a trial in a criminal court is a prosecution);
(c) identify the relevant law — this means firstly identifying the broad area (e.g. the tort of negligence), then making careful selections of the issues involved: the question is not inviting the candidate to write all about the branch of law in question;
(d) consider whether there would be defences available;
(e) identify any relevant cases;

(f) after applying the relevant law to the relevant facts, give the advice.

All these matters should be thought through before fully beginning to write. Reasoning should lead up to decided cases which appear relevant, not argued back from the cases: answers which merely state, 'The plaintiff will win because the facts of this case are just like one decided last week' will gain hardly any marks even if the case is fully identified! Incidentally, it is rarely useful to give a lengthy account of a particular case: the art is to indicate the relevance of the case tersely but accurately.

Advice should be given in the third person — not in the form of, for example, a letter to the accident victim.

In management papers candidates may expect to be asked to advise senior management on how to avoid running foul of the law. For example, 'Advise your employers of the liabilities they may incur in respect of the conduct of Bill, an employee who refuses to wear safety boots when working on construction sites'.

The examples given here are terse: in practice, a problem is likely to extend over a number of lines and include a considerable amount of factual information. This is to identify whether the candidate can separate the relevant issue(s). The candidate must answer the question fully on the facts supplied: it is unwise to 'fill in' extra facts. On the other hand, the candidate may not declare that shortage of facts prevents an answer being provided! The most the candidate can do is comment on lack of what seems relevant information (e.g. 'The outcome might be different if the employer knew that incidents of this kind had occurred before').

In the exam the candidate should not waste time in rewriting the given facts in full, but there may be points in the answer where it is relevant to refer expressly to a phrase to indicate the significance of it to the answer. For example, 'As we are told Jim had been "trained by the employer", we can, for present purposes, assume that the training he had received was adequate'.

A word of warning seems appropriate here. There are a number of important differences between cases given in the examination room and real-life occurrences. Firstly, the examination problem is related to the syllabus; secondly, the facts are given. In practice, there is no reason why incidents at the workplace should actually be related to hazards at that workplace and secondly, the account given by the third party must always be investigated carefully to ensure that it is a complete and accurate account.

Alternatively, if required to express an opinion on given facts, the writer should (outside the exam room) set out fully the facts relied on and make it clear that the opinion expressed is related only to those facts.

Preparing for the examination

Preparation for the examination begins when the course begins! Preparation for any examination always has two aspects: firstly, the acquisition of knowledge and secondly, developing the technique of analysing and applying that knowledge, including writing the answer in a form which does justice to the mental processes which have been involved.

The development of the power to analyse a situation and apply knowledge to it is probably more important than the acquisition of the knowledge itself. This is one reason why it is unwise to mark printed texts: marks made at an early stage of understanding may well inhibit subsequent re-evaluation of the material highlighted.

In other words, examination preparation is a developmental process carried on throughout the length of the course of study.

Last minute revision
It follows from the previous paragraph that it is not sensible to try to absorb the syllabus for the first time shortly before the examination: it is doubtful whether the examination can be passed in this way — it is certain little of the knowledge thus acquired will be retained for long.

Revision should be carried out in short, sharp bursts, not by sitting long over the texts. The most effective revision is for candidates to make brief notes of what they know and check these notes against the text. It is more valuable to understand the framework of the subject than to master all the detail.

Past examination papers are useful aids to revision. They indicate the style of the examination. Making rough plans of answers to individual questions is a good way to revise. It is not generally helpful to devote time to writing out model answers in full. This is not an economic use of time, though it is a good idea to do one or two timed questions just to get familiarity with how much can be tackled in the time allowed.

Conduct in the examination room

1. Read the rubric carefully: note how many questions have to be answered — how much time is allowed, whether all questions are of equal weight, whether any questions are compulsory.
2. Allow at least ten minutes to read the whole paper and decide what questions to answer.
3. Divide the remaining time equally between the questions to be answered. Do not devote too much time to any one question — it carries a limited number of marks. If the allotted time runs out before a question has been completely answered, leave it and go on to the next: it can be finished later if time allows (but leave adequate space for this).
4. Plan each answer before starting to write: do not be afraid to show your plan on the script. In any case, you may have to hand it in since most exam room regulations prohibit removal of even rough notes from the exam room. Do not be afraid to spend ten minutes or even more on fully planning each answer before starting to write. In the planning phase constantly refer back to the question paper to safeguard against careless misunderstandings of the question asked.
5. Try to keep the script legible and orderly, remembering to number questions and, if necessary, answer sheets. Examiners are patient, but they are human!
6. Try to allow five minutes at the end of the paper to check it through and make sure it is presented in an orderly fashion.
7. Never leave before he end of the allotted time — spare time should be spent in checking the papers: both the question paper and the script. Rewrite if necessary.
8. Avoid making marginal notes: the margins belong to the examiner and anyway such notes are often hard to read back into the text by an examiner who has to work quickly.

Index